FAITH AND RELIGION IN CUMBRIA: FROM PREHISTORIC TO MODERN TIMES

Volume One
From Prehistoric Times to the
Seventeenth Century

Recent Publications by Michael A. Mullett

A New History of Penrith, Book I: From Pre-History to the Close of the Middle Ages (Carlisle: Bookcase, 2017).

A New History of Penrith, Book II: Penrith under the Tudors (Carlisle: Bookcase, 2017)

A New History of Penrith, Book III: Penrith in the Stuart Century, 1603-1714 (Carlisle: Bookcase, 2018).

'Lancaster Castle and the British Civil Wars, 1642-1651', *Contrebis A Bulletin of Archaeology and History for Lancashire and the North West*, Vol. 37 (2019).

'The Towneleys and Catholic Recusancy in Early Modern East Lancashire', *North West Catholic History*, Volume XLVI (2019).

A New History of Penrith Book IV Penrith in the Eighteenth Century, 1715-1800 (Carlisle: Bookcase, 2019).

A New History of Penrith, Book V: Penrith in the Nineteenth Century, 1800-1901: Chapters on the Victorian Town (Carlisle: Bookcase, 2020).

'"Your Majesty's Loyal and Dutiful Subjects": Carlisle and '"Papal Aggression"', *Transactions of the Cumberland & Westmorland Antiquarian & Archaeological Society*, Third Series, Vol. 20 (2020).

With Lorna M. Mullett: '"The Bill, the whole Bill and nothing but the Bill"': The 1831 General Election in Cumberland', *Transactions of the CWAAS*, Third Series, Vol.21 (2021).

'Demistifying a dean: more on "Papal Aggression"', *Transactions of the CWAAS*, Third Series, Volume 21 (2021).

A New History of Penrith Book VI Penrith in the Twentieth Century, 1900-1974 Essays on the Public Realm (Carlisle: Bookcase, 2022).

Carlisle in Revolution and Restoration, c. 1648-1688 (Kendal: CWAAS, Tract Series Vol. 30, 2022).

A Guide to the Catholic Church of St Catherine of Alexandria, Penrith (Penrith: Parish of St Catherine of Alexandria, 2022).

'Catholics in the United Kingdom, 1800-1820', in Liam Chambers, ed., *The Oxford History of British and Irish Catholicism Volume III: Relief, Revolution and Revival, 1746-1829* (General Editors James E. Kelly and John McCafferty, Oxford: Oxford University Press, 2023).

Copyright: Michael A. Mullett
First edition 2024
ISBN 978-1-912181-71-1
Published by Bookcase, 19 Castle St., Carlisle, CA3 8SY
01228 544560   bookscumbria@aol.com
Printed by The Amadeus Press.

FAITH AND RELIGION IN CUMBRIA: FROM PREHISTORIC TO MODERN TIMES

Volume One
From Prehistoric Times to the Seventeenth Century

MICHAEL A. MULLETT

In Memoriam: James Edward Mullett

BOOKCASE

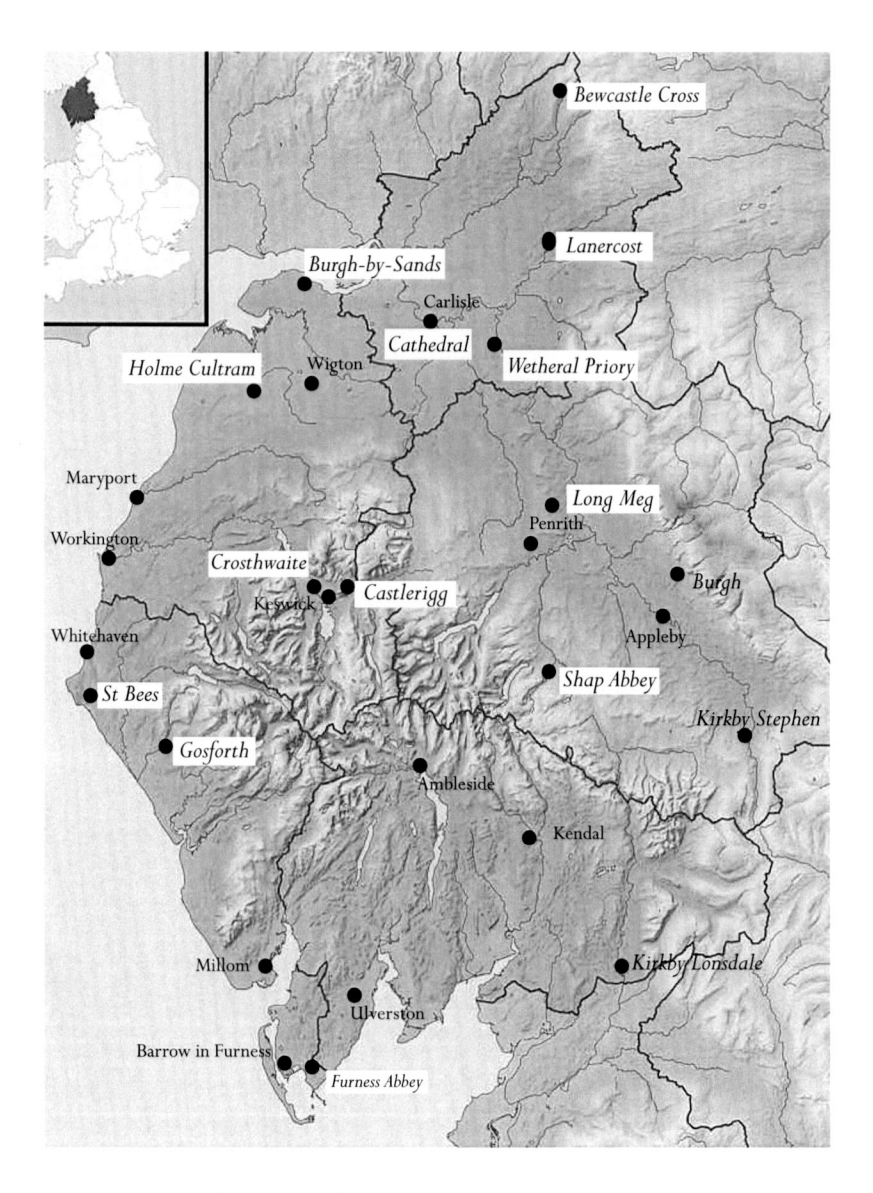

Cumbria showing early religious sites

Contents

Introduction	5
1: Prehistoric Prelude	9
2: Religion and the Romans in the Lake Counties	14
3: Religion in the Post-Roman Lake Counties	23
4: Faith and Religion in the Early Medieval Lake Counties	36
5: Faith and Religion in the Medieval Lake Counties	50
6: Faith and Religion in the Late Medieval Lake Counties	73
7: Faith and Religion in the Medieval Lake Counties: An Essay in Iconography and Instruction	84
8: Reformation and Resistance in the Tudor Lake Counties, 1485-1603	126
9: Faith and Religion in the Stuart Lake Counties, 1603-1689	171
Endnotes	247
Index	283

Volume Two

10: The Church of England in the 18th-Century Lake Counties
11: Religion and Society in the 18th-Century Lake Counties
12: Faith and Religion in the 19th-Century Lake Counties
Conclusion
Endnotes
Index

Acknowledgements

As always is in my research and writing in Cumbrian regional history, I have been reliant on the plentiful Local Studies resources of the Penrith Branch of Cumbria Public Libraries - and am deeply grateful for the kind helpfulness of the town library's staff. I have also leaned on the Cumbrian studies literature that we have built up at home over the years of our residence in Penrith, and in particular I have had, within easy reach and in a sometimes difficult time for travelling to major libraries, accumulated volumes of the *Transactions of the Cumberland and Westmorland Antiquarian and Archaeological Society*, as well as those of the journals *Northern History* and *North West Catholic History*: without those published sources this book could not have been written.

    The writing of history is a collective exercise, and it has been my privilege in the research and writing of this book to draw in particular on many deeply and specialist *CWAAS* articles and 'notes', published by the Society over its many decades of cherished service to regional history and archaeology: I have endeavoured to weave these many closely focused and impeccably researched papers into a broader synthesis.

    Those who have generously made the fruits of their research directly available to me include Scott Sowerby, Anthony Cousins, Jane Platt and my wife Lorna. Lorna has been my authorial editor and guide through the many months of putting this study together - always vigilant over the text, always encouraging, always uplifting.

    Timothy Sykes has been my lynx-eyed copy editor as well as the ultra-generous lender of research material from his renowned library, and Stephen Matthews is my omnicompetent manager.

    A stylistic note: where these are available, life dates are given in parenthesis for persons mentioned in the text, with regnal date for monarchs ('r.') and pontifical dates for popes (also ('r.').

Michael A. Mullett
Pentecost, 2024

Introduction

What follows in this book is my most ambitious authorial undertaking in over four decades of historical publishing: as an historian once pigeonholed into the two centuries of the 'early modern' 16th-17th- century period of British and European history, I have now been seduced 'to boldly go' into a timescale of two millennia, guided, though, by the work of the many specialist researchers whose cumulative scholarship in history and archaeology I have gratefully recognised in my Acknowledgements, above.

This audacity over chronology is balanced, however, by my more concentrated approach to geography, as I limit myself to the study of the two counties of the English far north west. Though they were bracketed together as 'Cumbria' only as late as 1974, these shires (with their southern, Lancashire, appendage), have always had a shared identity, especially in civil government, while historically they have shared in the poverty bequeathed by a harsh climate and inhospitable terrain.

To begin at the beginning, in chapter 1 a study of a wealth of prehistoric stone monuments in this area has made possible hypothesising on the religious beliefs and rituals of the first Cumbrians. Then, the military presence of the Romans in this, the ultimate north-western outpost of their vast empire, left a treasury of artefacts and monumental inscriptions recording the spirituality of the imperial personnel: the elastic capacity of Roman religion to absorb elements from other belief systems meant that fusions were made between international cults of the Empire and indigenous Celtic forms of faith. This area also participated in the gradual Christianisation of the Roman Empire that took place before its demise: Christian continuity is the theme of the centuries before and after the fall of Rome, while the missionary efforts of the charismatic evangelists Ninian, Kentigern and Cuthbert awoke a post-Roman Christian revival. Within the Lakes area, which became a zone of Scandinavian immigration, artistic themes from Norse iconography were freely borrowed to furnish stone monuments in order to bolster the essentials of faith and hope in Christ and the Trinity.

From the late 11th century onwards, the inclusion of Lakeland in the new Norman English kingdom led to a large-scale make-over of religious life: the former Roman base at Carlisle acquired a new dignity as the seat of a cathedral - a distinctively royal one - and a diocese, while Norman-French barons became the patrons of new forms of monastic life imported from the Continent, of which Furness Abbey became the archetype.

Poverty - with never enough parish churches, never enough properly trained parish priests - was the fact of regional life with which a succession of medieval bishops of Carlisle strove to cope,while matters were made worse in the Anglo-Scots wars of the 14th century, when the Lakes region became a battleground and many churches were ruined. Even so, Carlisle Cathedral became a place of religious instruction and pilgrimage. Its rich iconography - the 'books of the illiterate' - was deployed to teach the basic data of Christian faith. Above all, while Lakeland may from one point of view have been regarded as 'remote', plentiful evidence, much of it archaeological, shows that the region's religious life was suffused with themes derived from medieval European Catholic culture.

A more settled social life in Cumberland, Westmorland and north Lancashire from the 15th century onwards was the context for a late medieval Cumbrian Catholic renaissance of 'traditional religion', which subsequently put up a popular barrier against religious innovation and Reformation in the 16th century. That was when this region staged a military offensive and popular revolt - the 1536-7 Pilgrimage of Grace - against the crown's suppression of the monasteries.

Thereafter, the decades-long campaign by the Tudor, then the Stuart, state and the Church of England to turn the English into a Protestant people also met with eventual success in the Lake Counties, as ancestral Catholicism became confined to a few gentry manor houses. Then, though, following the British civil wars of 1642-51 the collapse of an attempt to impose a monolithic puritan and Presbyterian ascendancy on Cumbria released an opposing new pluralism: worship according to the banned Anglican Book of Common Prayer went underground, to await its open return with the restoration of the monarchcy in 1660; the Catholic gentry survived; new, more radical forms of puritan faith arose; above all, Westmorland became the birthplace of a novel Christianity, nursed in the hearts of the independent-minded men and women of the upland peasantry, people well used to forming their own spiritual lives in the absence of the often distant parish churches: the Quakers.

Efforts after 1660 to reimpose a single religious form inevitably failed, nationally and regionally, and the 1689 Toleration Act partly liberated most styles of churchmanship. Nevertheless, in Cumbria the Church of England remained largely in control of the religious landscape, retrieving and repairing the half-ruined parish buildings, erecting magnificent Georgian churches to serve the market towns. When the Methodist founder John Wesley approached those settled urban communities, with their plentiful existing religious provisions, he encountered rebuff or indifference, but when he targeted

Whitehaven - a port - new, industrial, trading world-wide, perhaps a little raw, open to novelty, a place of immigrants - he found his Cumberland response. Early in the 19th century the working-class-based Wesleyan reformation known as the Primitive Methodists created a Great Awakening in Alston and Nenthead.

The results of the national Religious Census of 1851 shocked many contemporaries with its disclosure that England was only partly a church-going society: the pattern of attendance at the churches and chapels of this region reflected its complex patterns of church provision and social strafication. Meanwhile, the Cumberland Catholic population mirrored the 19th-century English Catholic Church's transformation from a tiny rural sect, led by squires, into a large denomination, immigrant, Irish, industrial, urban, proletarian, directed by its priests. The sudden arrival of 'popery' in Victorian west Cumberland aroused violence, but then religion sometimes does that.

Chapter 1:
Prehistoric Prelude

Whatever 'religion' means - as the *New Oxford Dictionary of English* defines it, 'the belief in and worship of a superhuman controlling power, especially a personal god or gods' - the Lake Counties' rich stock of prehistoric monuments arose directly from religious beliefs and practices that were present in the remote past, our ancestors being 'driven by an enormously powerful belief system that brought order and meaning to a dangerous and potentially chaotic universe'. The arrangement of 'one of the most remarkable and accessible groups of prehistoric monuments in the County', the stone circles on Moor Divock, to the east of Ullswater, 'can be related to and inform discussion of how prehistoric people saw their landscape and invested it with meaning, mythology and lore'. A 'long sequence of ceremonial activity' and 'a long history of religious and ceremonial associations', focused on human cremations, characterised the ritual site at Oddendal, near Shap.[1]

Archaeological investigations are facilitated by the profusion of such sites in the Lake Counties, for no fewer than 18 stone circles have been enumerated in the region, headed by the four most famous of them - Swinside, near Millom, Castlerigg, near Keswick; Mayburgh at Eamont Bridge, south of Penrith; and Long Meg and Her Daughters, the plinth and its satellites which stand at Little Salkeld, six miles north-east of Penrith. It is clear that the 'stone circles of Cumbria are ... sufficiently numerous to be of national importance ... as well as

Long Meg and her Daughters
Swetten, 1848

Castlerigg Stone Circle
James Baker Pyne, 1853

a major feature of local prehistory ... worthy of serious consideration'.[2]

The scale of these structures continues to impress the visitor. At Shapbeck, near Shap, three concentric circles of stones stand, with 28 forming the outer disc and 18 making up the second ring. Mayburgh, at Eamont Bridge, is an exceptional Cumbrian example of the genre, with its great banks of cobblestones reaching 15 feet in height. The circle takes in more than an acre, and one immense stone stands about nine feet above ground. It is partnered by the superb henge - a ring-shaped bank with a ditch inside the bank and known locally as King Arthur's Round Table. Castlerigg, near Keswick, has '39 huge stones in a brooding circle', the largest seven feet tall and weighing several tons, with a subsidiary group forming an inner sanctum. Swinside, near Millom in south-west Cumbria, is 'perhaps the most perfect example in the region'. Long Meg is seen as 'in some ways the most dramatic of all these sites'.[3]

The most appreciative early admirer of the Long Meg complex was the topographer William Hutchinson (1732-1814) who thought it 'the greatest and most extraordinary piece of antiquity ... in the world, of its kind'. Hutchinson described the site as a combination of law court and parliamentary gathering - 'a court of judicature; and place of public assembly for the disposing of justice'. He shared the conviction of his contemporaries that such edifices were creations of the Druids, the priestly caste who arose in Celtic Gaul in around 200 BC, many centuries later than the Neolithic age, of the fourth millennium BC, that witnessed the creation of the stone circles. Hutchinson imagined Long Meg as combining its function of a 'druidical court of justice' with that of 'a temple for religious worship'.[4]

Long Meg was indeed conceived as a site of worship, the

religion being directed at the sun, for Long Meg acted as a '"marker" for the mid-winter sunset, and is also carved with symbols of a type which have been linked with some early form of early sun-worship'. This purpose dictated the timetable of the construction of the site, since 'the Long Meg stone must have been in place before the circle was built in order that the stones of the circle and its portal could so accurately facilitate the [solar] shadow .... Long Meg was standing before the circle stones were put in place'.[5]

The sixth largest stone circle in Britain, Ireland and Brittany - 25-times larger than the average specimen - the Long Meg edifices would have required a construction team of at least 135 and, when completed, could have accommodated over 1,500 worshippers, both locals and outsiders, convoked by a seasonal solar calendar, in the year's 'shortest, darkest days to supplicate the return of summer, light and warmth'.[6] A high degree of social, religious and political organisation would have been required to mobilise the construction and utilisation of this ritual site.

Near the south-west coast of the county, and part of the Millom 'Lacra' complex, the late Neolithic to early Bronze Age structure at Kirksanton, known as the Giant's Grave, has two upright stones, ten and eight feet high respectively, the larger of the pair having cup marks, measuring three inches across and 1½ inches deep. The 'religious' theme in this case is that of rituals surrounding the burial of the dead: 'there was both time and space in the north of England to allow of the building of substantial funerary monuments of more than one kind', and at Skelmore Heads, Ulverston, burial deposit would probably have been placed between the two tall stone uprights.[7]

Stone structures are not the only objects surviving from the prehistoric era that might have had spiritual significance. One possible reason for the wide distribution of stone axes produced at the Langdale 'factory', in Great Langdale, is that, alongside their practical utility, they possessed a supernatural allure, enhanced by the cup- and-ring markings they were given. In 1774 in Ravenstonedale, in Westmorland, a vessel was discovered,'sound and intire, the diameter whereof at the bottom is 8 inches … it contains about 8 gallons and an half made of three plates of copper neatly joined together'. Dating from the final phase of the Bronze Age - the eve of the Iron Age - this finely made artefact formed part a 'ritual deposit' associated with cultic performances.[8]

A stone at a circle in Dean, near Cockermouth, may show 'the influence of entropic [message transfer] imagery on the designs. The effects of hallucination have been considered and common ethnographic [the scientific description of cultures] descriptions of trance have also been deliberated'.[9]

Chapter 2:
Religion and the Romans in the Lake Counties

The Roman conquest of Britain, which began under the Emperor Tiberius Claudius Drusus Germanicus (Claudius, r. 41-54), advanced into the Lakes region during the governorship of the province of Quintus Petillius Cerialis (c.30- after 83), who was appointed in 71. The conquest in the far north was consolidated in the building of Hadrian's Wall, which was commenced in 122. For as long as the Roman occupation lasted, which was until the early 5th century, this north-western zone remained militarised, with a largely un-Romanised indigenous Celtic population. Carlisle (*Luguvalium*) was primarily a frontier fortress and garrison, though gradually developing commercial, administrative, religious and political structures.[10]

The prominence of a military presence and ethos in this part of the Roman world is reflected in the Latin inscriptions that troops left behind them. Roman soldiers, in their dangerous lives, put themselves under the protection of the chief god, Jupiter (Iupiter, or Jove). This figure was not only the head of the Roman pantheon - 'Best and Greatest, *Deo Optimo Maximo*' - but was also the special deity of the Empire and its army. Thus the writing on a convex disc uncovered in Carlisle in 1983 translates as 'Best (and) Greatest, protect us, a troop of fighting men all'.[11]

In dedicating altars to Jupiter, troops also celebrated their regimental *esprit de corps*, which was partly based on their regional origins within the Empire, as well as on their fealty to officers, who fostered their piety. At Castlesteads, or

14

Roman Inscriptions: A: Iupiter Optimus Maximus, Castlesteads; B: Iupiter Optimus Maximus erected by M. Censorius Cornelianus, Maryport; C I.O.M erected by Valeria Victrix Antoniana, Carlisle; D Tombstone of Aurelia Aureliana, Carlisle E: Cocidius, Netherby; F: To Belatocadrus, Kirkbride

Camboglanna, betweeen the Wall forts of Birdoswald and Stanwix, an offering was made:

To Jupiter, Best and Greatest, the Fourth Cohort of Gauls, part mounted, (set this up) under the command of Volcacius Hospes, prefect of cavalry.[12]

The links between Jupiter, the Roman Empire and its army are also celebrated in a mid-2nd century intaglio - a design engraved into backing material - from Carlisle, displaying the god, nude and holding a sceptre, with the imperial and military symbol of the eagle - 'Jupiter's bird'- gazing up at him.[13]

A manifestation of this deity as 'Iupiter Augustus' was evoked in an altar, unique in Britain, set up by an acting commander (*praepositus*), M. Censorius Cornelianus, of the 1st Spanish Cohort, which, it is assumed, occupied Maryport (Aulana) in the reigns of the Emperors Marcus Ulpius Trajanus (Trajan, r.98-117) and Publius Aelius Hadrianus (Hadrian, r.117-38).[14] On a tombstone at Brougham, originally Brocavum, near Penrith, the 'O' in 'D.O.M.', part of the 'D.O.M.' in 'DEO OPTIMO MAXIMO', has been re-shaped into a depiction of a pine, a Roman symbol of immortality - his parents' commemoration of the premature death of their son, the youth Crescentius.[15]

The imperial cult was celebrated in a number of individual objects present in this region. Probably from the Roman fort site at Kirkbride, on the Solway Plain, a rare and beautiful plaque representing Claudius 'could have been made specifically for a religious shrine to be placed alongside busts of other deified emperors'. The Senhouse Museum at Maryport houses a dedication 'To Jupiter, best, greatest', commissioned by Postimius Acilianus, prefect of the First Cohort of Dalmatians,'for the welfare of Antoninus Augustus Pius' - the

Emperor Titus Aurelius Fulvus (Antoninus Pius, r. 138-61).[16]

The 'Community of the Carvetii' (*Civitas Carvetiorum*] set up an eloquently inscribed milestone at Langwathby, north-east of Penrith, datable to 223: 'For the Emperor, Caesar ... Severus Alexander (Alexander Severus, r. 221-35), Pious, Favoured of Fortune, Augustus, Chief Priest, in the Second Year of his Tribunician Power, Consul, Proconsul, Father of the Country'. The year 223 marked a key stage in the establishment, during Alexander Severus's rule, of the *civitas Carvetiorum* as a part-Romanised society based on Carlisle.[17]

An altar dedicated to Jupiter and to the god of fire Vulcan (Volcanus), erected at Old Carlisle (Olenacum) for the welfare of the Emperor Gordianus Pius (Gordian III, r. 238-44), was funded with money collected from the *vikani*, or *vicani* - the villagers, the locals - by *magistri* - the masters, who were perhaps 'leaders of the townspeople in matters pertaining to religion'.[18]

More deities from the Roman pantheon - culminating in a comprehensive round-up of its members - feature in the dedication on a Carlisle altar: 'To Jupiter Best and Greatest, to Queen Juno, to August Minerva, to Father Mars, to Victory, to all the other gods and goddesses'. The offering was made by Marcus Aurelius Syrio, a military tribune of the 20th Legion, *Valeria Victrix Antoniana*, 'from the province of Thrace'. Yet though the name of the dedicator is given, this dedication was not 'an act of private devotion' but the memento of a public 'votive ceremony': the officer was acting, not as an individual *dévot* but as a ritual represesentative of his unit of command.[19]

A dedication to the deity Victory at Birdoswald on Hadrian's Wall 'need occasion no surprise. Victory appears as a goddess in her own right ... as a personification of virtue of the Emperor'. At Lodge Crag, about a mile south of Milecastle 51 on the Wall, the soldiers of Legio VI Victrix had verse in tribute to their

legion's triumphs carved on to an altar:
> *aurea per caelum volutat Victoria pennis-*

'Through the sky on her wings flies golden Victory.'[20]

At Papcastle (Derventio), near Cockermouth, a small winged figure, 'male, nude and incomplete', is thought to be the god of love, Cupid. A bust, from Kirkby Thore, between Penrith and Appleby, made of copper alloy, helmeted, is probably the goddess Minerva - but may be a youthful Mars.[21]

This archaeological thesaurus, then, clearly reveals the richness of Roman cultic observance in this region. From excavation in the bath-house at Bewcastle Fort, on the Wall, a building of 2nd-3rd century dating - an image of the goddess of luck, Fortuna - shows 'a seated figure of Fortune carved in the round from a block of red sandstone and holding a cornucopia [the horn of plenty] in her left hand'. Among the antiquities assembled at Scaleby Castle, near Carlisle, by the Cumbrian historian W. G. Collingwood (1854-1932) is a dedication to the deity of water and the sea: 'To the god Neptune Reginius Justinus, the tribune, willingly and deservedly fulfilled his vow'(to dedicate a thanksgiving).[22]

At Castlesteads, between Birdoswald and Stanwix, a centurion repaired a temple, dedicating it to 'the Mother goddesses of all nations', the Mother goddesses being particularly venerated by legionaries. Dedications to the Mother goddesses are also located south-west of Milecastle 73, set up by the Sixth Legion Victrix Fidelis, and east of Milecastle 79 by unidentified 'Soldiers'. From Carlisle, a 'delicately modelled' incense container in the shape of the god of revelry, Bacchus (or Dionysius), is similar to others found in Roman graves in the Netherlands, Spain, Germany and Austria. This object played a part in funerary rites, taking account of the role that this deity had 'as a provider of bliss in the afterlife'.[23]

Inscriptions marking funerals commended the departed to the custody of the community of the deceased, the *Manes*, the shades of the dead, the 'good people', belonging to the lower world. Thus an inscription from Brougham translates as 'To the spirits of the departed. [...]alis lived 80 years. [...]us set up the inscription to his uncle'. At Old Carlisle, near Wigton, the daughter of Flavius Martius, councillor in the *civitas Carvetiorum*, set up the inscription 'To the spirits of the departed' and to her father. Two 'modest monuments', from Ambleside (Galava), of late 2nd to early 3rd century dating, commend to the *manes* two soldiers who may have been father and son, the younger, Flavius Romanus, at the age of 35, having 'been killed in the camp by the enemy'. From the Roman cemetery on London Road in Carlisle, a headstone can be translated as 'To the spirits of the departed - Aurelia Aureliana lived 41 years. Ulpius Apolinaris set this up to his very beloved wife'.[24]

Originating in Persia, worship of the sun god Mithras was one of the Roman Empire's newer 'mystery' cults that stressed individual experience and personal redemption over against the more formal social worship of the official pagan pantheon. The adoption of Mithraism by soldiers facilitated its spread, from the 1st century onwards, through the militarised frontier provinces of the Empire, such as Britain, where, probably, a Mithraic temple was set up east of the fort at Maryport. At Naworth, north of Brampton, the inscription on an altar translates as 'To the unconquered Sun-god Mithras, Marcus Licinius Ripanus, prefect, has fulfilled a vow'. At Castlesteads, which had at one time a 500-strong command, an inscription, aligning Mithras with the 'unconqered Sun (*Sol invictus*)', translates as 'To the Invincible Sun-god, Sextus Severius Salvator, prefect, willingly and deservedly fulfilled his vow'. Also at Castlesteads, an altar inscription near Milecastle 59, referring to the 'genius', or spirit, of Hadrian's Wall ,suggests that some legionaries serving on that posting may have believed 'that the border itself had a spiritual identity'.[25]

The profusion of the Roman epigraphic material being investigated in this chapter may have the effect of distracting attention away from the survival of Celtic culture and religion in Britain. This area, however, retained Celtic cultic patterns, as, for example at Netherby, on the Scottish border, where:

> The presence of a wheel classifies the ... relief as representing a Celtic deity whose main identifying symbol is the wheel ... and it is possible to identify a Celtic celestial divinity whose specifically solar power is indicated by the presence of a spoked wheel representing the central sphere, nimbus and rays of the sun. [The figure] is unique in British contexts in that it appears to provide evidence of an identification or collation between a Celtic sky and solar god and the symbolism associated with protection, prosperity and well-being.[26]

Stone heads, coming from south-west Cumbria and datable to the later Iron Age or to the post-Roman conquest period of Roman and Celtic co-existence, 'represent part of a pan-European belief in the head as an important spiritual symbol.' One of several 'crude heads of Roman period date, fashioned from local sandstone and associated with nature cults', has been recovered in the south-west of the region'. Probably of 1st to 3rd century date, a red sandstone head was discovered in 1977 at Rickerby Park, Carlisle. Placed near the centre of a cairn at Santon Bridge, north-east of Ravenglass, a 'circular waterworn cobble', inscribed roughly with a pair of eyes and a mouth, may have been a 'cult object'. A bog body from Seascale Moss 'contains various points which could link it to the widely accepted tradition of Iron Age and Romano-British ritual sacrifice and burial in peat which seems to have occurred across Northern Europe'. A chiselled sandstone block containing a small male head, disinterred from the Eden at Carlisle may indicate a river god - which, in turn, may point to a local or indigenous, rather than pan-imperial, cult.[27]

Roman religious practice often deployed syncretism, which is the adaptation by one religious system of the beliefs and/or performances of another or others. Because, as has been seen, Roman deities were ascribed specialist functions or characteristics, when those aptitudes were identified in other, non-Roman, gods, the latter might be aligned with the Roman original. Thus, for example, the Roman Vulcan, as the god of fire, could be readily assimilated to native Celtic 'Smith gods'.[28]

A major instance of this kind of transference took place in the case of the Celtic god Cocidius, who, with his specialisms in war and hunting, was appropriated to the Roman war god, Mars. Eight out of 15 named dedications on altars found at or near the sites of milecastles on the Wall are to Cocidius, one of them collated to 'Mars Cocidius'.[29]

At a number of forts along the wall legionaries twinned veneration of Cocidius with that of another Celtic figure, the horned martial god Belatucradrus. Though adopted by soldiers, the cult of Belatucradrus had its origins with the Carvetii, for, of 28 inscriptions involving him, 'the distribution ... is very firmly in line with what might be expected of a deity associated with a tribal group [the Carvetii] based on the lower Eden valley and having its *civitas* capital at Carlisle'. Four altars were devoted to this god at Brougham. The items put together by Collingwood at Scaleby Castle include the dedication: 'To the holy god Belatucradrus Ullinus gave this small altar with his vow fulfilled'. An altar in honour of this 'locally popular god' was at some stage recycled as part of a garden wall in Wigton.[30]

It is clear that, as the Roman Empire developed a Christian identity in its later centuries, culminating in toleration of the Church in 313, the province of Britain shared in the spread of the new faith: epigraphic evidence at Maryport, Carlisle, Brough-under-Stainmore and Bowes and a tombstone fragment from Maryport containing the Greek cryptogram for Christ's name *chi-rho* provide only some of the early evidence for what had become an established Christian status quo in Britain under the later Empire.[31]

Indeed, the Christian faith had clearly become such a familiar feature of the religious scenery in this province of the Empire that it may have engendered highly advanced unorthodox trends there: the influence of an erudite heretical movement which originated in Continental Europe in the 2nd century, Gnosticism, teaching that the world was governed by a minor deity, the demiurge, may be traceable in 3rd-century art work - an intaglio from Castleheads which 'might have been interpreted in a Christian or in a Christianising Gnostic manner'.[32]

Chapter 3:
Religion in the Post-Roman Lake Counties

The fragmentary and elusive epigraphic and artefactual evidence cited towards the end of the previous chapter to document the establishment of Christianity in the north west does not do full justice to the institutional solidity which that ecclesiastical settlement had acquired by the end of the Roman period. The fact that bishops from York and other Romano-British urban locations were present at the Church Council of Arles in Gaul in 314 'shows the structure which already existed within the province: these bishops will have had churches and a flourishing congregation'. The north-western church-sites at Heysham Head, Urswick and Aldingham suggest established Romano-British Christian centres.[33]

Subsequently, Christian survival was to be converted into a post-Roman Christian *re*-vival and missionary renewal, with the imperial urban centres nurturing the extant tradition, prior to its re-awakening at the hands of a trio of compelling evangelists, Ninian, Kentigern and Cuthbert. At Carlisle:

> as one of only ten Roman towns in Britain partly to conserve its Roman name, continuity of some sort on the spot is highly probable, if the recent dating of the sub-Roman period of the structural fragments of a Christian building ... is any guide. Moreover, ornate ecclesiastical construction work was to be found in the vicinity of the old city at this time.[34]

Continuity between a Christian presence in the Lakes region on either side of the withdrawal of the Romans in the early 5th century, along with the persistence of the Christian legacy being transformed into a vigorous missionary re-birth, eliminating pagan survivals, were strongly evident in the career of Ninian (c. 360- c. 432), who led the way in both retaining and re-building British Christianity's links with its western European origins and with the vibrant ecclesiastical and monastic Christian renaissance taking place in 4th-century Gaul. Consecrated a Bishop in Rome in 394, Ninian was commissioned to evangelise in Scotland. In Tours he met the Bishop of the city, Martin (c. 316/17-c. 397), who had established Gaul's first monastery and whom Ninian was to make the pattern of his own evangelism in the north-west.[35]

The Martin whom Ninian encountered was already the focus of a popular devotion: huge numbers were present at his funeral and many miracles were attributed to him. Ninian introduced Martin of Tours into north-west Britain as a patronal figure, dedicating to him the missionary focal point - the White House, or *Candida Casa* - that he built at Whithorn, in present-day Dumfries and Galloway. The dedication to St Martin of the original church at Brampton also has 'local features associated with St Ninian'. The church of St Martin at Martindale, south-east of Ullswater, is another local example of such a tribute.[36]

From Candida Casa, Ninian launched a mission into Cumbria, setting up a church or preaching station at Brocavum (Brougham), where a small population lived on in the abandoned Roman fort. In line with the austere monastic practice of Martin at Tours, who placed his monastery two miles away from the city and its temptations, Ninian's church at Brocavum - today's 'Ninian Nine Kirks' - was sited over a mile from the lay settlement, and it is suggested that the local caves, known as Isis Parlis, which are set into the sandstone bank of the river Eamont before it joins the Eden, were the location of a monastery of hermits.[37]

The second in a succession of evangelists in Cumbria in the first Christian millennium was Kentigern (or Mungo, d. 603). The hagiographer Jocelyn of Furness (fl. 1175-1214) related how on one occasion Kentigern was informed in Carlisle of paganism still prevalent in the region's highland core - 'many among the mountains given to idolatry, or ignorant of the Divine Law'.[38] The immediate missionary solution was not, initially, to put up church buildings but first to create convert communities made up of members who were introduced into the faith by being baptised.

Consequently, this region has a large number of places which have Kentigern associations and dedications, along with natural sources of water for baptisms: Grinsdale, on the river Eden, near Kirkandrews-on-Eden; Irthington, near today's Carlisle airport, 'with its Mungo spring'; Kirkcambeck, with its beck, north of Lanercost Priory, near Brampton; Caldbeck, near Hesket Newmarket, with another 'Mungo spring'; Mungrisdale, north of the Penrith-Keswick A66, whose church is dedicated to Mungo; the 'great Kentigern centre' at Crosthwaite, Keswick, where, according to Jocelyn of Furness, Kentigern erected his preaching cross; St Kentigern's in Bromfield, south-east of Abbey Town, which possessed a covered well; St Kentigern's in Aspatria, which has a well in the churchyard; and St Mungo at Dearham, between Cockermouth and Maryport. These 'all have an obvious and usually identified adjacent baptismal site associated with the name of Kentigern', based on 'strategic planning aimed to reach those around the mountains of central Cumbria'. These 'Cumbrian commemorations are in places which Kentigern visited, where he personally preached the Gospel, and where churches [i.e. congregations] were first gathered'.[39]

The third in a succession of founding fathers of Cumbrian

Christianity in the first millennium was Cuthbert (c. 636-87), Bishop of Lindisfarne, the 'indefatigible' 'travelling priest spreading the Christian message to remote villages', to whom the Anglian King Ecgfrith (r. 670-85) of Northumbria made an award of 'the land called Cartmel and all the Britons in it', Cuthbert discovering that this Celtic area housed an already well-established monastic community.[40]

Cuthbert was 'no stranger to Carlisle', and, towards the end of their lives, he acted as 'spiritual counsellor' to the Derwentwater hermit Hubert (d. 687). Testimony to devotion to Cuthbert in what is now Cumbria is the fact that in the area of Appleby and Penrith seven churches are dedicated to him.[41]

The steady progress of Christianisation in the Lakes region propagated by the preaching and charisma of Ninian, Kentigern and Cuthbert is reflected in the area's exceptionally rich stock of stone monuments from its first post-Roman Christian period, comprising 21 early crosses from west Cumbria and 'hogback' tombstones - two in Gosforth, plus others in Appleby St Michael's, Crosscanonby, on the coast north of Maryport, Kirkby Stephen, Lowther, near Penrith, Penrith St Andrew's and Plumbland, south of Aspatria. As with Kentigern's temporary baptismal sites, it is possible that crosses were put up as provisional preaching stations pending the eventual building of durable churches.[42]

The group of crosses in west Cumberland stretching from Waberthwaite to Bromfield and Aspatria were set up in prominent positions on important routes, cross-roads and fords. Waberthwaite has two crosses, one probably early 10th-century Anglian and the other Anglo-Danish in styling. At Muncaster two or three monuments were set up, one a Gaelic-Norse cross of c. 1,000 on the old road from Waberthwaite to Muncaster, while at the intersection of pre-historic tracks at Irton an early 9th-century

Irish Celtic cross was erected. Beckermet St Bridget's has a red freestone stump with small Gaelic figuring, plus a 'headless shaft of a white freestone cross'. Beckermet St John's has five or six 10th to 11th century crosses, with stylistic similarities at Distington, Workington, Aspatria, Bridekirk, Bromfield, Crosscanonby and Dearham. Several late 10th or early 11th-century cross fragments were set up at Haile, along with cross fragments in white freestone at the Benedictine Priory of St Bees (1125), plus one or two 10th-century white freestone crosses at Distington. Harrington hosted a white freestone cross head, and Workington white freestone cross fragments of 10th or 11th century workmanship, in an unusual key pattern which Collingwood suggested was from Ireland or was the 10th or 11th-century 'work of Irish Vikings'.[43]

Early Anglian carved stone crosses also survive at Dacre, Addingham, north of Penrith, Brigham, just outside Cockermouth, Carlisle, Irton, near Seascale, Waberthwaite, Kendal, Kirkby Stephen, and Heversham, north-east of Grange-over-Sands. From later in the Anglian period, there are crosses at Burton-in-Kendal, Beckermet, near Egremont, St Bees, Bromfield, Workington and Dearham. However,'the earliest and finest example of Anglian workmanship stands in St. Cuthbert's churchyard at Bewcastle, north-east of the border town of Longtown. Of this superb 4.5-metre sandstone structure Nikolaus Pevsner wrote that, along with the Ruthwell Cross, just over the border, there is 'nothing as perfect as these two crosses of comparable date in the whole of Europe'.[44]

Missionary and teaching functions were the purpose of these edifices, including images setting out doctrines of the eucharist. A cross fragment, of the Anglian period, from Beetham near Arnside in south Cumbria, which displays the loaves and fishes from the prefiguration of the eucharist in Mark 6:34-44,

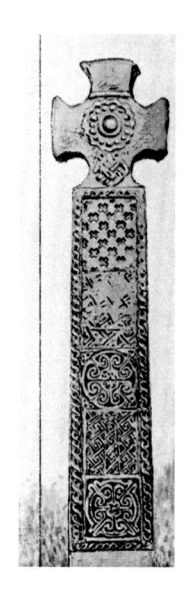

The Crosses at Dearham (top right) and Irton (top left) and the fragments at Dacre (bottom) as drawn by W G Collingwood in 1899

Matthew 14:14-21 and Luke 9:12-17, projects such an analogy. The Bewcastle cross carries an image of the vine, a motif of Mediterranian origin, the source of the eucharistic wine, a symbol also found in a cross fragment at Eaglesfield, near Cockermouth.[45]

A further doctrinal message is embedded at Bewcastle's western face, which has four panels, the top one depicting John the Baptist carrying Christ as the 'Lamb of God'; below it is one of this country's earliest images of Christ: a conqueror over sin and death, He stands upon a lion and a serpent. It is probably St John who again appears at the foot of the structure.[46]

Complex theological content features in a stone shaft at Dacre, which Collingwood dated to the Viking period. The lowest panel displays the Fall of Man in the persons of Adam and Eve and is a rare example in English sculpture before the Norman Conquest of the depiction of this theme. As a counterpoint to the Fall, an upper panel discloses the Sacrifice of Isaac in Genesis 22:1-18. Early scriptural commentators interpreted Isaac's sacrifice as a pre-figurement - a 'type' - of Christ's, an interpretation that was widely understood in England in that period. Something more complex, however, is going on in the Dacre shaft, for in some Christian thinking of the period Isaac's sacrifice was itself intensely and inherently positive in its significance, since Abraham's surrender to God's will brought about a kind of early closure to the estrangement between God and humanity that the Fall, which is depicted in the lowest panel, had initiated. There is also a panel displaying the subject of the hart and hound which 'can be interpreted as a Christological image, as a symbol ... of the same redemptive sacrifice to which the Isaac scene alludes'. This series contains sophisticated theological Scriptural and typological thinking that might be expected to survive in one of the 'three known pre-Viking

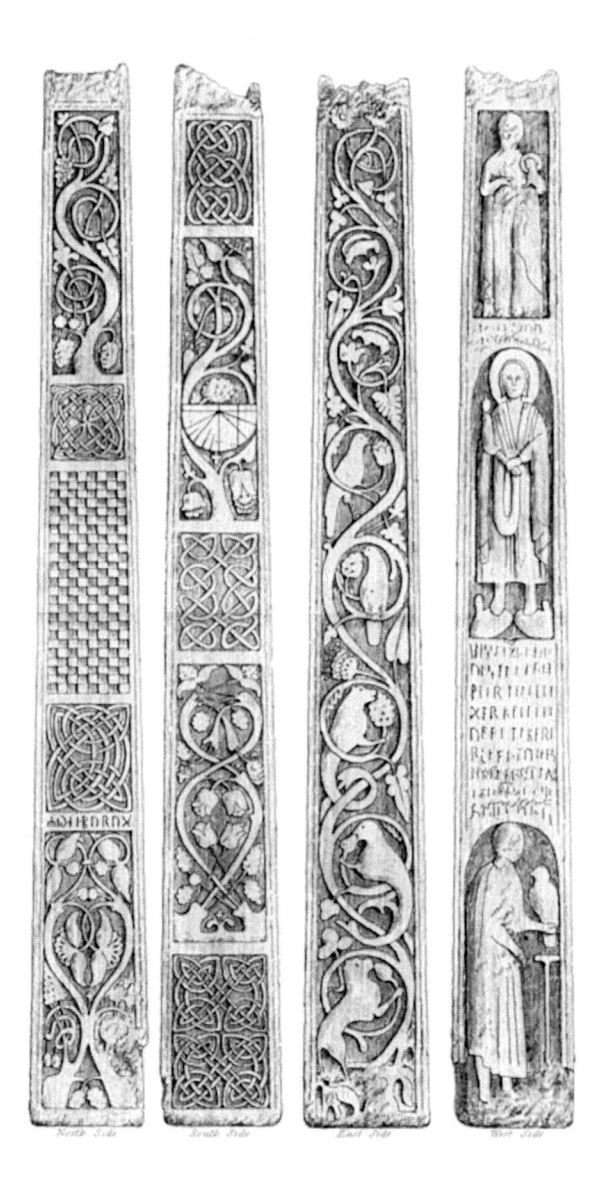

The four faces of the Bewcastle Cross

monasteries in Cumbria'.[47]

By the later 9th century what had begun as Scandinavian invasion in the Lakes area had been transformed into Norse migration, with new pastoralist farmers, often secondary 'Norse-Irish' migrants from eastern Ireland and the Isle of Man, taking to the higher dales and fells - Patterdale, at the southern foot of Ullswater, was settled by a 10th-century Norse-Irish immigrant named Patraic [48] - while the agriculturalist Anglians remained in the fertile lowlands, such as the Eden valley. The literary, religious and artistic traditions of the newcomers were rooted in Norse paganism and its pantheon, so that a complicated artistic negotiation was required to establish an intelligible relationship between the Christian faith that had been established in this region and the religio-cultural legacy of the 'new Cumbrians'.

The best-known attempt at forging a synthesis between these two traditions was made in the 10th century, in the form of a sandstone cross, 4.5 metres in height, the great wheel-headed structure at Gosforth, full of drama and incident. In its various narrative instalments, themes from the Norse pre-Christian oral tradition predominate. The south face presents a creature resembling a seal; a wolf leaps in the air; a stag perhaps represents Odin, god of magic, wisdom, farming, battle and poetry, along with the giant-god Mimir whose fountain, filled by a spring flowing from the great ash tree Yggdrasil, gave Odin his wisdom; the wolf Garm may be present; there is a snake consuming its own tail and another snake, in knots; Loki, the god of conflict and evil is depicted, with his conqueror Sigyn, holding a poisoned chalice; a rider appears, upside down, and a figure aligned with Heimdall, the god of light who keeps watch over the rainbow bridge; wolves with twisted torsos and a dragon surmount this face.[49]

Clearly, the composer or composers of this statuary

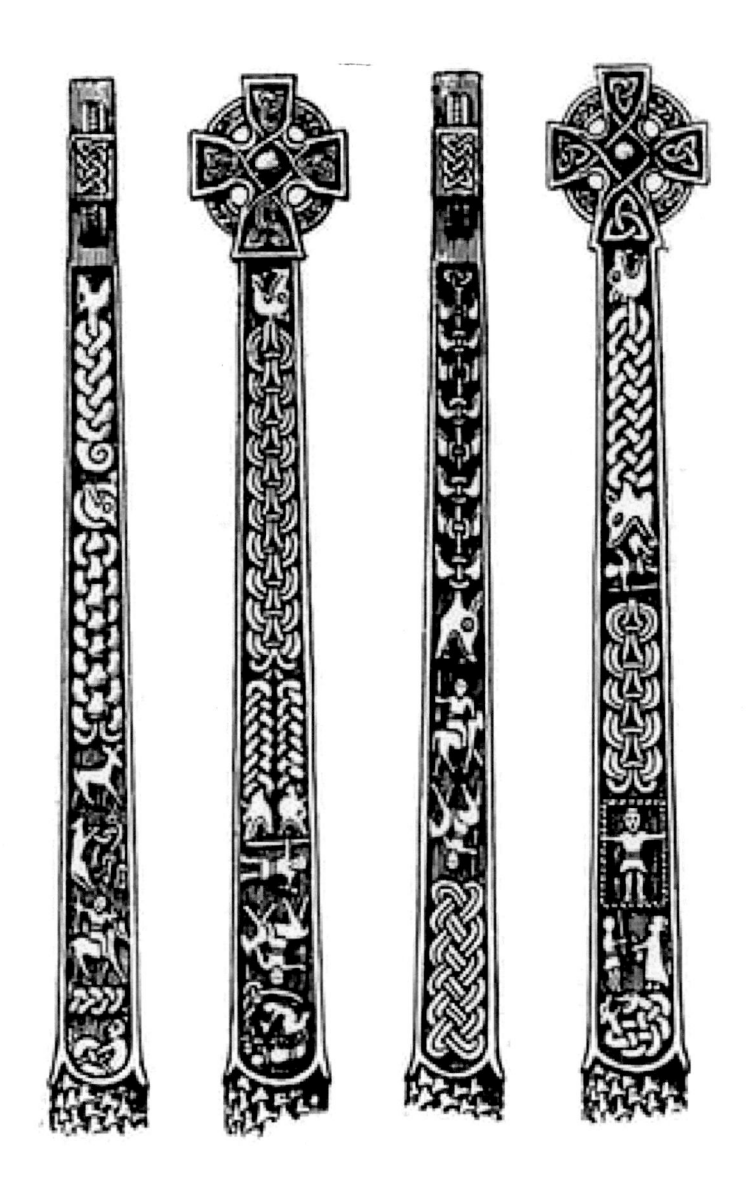

The four faces of the Gosforth Cross

possessed deep familiarity with the complexity and richness of the inherited Scandinavian belief system and its key figures but although in this monument 'distinctly Christian emblems are curiously mixed up with emblems as distinctly heathen', across the entire composition the identifiable Christian elements are in the minority: 'Only the cross-head, small and ringed, with triquetra on both sides, and *the Crucifixion on the E* [my emphasis], are Christian'.[50]

That 'Only' however, is highly significant. The ringed 'wheel cross at the summit of the monument is a Christian symbol and each of its four arms contains the Triquetra, often used in Irish art to signify the Trinity'. As with the Mediterranean vine motifs in crosses at Bewcastle and Eaglesfield, the triquetra symbol points towards a faith that was *katholikos* - universal. For the purpose of the Gosforth structure was that of asserting the triumph of Christianity over its pagan rivals - a process narrated in the Norse work known as the *Völuspá* - the 'Witch's Prophecy'.[51]

In the centre of the east side of the Gosforth statuary, Christ's own victory is announced in His manifestation as the universal *Salvator Mundi,* Saviour of the World, shedding His redemptive blood for the whole of mankind; the centurion thrusts his spear at the moment of Christ's redeeming death and conquest, and Mary Magdalene acts as the delegate of saved humankind, while around this victory of the cross the Norse deities are consigned to a *Götterdämmerung* - the 'downfall of the gods', 'the story of Ragnarök and the doom of the Old Norse gods'.[52]

The Gosforth wheeled cross is also part of a suite of regional Christian doctrinal proclamations in stone statuary, another example of which is to be found in the cross known as the 'Giant's Thumb' in St Andrew's churchyard in Penrith. There the wheel-head, as is the case with the specimen at Knockross,

The Giant's Grave, in the Churchyard, Penrith, Cumberland, drawn by Thomas Allom, 1835.

Bowness-on-Solway, is 'of the type seen across much of the northern part of Cumbria and the west coast, extending southward into Cheshire'. These individual works, however, belong within a coherent educational and artistic programme, linking the sculptures in Penrith churchyard 'with more distant instances of the genre to the north and west of Penrith itself, as at Aspatria, Bewcastle, Beckermet and Gosforth' - a 'corpus of known pre-Conquest sculptures ... parts of complex sculptural groups'.[53]

In the Penrith and Gosforth works, it was representations of the person of Christ that guided the artistry A stone statue unearthed in Nether Denton, 12 miles from Carlisle, where a church existed in 1170, is about two feet long and 15 inches across and has a carved figure, 19½ inches long and 4½ inches across. Standing out in high relief from the cross as a background,

The figure of Christ from St Cuthbert's, Nether Denton

the figure is 'full length, apparently bearded, dressed in a simple double-breasted robe and holding a sceptre or rod' - a 'fine, smallish Norman figure ... with sceptre (?), set against a cross with arms extending Maltese fashion beyond a small central circle ... a very good piece, and ... reminiscent of the French mid C12'.[54]

This figure is of Christ, in a triple projection of Him as 'priest, prophet and king' - '*Majestas*, Christ in Majesty', grasping the sceptre, 'reigning from the tree' of the cross, triumphant over death, '*victor rex*' - 'victorious king'- as the Easter hymn expresses it, Lord of Creation, *Pantocrater*. Then, as this intricate work unfolds its meaning, the figure is revealed, vested as a priest, Jesus the 'High Priest', as in the Letter to the Hebrews, chapter 5, his clothing resembling that worn in the serene representation of the Crucifixion, in a processional ivory crucifix of 1063, in the church of San Isidro de Léon (Madrid Archaeological Museum) or by Giovanni Cimabué (c. 1240-c. 1302) in the church of S. Domenico in Arezzo.[55]

Over the course of the post-Roman centuries of preaching and mission in the north-west, a focused cult of Christ the Sovereign Redeemer had been inculcated, set out iconographically and didactically in the monumental assemblage that has been studied in this chapter.

Chapter 4:
Faith and Religion in the Early Medieval Lake Counties

As far as the English north-western border region was concerned, the Norman Conquest that began with the victory of William I (r. 1066-87) at Hastings in 1066 saw an acceleration of the process of church settlement that had begun before the Conquest, while there was extensive continuity in ecclesiastical life in this region as between the periods before and after 1066. Sited on its 'low rounded eminence' in the heart of the town, Penrith's St Andrew's church is 'clearly of ancient origin', with its 9th-10th century sculptures in the churchyard, while the 'fact that the Bishop's Row was granted to the diocese of Carlisle at the creation of the see in 1122 perhaps suggests that this entity was an ancient block of church land' - but also a continuing 'parochial centre from the medieval period onwards'.[56]

A link between the pre-Conquest Scandinavian Christian legacy and the post-Conquest Norman hegemony is present in Bridekirk, with its Norse suffix *kirka*, 'a church' - Bridget's church - 'standing in an area thickly populated by the Vikings who landed on the Cumbrian coast'. Adopted as a Norman establishment, it was donated to Guisborough Priory in Yorkshire in the mid-12th century, followed by extensive re-building.[57]

Morland church in Westmorland provides a further example of such continuity, since it 'includes the remains of the finest Anglo-Saxon structure in Cumbria, comprising what seems to be an eleventh century, very strongly constructed free standing tower with high plinth'. However, alongside such survivals is the fact that 60 Cumbrian churches display post-Conquest Norman work, while in 21 other cases documents prove a Norman origin: Gosforth has Norman building; Ulverston is basically a Norman church; Kirkby Lonsdale gives us one of 'the finest and most complex of the region's Norman churches'; there is further Norman work at Kirkby Stephen and Sedbergh; at Crosby Garrett and Crosby Ravensworth durable church buildings may have replaced pre-Conquest preaching crosses; at Appleby, St Lawrence's, contains Norman features, as do Kirkby Thore and Milburn churches, and there are Norman origins at Dacre, Barton, Denton and Kirklinton. The post-Conquest building programme was accomplished with considerable speed: about 80 churches in the Cumbrian lowlands are datable to before c. 1200.[58]

Alongside this post-Conquest revolution in Cumbrian church building, there was a strong continuity of clerical personnel, with the Celtic stratum surviving markedly, as revealed by the number of west Cumberland priests in the early and mid-12th century whose names begin with the Celtic prefix *Gille* - disciple or *dévot*, such as the priest Coremac Gille Becoe - Cormac, follower of St Bega - at St Bees.[59]

Where *dis*continuity did take place in post-Conquest Cumbria, and with massive consequences for the religious character of the region, was in the settlement, which was at first hesitant, of a new French-speaking military baronial caste endowed with vast estates by successive Norman kings. The delayed Normanisation of this region and its inclusion in the Norman-English kingdom - rather than that of the Scots - was accomplished in 1092, when William II Rufus (r. 1087-1100) brought his army to Carlisle, evicting the Scottish ruler, Dolfin, and constructing a castle.

The Norman kings' feudal barons were eager to endow the Church. William Rufus made over to his steward, Ivo de

Taillebois (d. c. 1094), the barony of Kentdale - Kendal - as well as the lordship of Kirkby Stephen. In turn, in the 1090s de Taillebois transferred Kirkby Stephen church and its revenues to one of the most important monasteries in the north, St Mary's Abbey in York, along with Kendal, Heversham and Kirkby Lonsdale churches, embracing these within the wider ambit of European Benedictine monasticism.[60]

The originally Anglian church at Kirkby Lonsdale had been destroyed in the invasion by William the Lion (r. 1165-1214) of Scotland in 1173; re-built and presented to St Mary's Abbey in 1240, it remained, nonetheless, in the possession of the parson Adam, protected by aristocratic patrons.[61]

From 1120 Randolph (Ranulph, or Ranulf) de Bricquessart (d. c. 1129), *vicomte* of Bayeux and earl of Chester, known as le Meschin, lord of Cumberland and Westmorland, established the small Benedictine Priory at Wetheral, while his brother William le Meschin (d. c. 1134) founded the Benedictine Priory at St Bees in about 1125.[62]

Members of the family of the Norman William de Lancaster I were major benefactors of St Bees. William was related to Ketel Eldredsson (c. 1094-1120), who presented the churches of Morland, Bromfield and Workington to St Mary's Abbey, the Benedictine mother house of St Bees. In c. 1170 William de Lancaster II (d. 1180) donated 'the whole of the land in Newby' in Kendal to St Peter's Hospital in York.[63]

In c. 1150 Alan, lord of Allerdale, gave to the Augustinian Prior and convent of Carlisle the new Norman church of Ireby, near Skiddaw, in the Caldbeck Fells. The donation was accompanied with that of a relic of the True Cross, and the Priory appointed non-monastic ('secular') priests as chaplains to conduct services.[64]

The architectural quality of early medieval Lakeland

churches varied considerably. Some rural chapels must have been 'only simple structures put up by the people themselves'. Even so, increasingly elaborate embellishments were being made to local churches, including finely worked grave slabs. One that has made an escape from the churchyard of Distington's Holy Spirit features a sword, a cross, six annulets (signifying chainmail rings) and 'Calvary steps' (a Latin cross mounted on three steps), all in a tradition linking the design with the Crusader Adam de Yrton.[65]

In Cumbria's challenging geography and climate, central parochial churches generated subordinate rural chapels of ease, giving parishioners access to the Church's services without arduous journeys to mother churches, especially in winter. Kentigern's great church at Crosthwaite commanded a vast parish that 'once stretched from the top of Bassenthwaite Lake to Dunmail Raise, with five chapels run from one church'.[66]

The main institutional barrier to the convenience of having these locally-situated subsidiary chapels was a 'hardening' of parochial 'vested interests, since the grant of parochial rights to a chapel meant the loss of valuable fees to the incumbent of the mother church'. Those pecuniary rights centred on burials, on which fees were claimed by mother churches, though, after about 1160, Hawkshead, a dependency of Dalton-in-Furness, had its own funerary rights, without which 'Christian burial would often have been impossible', resulting in a horrific situation where 'the inhabitants were compelled in bad or wintery weather to allow their dead to remain unburied, or to deposit their bodies in woods, streams, or lakes'. In Cumbria, the chapel of ease system shows 'how well the medieval Church served these remote hamlets', bringing to 'the people the ministry of the Church'.[67]

Overseeing these parochial arrangements, in the 12th century the Cumberland diocese of Carlisle and the city Priory of St Mary were established, the latter on the basis of a pre-Conquest city church, with a dedication to the Blessed Virgin Mary. The establishment was served - the only one in England - by Canons Regular of the Augustinian Order, the 'Black Canons' - priests living in community and observing the daily choral 'office', though not monastic, and able to take on pastoral responsibilities.

There has been some discussion of the chronology of the foundation of the Priory. H. S. Offler drew attention to a late 13th-century tradition, recorded in the *Liber de gestis Anglorum* - ' The Book of the Deeds of the English People' - that, in 1101 or 1102, King Henry I (r. 1100-35), encouraged by his pious queen, Matilda (1079/80-1118), introduced an unspecified group of Canons Regular into Carlisle. Henry was said to have appointed the priest Walter, a long-standing Norman royal servant, who founded the church of the city just before his death, upon which the king awarded his lands and goods to the Augustinian Canons Regular, promoting Adelweld, prior of Nostell in the West Riding, as their Prior. Evidence concerning Walter the Priest, however, indicates 'that the veracity of the 1102 date is very doubtful and that this "unspecified" community did not exist'.[68]

The present consensus, then, is that the 1122 dating is pivotal, since it marked Henry I's decisive move to inaugurate the diocese, priory and foundation of Canons Regular, with his visit to the city in 1122, part of a move made in order to advance his strategy of fortifying the frontier with Scotland, resisting the expansion southward of the diocese of Glasgow. Henry was determined to ensure that the Cumberland diocese would come under the jurisdiction of the northern English metropolitan, the Archbishop of York, of which it would become a suffragan see: 'a politically crude anti-Scottish political manoeuvre to elevate an obscure struggling house of canons into the cathedral of the new diocese of Carlisle'. The new bishopric took in northern Westmorland and the tracts of Cumberland to the north of the river Derwent, together 'the area long claimed by Scotland'. The rest of Cumberland and much of south Westmorland were devolved to the diocese of York and its immense archdeaconry of Richmond. Coupland, Furness and Cartmel, and Lancashire north of the Sands, were left out of the new creation, as was the 'anomalous' enclave of Alston.[69]

The construction of Carlisle Cathedral, beginning in 1133, absorbed the pre-Conquest parochial church of St Mary. The last of the English cathedrals to be built during the middle ages, and one of the smallest in the country, the 12th-century Romanesque (or Norman) edifice was also to be the first of four phases of building over the course of the medieval centuries. The initial programme would have been speeded up by the availability of already worked Roman masonry. Its layout, which was 'of moderate dimensions and simple details, displaying no unusual features', was cross-shaped, with a eight-bay nave and a tower at the cross-over between the north and south transepts.[70]

For contemporaries, the new Cathedral must have suggested a renaissance in Carlisle's fortunes - 'the first stone building of any size to be created [there] since the Roman occupation ... a source of pride and satisfaction to its builders and contemporaries'. The border settlement was now transformed into 'a major religious centre in the outer zone of the medieval kingdom of England'. Carlisle now had ecclesiastical administration as one of its leading functions, a role unfolding over the course of time in the creation of a succession of urban churches, hospitals and friaries. The Cathedral apart, Carlisle's religious renewal was led off by the royal-sponsored restoration of the Cathedral's near neighbour, St Cuthbert's church. Linked with Cuthbert's visits to the city in 685-6, it had been destroyed by the Vikings in 876 and left for some time in ruins, until William II ordered its rebuilding from c. 1095 onwards.[71]

Beyond the city, the Augustinian Canons' non-monastic status gave them a flexible ministry which included parochial and hospital work within the diocese. Between 1154 and the 1180s, Gamel de Pennington, lord of Pennington, with assistance from William de Lancaster I had founded Conishead Priory as a hospital run by the Augustinian Canons in aid of 'poor decrepid, indigent, and lepers in the environs of Ulverston'. The Canons also had the care of St Leonard's Hospital in Kendal, as well as providing guidance over the dangerous tidal sands of Morecambe Bay. The Priory was endowed by de Pennington with the churches of Pennington and Muncaster and owned a minor estate at Langdale.[72]

Based initially in the Carlisle Priory, the Augustinian Canons proceeded to bring about a major extension of the range of endowed religious houses in Cumberland. Between 1165 and 1174, by a gift of Robert de Vaux, or de Vallibus (d.1195), lord of Gilsland in c. 1165, sheriff of Carlisle in 1174 and of Cumberland between 1175 and 1185, the Canons were established at Lanercost, on the river Irthing, near Brampton. In line with Augustinian custom, the priory was dedicated to the symbol of penitence, Mary Magdalene, whose image still surmounts the west door of the church. The building work may have begun in c. 1175-80, using stone from Hadrian's Wall.[73]

A list dated 1181 gives, as churches belonging to the Priory, Walton, Irthington, Brampton, Carlattton, Farlam, Grinsdale, Denton and Distington, and, thanks to other donations from Robert de Vaux, member of his family and other magnates, by 1220 the house possessed the Irthing valley on both of its banks. Even so, much 'of this land was marginal and just about cultivable and it was the task of the canons, *conversi* [lay brothers], villeins and paid labour to explore and exploit its potential'. Lanercost 'was never a very large or important house', unlikely to have ever housed more than 12 Canons.[74] Even so, its proximity to the border as the region's northernmost religious house bestowed on it both insecurity and prestige as a strategic centre which was to be visited by King Edward I (r. 1272-1307).

In 1186 William Marshall (c. 1146-1219), 1st earl of Pembroke and Strigul, was awarded the crown estate of Cartmel, west of Grange-over-Sands, in Lancashire 'north of the Sands', and proceeded in c. 1189 to award it to a community of Augustinian Canons from Bradenstoke Priory in Wiltshire, granting them all the land of Cartmel, as far north as the east bank of Windermere, plus properties in Ireland, though, for whatever reason, 'with a clause that it should never be erected into a priory'.[75] In the annexed church of St Mary and St Michael the Canons made provision for local parish worship.

By 1201, after migrations involving Cockersand in Lancashire and Preston Patrick in Westmorland, Canons Regular of the Premonstratensian Order, founded by Norbert (c. 1080-1134), Archbishop of Magdeburg, had settled at Shap, in the Lowther valley in Westmorland, on land donated by Thomas de Workington (d. 1200), with dependent churches in Shap, Warcop and Bampton.[76]

One of Shap's dependent churches, that of St Margaret and St James, at nearby Long Marton, granted in 1170, acquired two remarkable tympana - a tympanum being the 'surface between a lintel and the arch above it or within a pediment'. As Rita Wood has shown, these 'forceful and barbaric' features, 'carved in shallow relief', include a 'winged dragon with a knotted tail, a quadruped with a wing on its neck and a tiny head, and a winged shield'. St Michael, 'champion of mankind', is depicted, along

Cartmel Priory: Samuel and Nathaniel Buck, 1737

with the Trinity and angels. A boat, standing for the Church, is steered by the Apostle Peter, the fisherman believed by Catholics to have been the first pope. The elaborate doorway and the tympana had particular liturgical use in the Palm Sunday processions at the opening of Holy Week [77] - this church's relationship with Shap Abbey probably enhancing the solemnity of its ritual.

At some point during the reign of Henry II (r. 1154-89), Torphin, son of Robert, made an award of the manor of Ravenstonedale, near Kirkby Stephen in Westmorland, to the Priory of Watton, in the East Riding, of an establishment of a master and three Canons. The convent was made up of Gilbertine Canons Regular, of the Order founded by Gilbert of Sempringham (c. 1083/9-1189), the only indigenous English medieval religious order. Through the 13th century Watton retained the small cell housed on the north side of the parish church, but by 1405 there had been no incumbent for some time. In 1539, as part of Henry VIII's (r. 1509-47) Dissolution of the Monasteries, the property was transferred to the Archbishop of York, later to Sir Thomas Wharton (1495-1568) and eventually

Long Marton Tympanum

to the Lowther family of Lowther.[78]

As the presence of the orders of Canons Regular thus expanded in the Lakes region, the more purely contemplative monastic life, centred on the *Opus Dei* - 'God's work', that of prayer - flourished from the 12th century onwards. Leading the post-Conquest monastic foundations in the region was the establishment by Randolph, or Ranulph, le Meschin , perhaps in 1106, but no later than 1112, of the Benedictine Priory at Wetheral, in the Eden valley just north of Carlisle, conveying it, with its 12 incumbents, as a cell or dependency of St Mary's Abbey, York; he added to the Priory's endowments the two churches in his town of Appleby, a grant confirmed for St Michael's by Pope Gregory IX (r. 1227-41). Henry I awarded a mill, a fishery, woodland and a chapel at nearby Warwick and two ploughlands in neighbouring Corby.[79]

In 1124 Stephen of Blois (1097?- 1154), count of Mortain and Boulogne, made a grant of land near Preston to members of the French monastic order of Savigny, in Normandy. In 1127 the group of 12 of the Savigny brethren, led by their Abbot, migrated to the 'Valley of the Deadly Nightshade', on the outskirts of modern Barrow-in-Furness, and began building their monastery, quarrying the red sandstone from the cliff sides and establishing at the site the leading English Savigniac Abbey. In 1148, the Abbot of Savigny united his order with that of the Cistercians, who had been established at Cîteaux in Burgundy in 1098, dedicated to strict observance of the monastic Rule of St Benedict of Nursia (c. 480-c.550): Savigniac Furness was thus incorporated into the Cistercian family.[80]

At the end of 1149 or the beginning of the following year, a party of Cistercian monks from Melrose Abbey in Roxburghshire, set up as a Cistercian house in 1136, established the new Abbey of Holm Cultram, near Wigton in west Cumberland. The patron was Prince Henry of Scotland (c. 1115-53), earl of Huntingdon, younger son of Scotland's King David I ('the Saint', r. 1124-53), supported by Alan, son of Waldeve, lord of Allerdale, and giving the Abbey the lordship of Holm Cultram. This was a distinctly Scottish foundation, a daughter of Melrose, set up during a brief re-occupation of the area, and the Scottish link was confirmed by Henry II when he resumed English control of the region in 1157. In 1179 Holm Cultram received a grant of land allowing it to set up a grange at Haile, south of Egremont, while urban property in Fisher Street in Carlisle came into the possession of the Abbey.[81]

In January 1134 12 Savigniac monks of Furness, led by their Abbot Gerald, received from William le Meschin (d. 1134), as lord of Copeland, land at Calder (near Sellafield), close to the centre of William's lordship at Egremont. Three years later, they were driven out by Scots raiders, were refused re-admission to Furness, where Gerald attempted to retain the status of Abbot,

Holm Cultram: Samuel and Nathaniel Buck, 1739

and settled at Byland in north Yorkshire until, in 1143, the Abbot of Furness sent a second group back to Calder, led by Abbot Hardred. As seen earlier, in 1148 the Order of Savigny was merged with the Cistercians, Calder, Furness and Byland, being incorporated into the unification. Extensive donations to Calder followed, including, in c. 1155, from Cicely, countess of Albemarle, a house in Egremont, two coastal saltworks, fisheries on the river Derwent, forestry and pastures, while William de Esseby and his wife made over to Calder the village of Beckermet, with pastures, a mill and fishery. A map shows over 20 estates in west Cumberland, from Millom in the south to Gilcrux in the north. Even so, 'Calder remained poor and obscure', its limited finances restricting its building plans.[82]

The saint's cult from which the coastal Benedictine Priory of St Bees took its name was that of 'the shadowy and hypothetical saint', the refugee Irish princess and virgin Bega, who was reputed to have spent time as a hermit at the site and was associated with a wonder-working ring or bracelet. In about 1125, a Benedictine Priory dedicated to Bega was established thereabouts as a daughter cell of St Mary's Abbey, York. The

St Bees: Samuel and Nathaniel Buck, 1739

Priory also had oversight of chapels at Loweswater, Wasdale, Ennerdale and Eskdale.[83]

In c.1190-1200, the female Benedictine contemplative life was established, probably by a grant of Henry Fitzarthur, lord of Millom, at Seton, alias Lekeley, near Bootle in south-west Cumberland, in a small Priory, dedicated to the Blessed Virgin Mary. Though the house was granted the income of the church of Irton and the leper hospital of St Leonard in Lancaster, it was very poor: on the eve of the Dissolution of the Monasteries betwen 1536 and 1540, only 17 out of 72 Benedictine nunneries in England and Wales had incomes worth less than its sum of under £314 pa. Scandal struck the little house in c. 1381, the case being taken up to the highest ecclesiastical levels, when Margaret Prestwich petitioned to the effect that 'certain of her friends compelled her against her will to enter the the Priory of Nuns of Seton ... . She remained there as in a prison for several years, escaped and was married'. Although by deputation from Pope Urban VI (r. 1378-89) the Bishop of Coventry and Lichfield 'released her from her observance of the ... Order or any other', the dispute dragged on into the 1390s.[84]

In 1480 the small number of Benedictine sisters of Armathwaite, mid-way between Penrith and Carlisle, aiming to invent a greater antiquity and value for their establishment than it in fact possessed, decided 'to reinvent their own charter, spuriously dating their foundation to 1089 and to William Rufus' (William II): the forged charter, whose validity was upheld by the crown, claimed that King William had made over to the nuns extensive land grants, including 216 acres in Inglewood Forest, a rent of £2 pa. from royal property in Carlisle and freedom from tolls throughout the kingdom.[85]

Although the instability of the border region made the female conventual life largely insupportable, the first Norman century in Cumbria saw the implementation, thanks to baronial land grants, of the corporate religious life, in the forms of the Augustinian, Premonstratensian and Gilbertine Canons Regular and the contemplative Benedictine and Cistercians monks, a structure that would remain in place until the Dissolution of the English religious houses in 1536-40. A structure of parishes and their churches was laid out. Other additions to organised religion in the medieval Lakes region such as the development of Carlisle Cathedral and the addition of parish churches, the setting up of charitable hospitals, the further evolution of the monastic system and the arrival of the Mendicant preaching friars in the 13th century, will be dealt with in the next chapter.

Chapter 5:
Religion in the Medieval Lake Counties

The relatively peaceful and prosperous 13th century formed a period of renewal, religious creativity and reform in Europe, one of its features being the construction of the great Gothic cathedrals such as Amiens (begun 1220), Chartres (mostly 1194-1260), Cologne (begun late 13th century) and Salisbury (begun 1220).

Carlisle's place in this building wave was marked by the replacement of the Cathedral's early, and plain, eight-bay Romanesque structure. In 1218 the Cistercian Abbot Hugh de Beaulieu (d. 1223) became Bishop of Carlisle and in c.1220 commenced work on the new structure, designed in the variant of the medieval Gothic style known as Early English. Twelve feet wider than its predecessor, with additional space for Mass altars, the building had as its centrepiece a much enlarged choir, which was burned down in the city fire of 1292, a catastrophe requiring a second re-construction.[86]

The dynamism of Bishop Hugh in initiating the rebuilding and of Ralph de Irton (Bishop, 1280-92) in raising the funds for the completion of the work offers a reminder of how important the personality, character and ability of a Bishop were in managing a medieval diocese, not least one as remote, impoverished and embattled as Carlisle was. Following Henry II's recovery of Cumberland, the see remained vacant, until in 1204 King John (r. 1199-1216) appointed to the vacancy the 'Serbian émigré', Bernard, Archbishop of Ragusa, providing him with an allowance of £13 13 4d pa. In the meantime, the Priory had gained some endowments, but when Hugh of Beaulieu succeeded the bishopric remained poor, with small number of appropriated Northumberland churches, plus a few in and around Carlisle. Further, the diocese seems to have become accustomed to not having a head, and standards of clerical discipline were low, with priests resorting to 'judicial combat'- trial by battle - and benefices being inherited by relatives of incumbents.[87]

The endemic poverty of the Carlisle diocese - in 1292 it was the second poorest in England, with an income of £127 pa. - meant that there was an undertow of conflict between bishops and the Priory over scarce resources, quarrels which Beaulieu's successor, Walter Mauclerk (Bishop 1224-46), tried to avoid by acquiring property, in nearby Dalston and in Horncastle in Lincolnshire, that was not claimed by the Priory. Mauclerk's successor, Silvester de Everdon (Bishop 1247-54), had a distinguished career in the royal service of Henry III (r. 1216-72) and, as 'the lord King's faithful clerk [cleric], dear and close', a 'trusted and efficient' agent, de Everdon was elected to the see by direct royal intervention, though initially declining it before taking it up: he may have been influenced by the contemporaneous movement of Catholic Church reform, which drew a sharp distinction between the pastoral dimension of the Bishop's role and its political aspects as an office under the crown.[88]

A major challenge that de Everdon faced was that of resolving the long-standing discord with the Priory over income, the Canons insisting on having their own means, rather than simply sharing resources with the Bishop. In 1248 the Canons obtained a papal prohibition on the Bishop's disposing of their property without their consent, but over the following year de Everdon worked out a distribution of property that was acceptable to both sides and which proved durable. This and

Carlisle Cathedral: Kip, 1702

others of Bishop de Everdon's negotiations probably contributed to the release of funds that allowed the cathedral building project to continue.[89]

De Everdon, then, was 'a man who made things work ... [and] in that capacity he was a good Bishop. He settled disputes, made arrangements for the proper financing of vicarages ... [advanced] royal authority in north-west England ... and the king's control over the diocese itself', being noted for 'honesty, patience, conscientiousness and an eye for detail'.[90]

Within the city, the enrichment of religious provisions continued through the 13th century. While St Cuthbert's survived as a parish church, population increase required the building of Holy Trinity, probably in the northern Caldewgate suburb, to the west of the river Caldew. It was not, however, a durable institution, given its exposure to pillaging from across the border.[91]

From at least 1201 a new chapel, dedicated to St Alban, was brought into being on today's Scotch Street. In 1356 the chapel received vestments and liturgical vessels from a chaplain and 'continued to be favoured by the townspeople ... until it was ... extinguished between 1546 and 1549'.[92]

Benevolent foundations in the city followed, for the 13th century was the golden age of charitable hospitals in Europe, divided into three main types - the hospice or 'house of refuge'; the almshouse, providing relief for the needy, the aged and the mentally ill; and the leper hospital. W. G. Wiseman enumerated at least 17 medieval hospitals in this region.[93]

Carlisle's leper hospital of St Nicholas, first documented in 1201 in a letter of favour from King John, was, for sanitary reasons, set up outside the city walls, in the area of the present St Nicholas Street, and became 'the largest and richest of the medieval hospitals of Cumbria', occupying three acres of land and consisting of a house for the patients, known as brethren, a chapel, cloister and separate accommodation for the men and women assistants. Between 1218 and 1223 responsibility for its running was transferred from the Canons to the Bishop. By 1292 its role had probably 'changed to that of the long-term care of 12 infirm men under the direction of a master and chaplain', and in the following year its rules were tightened up by Hugh de Cressingham. The institution's vulnerable position as an isolation hospital beyond the walls led to its total destruction by John Comyn (d. 1313?), 3rd earl of Buchan, in a raid in 1296, though it was soon afterwards re-built, and in 1306 Edward I presented a gold brooch valued at five marks to the image of St Nicholas in the church. In 1340, however, a royal commission inspecting the establishment found it much run down.[94]

Further decline in this charity set in in the 14th and 15th centuries, for money was 'siphoned off' by an absentee master, and Carlisle's shrinking economy reduced donations from the citizens. In 1404 an episcopal enquiry was conducted 'into diverse defects in the houses and other buildings and the books, vestments and other ornaments through the negligence of the master and wardens and their ministers, the dissipation and alienation of the lands, possessions and goods and the diminution of divine services and other works of piety'. The hospital was transferred to the Prior and Canons in 1477 and then surrendered to the new Dean and Chapter in 1541, the remaining structure being badly damaged in the civil war siege of 1645, and 'altogther ruynated' by 1650.[95]

Another Carlisle hospital was dedicated to the Holy Sepulchre, perhaps to mark the gift to the Priory of stones believed to come from Christ's tomb and brought back from the Holy Land by a pilgrim or crusader. The hospital's existence was first recorded in 1220, and at some point in the 13th century it occupied five acres of royal demesne. However, having two such institutions in the city may have appeared to be something of a luxury, and it seems likely that, before the end of the 13th century, Holy Sepulchre was absorbed into St Nicholas's.[96]

Beyond the city, a steady progress of improvement and enlargement in the diocese's parish churches continued. In Caldbeck, the short chancel was extended in the 12th and 13th centuries and the inner doorway in the 13th century. In the southwest, Millom had a small Norman church in red freestone, 'very dark and draughty', with unglazed windows high up the wall. In c. 1228 William de Boyvill transferred the advowson - the right of appointment of a priest - to Furness Abbey and had a south aisle added. Windows at the east end may have been contributed by Furness Abbey, along with the 'hard, fine-grained red freestone octagonal font' which bears the arms of the Abbey.[97]

The records of Castle Sowerby church provide a chronicle of parochial development, from a 12th-century establishment onwards. The 13th century saw an upsurge of royal favour, both

English and Scots, towards this church, with a gift from King John and the appointment to it by Henry III of John le Franceys - John the Frenchman - and in 1294 John Balliol, king of Scots (r. 1292-6), installed a priest.[98]

(2) The Monastic System

Alongside this continuing programme of providing and improving parish churches, the monastic system became ever more fully entrenched in the regional scene.

Isolated on the coast, St Bees 'appears to have had little dealings with the ecclesiastical world in its papal or diocesan aspect', even though three former Priors became Abbots of St Mary's, York. In the mid-13th century the Priory masterminded the 'logical and enterprising' Rottington Beck scheme, an unusual example of 'medieval civil engineering which lasted for six centuries'. Endowments to religious houses from the landed classes continued to flow in: in the reign of Henry II Gamel de Pennington of Muncaster, lord of Orton, had appropriated Orton, Pennington and Muncaster churches to the Priory, an award that was confirmed by Bishop John de Ross in c. 1327. Conishead received from the widow Custance de Haile a quarter acre of land in Haile and the advowson of the church. In c. 1327 the will of William (d. 1457), 5th Lord Harington, bequeathed 100 marks to lead the roof of the Priory - along with £20 to Cartmel 'for its building', two sums of money to Carlisle friars and '10 marks for their prayers', plus sums of 20 shillings each to the friars of Penrith and Appleby.[99]

Holm Cultram was another recipient of a long series of lay awards: early in the 13th century Richard Gernun confirmed the grant to the Abbey of the church of Burgh-by-Sands; at some point in the second quarter of the century William, son of Gillecrist de Alnebank, ratified the right of the Abbey to fishery

Furness Abbey: Samuel and Nathaniel Buck, 1727

on the Alne, followed in 1273 and 1293 by the award of similar rights on the Derwent. In the later 13th century, Thomas de Multon endorsed the surrender of land in the vill of St Botolph: 24 acres in Distington, with pastures for 600 sheep, eight oxen, seven cows, a bull and two horses, as well as timber from Distington woods and six acres of arable and four acres of meadow land in Distington.[100]

In the mid-century John le Fleming and his wife Annabel granted to the Cistercians of Calder Abbey land in Millom or its equivalent in Beckermet, and in 1287 Sir John Hudleston (d. before 1306) made over to Calder pasture in Millom for six cows, four horses and 40 sheep, plus two acres of land at the Abbey's salt pans. Calder's economy, however, remained marginal, its properties being assessed at £32 in 1292, and it held in appropriation only the rectories of Cleator, Gilcrux and St John and St Bridget in Beckermet.[101]

The 13th and 14th centuries were a vital period in the consolidation of Furness Abbey as a great estate and an agricultural, industrial and commercial enterprise on a grand scale, controlling 'for almost four hundred years territories in the

Lake District that amounted almost to a kingdom'. The earlier decades of the 13th century saw extensive additions to the real estate that had been gifted to the Abbey in the previous era. In 1195 the heiress of the lordship of Allerdale, Alice (or Alicia) de Rumelli, had made over to the Yorkshire Cistercian house of Fountains the Watendlath valley and the low land between Bassenthwaite and Derwentwater, plus other properties. Then in 1209 Furness purchased from Lady Alice much of Borrowdale, from the head water of Derwentwater to Sty Head Pass. In Borrowdale, Furness now shared a border with its Cistercian sister, Fountains, so that 'a large segment of the central fells was used from the beginning of the thirteenth century by the two great Cistercian abbeys for the grazing of sheep and cattle'.[102]

In 1242 the Abbot acquired the vast 14,000 acres of Upper Eskdale, in exchange for the farm of Monkfoss, on the coast below Black Combe, as well as the iron furnaces in Langstrath. Royal favour continued to advantage the Abbey. Edward III (r.1327-77) made two grants giving the monks more independence in managing the Furness fells; in 1336 the Abbot was allowed free warren - rabbit hunting - in Hawkshead, Sawrey and Claife, and in 1338 a royal licence was issued to establish new deer parks in the woodlands.[103]

Workable freestone, lead and iron deposits, forestry and a sheltered harbour at Walney Island were all on hand in Furness Abbey's neighbourhood - and it was the large quantities of iron, rather than livestock, that were targeted by Scottish raiders in 1316. Three smithies and five water mills in High Furness exploited the rich iron deposits of the area.[104] Agricultural estates developed between Coniston and Windermere, with granges, such as the manor farm, still part of today's Hawkshead Hall, 'from which they controlled the affairs of the district', dominating 'the medieval economy of the Furness Fells'.[105]

Furness indeed became an archetype of the Cistercian agribusiness plan, second only to Yorkshire's Fountains Abbey in its economic capacity.

Sheep-farming was at the centre of this varied agricultural, commercial and industrial portfolio, even though, with its close control of livestock and denudation of woodland cover through grazing, it was basically incompatible with the favoured hunting pursuits of medieval monarchies and aristocracies. Even so, in 1284 the Abbey came to an agreement with Sir John Hudleston of Millom over the question of hunting as opposed to pasture: this environmental compromise harmonised the demands of sheep farming with those of hunting, even though the issue had already been settled in favour of the former.[106]

There was, then, to be a perfect fit between, on the one hand, this region's climate and its landscape, as it emerged in a treeless ecology, and, on the other, sheep ranching, which 'brought to the area west of Windermere the sheep farming and wool trading on which the wealth of the Cistercian order was founded'. As sheep farming was extended, managed by the highly-skilled semi-monastic lay brothers known as *conversi*, Furness took its prominent place in the emergence of the wool trade as England's largest export raw material, supplying the textile industries of the Continent. There was even good fortune, in that in the Scots raid of 1319 the flocks on the western slope of the Pennines 'seem to have escaped lightly'.[107]

The Abbey's territorial reach expanded in an apparently unstoppable process, giving it an Irish Sea outlet, with the acquisition of Kirk Michael and Kirk Maughold on the Isle of Man and the establishment of the Irish daughter house of Inislaunaght, part of the colonising advance that made eastern Ireland 'the granary of the abbey'. Meanwhile, located near the Morecambe Bay shoreline, the Abbey emerged as the seigneur of the bay, with fishing rights in that great tidal lagoon and the rights to dig peat and to dry salt on the foreshore; there were a harbour and a trading post on Foulney Island.[108] Across the water to the east, there was probably a grange on the coast at Slyne, north of Lancaster. Long-standing rights to tithes of salmon taken from the Lune underlined the link.

With this versatile and resilient portfolio, it is not surprising that Furness Abbey became wealthy, successive papal awards of 'freedom from payment of tithes, &c' conferring an enviable long-term tax break. The Abbey's monetary holdings of over £40 in 1292, derived from 'rentals, proceeds from livestock, pleas and mines', were topped by only four out of the 30 taxable ecclesiastical units in the deaneries of Coupland and Furness. There was further income to be raised from tenants who paid rents allowing them to cut ash branches to be made into mats, hoops, barrels, panniers for horses and charcoal containers.[109]

It might, then, have been tempting to concentrate the Abbey's activities, as a highly capitalised and economically diverse permanent corporation, on acquisition as its main purpose in life, with its Abbot a highly qualified chief executive, but 'scarcely distinguishable from the powerful marcher lords'. Such a person, however, might have received contrary guidance from certain warnings in the fundamental handbook of western monasticism, the Rule of St Benedict, to the effect that the abbot be not 'too solicitous about things transitory, things earthly, things perishable, closing his eyes to or too little weighing the salvation of the souls committed to his care ... not [to] complain of having too little worldly substance'.[110]

There were indeed a number of factors ensuring the primacy of religion in the Abbey's life and of a view of wealth as a means to a higher end. The *raison d'être* of a monastery was prayer, in the first place on behalf of the benefactors who endowed the lands that brought the institution into being and allowed it to survive, formal prayer taking the two forms of the celebration of Masses and of the choral recitation in Latin of the eight-part cycle of the daily 'office' of psalms, hymns, lessons and other prayers, ranging from one afternoon's Vespers to the following morning's Nones, and concluding with solemn sung Mass; all in an uninterrupted daily programme on whose perfect performance the Rule of St Benedict was most insistent.[111]

One reminder of the supremacy of Furness Abbey's religious obligations was its responsibilities for the parish churches under its care - its 'spiritual possessions' of Dalton and Urswick, Ulverston and Pennington, Kirkby Ireleth, Millom and its two Manx dependencies. In these, it was the Abbey's pastoral duty to ensure that Masses were celebrated on Sundays and holy days, to provide the laity with instruction in the faith and with the seven Sacraments of the Church and to see to it that infants were baptised, couples wed, the dying blessed and the dead properly dispatched. The predominance of the spiritual in the life of the Abbey was further guaranteed by its role as 'mother house' of a number of far-flung daughter houses, from Swinehead (1134) and Calder (1135) in England and Rushen (1138) on the Isle of Man to the Irish units of Fermoy (1170), Holy Cross (1180), Corecumruadh (1197), Wotherney (1198) and Inislaunaght (1240).[112]

The foremost factor, however, in ensuring that Furness Abbey's leading role as a pastoral and spiritual agency was not lost sight of in the quest for capital accumulation lay in the way that its territorial gains were made over the course of time, for the gifts of territory that various land-owners showered on the institution were not unconditional but were contractual in the sense that they were made on the strict understanding that their recipients would be engaged in offering a constant chain of prayer and Masses on behalf of their benefactors - a model similar to the contractual arrangements of military feudalism, in which vassals received landed fiefs in return for armed service to overlords.

Various land grants to Furness Abbey enshrined their donors' convictions that their surrenders of property were made in return for spiritual benefits to be won for them and their families, vicariously, by the mediation of their beneficiaries as *oratores* - men whose lives had to be dominated by the *Opus Dei*, 'God's work', the life of prayer. Thus, the 1127 foundation charter of Stephen of Blois made it clear that his massive award was issued 'providing for the safety of my own soul, the soul of my wife the countess Matilda', plus that of the king 'and for the souls of all the faithful, living as well as dead'. A later grant, in 1240, by William de Lancaster III (d. 1246), was made over 'for the health of my soul, the soul of Agnes my spouse, and the souls of all my predecessor and successors' (William required burial in the 'presbytery' - that is in the vicinity of the main altar, closest in space to the benefits of the Mass).[113]

A further directive to underscore an insistence that the Furness monks lived up to their profession as strictly reformed Benedictines was a confirmation document of the Cistercian Pope Eugenius III (r. 1145-53) to the Abbot and his brethren, who were 'professing a regular life [in which] you are engaged to serve God': the pontiff ordered 'the monastical discipline to be there observed at all times inviolably in the fear of the Lord, according to the Cistercian rule therein established'.[114]

There is also 'evidence of the rights of lay supervision claimed by a great baron in a monastic house which his ancestors had founded and also evidence of his interest in the fulfilment of the spiritual vocation by its inmates'. In 1524, Thomas, 2nd Lord Dacre (d. 1525) rebuked the prior of Lanercost because his building programme prevented him from having:

> tymes convenient and space to see the inward parte of yor chirche as to take hede and see the service of God contynualy maigteyned, the order of Religion wt the ceremoneys of the same wtin the Chirche, Closter, Dortor [dormitory] and frater [refectory] observed and kept so weale as nedeful it were.[115]

The ascendancy of spiritual values in the monastic culture of Furness Abbey is also evident in its building programme, beginning with the early construction of the church, planned in the Order's 'own standardized image', and completed promptly within the 12th century. Yet, and despite its eventual impressive size, the Abbey's church did not have diocesan, parochial or congregational functions but was an oratory for the recitation of the office and the celebration of Masses by the ordained monks, in the first place on behalf of their donors. This meant that 'the east end of the church contained five [Mass] altars, besides the high altar ... and probably there was a private altar in the sacristy'. The lay-out of the Abbey church was thus both that of an auditorium for sung prayer and a sanctum for the ritual of the Mass. When it came to elaborating features of the presbytery, the *piscina*, the drain in which the vessels of the Mass were washed, and the *sedilia*, the bench where senior brethren sat through lengthy parts of high Mass - out of these ritual features the brethren commissioned 'one of the best ensembles... anywhere in England'.[116] No form of architecture could have been more expressive of the central purpose of a Cistercian Abbey.

Likewise, since the monastic rule was the authoritative source for the Cistercian observance, the auditorium where an instalment of it was read out each day had to be a place of particular significance, calling for lavish embellishment. Dated 1230-40, Furness Abbey's centrally located chapter house is 'marked with ... elegance of Gothic sculpture... richly and multiply moulded ... Furness's particular showpiece ...[all] still lovely'[117] - the aesthetics of dedicated observance.

Finally, on either side of the entrance leading into the chapter house are the two deep tunnels that formed the abbey's library:

> Although only a handful of books are known to survive from the abbey, there is evidence suggesting a thriving intellectual culture and book production there between the 13th and 15th centuries. ... The presence of a substantial library at the monastery is indicated by the large book cupboards that flank the entrance to the chapter house and by the survival there of the abbey's two volume illuminated cartulary written in 1412 by the monk John Stell, which shows that the monastery remained capable of ambitious book production well into the later Middle Ages.[118]

In this literary concern Furness was following in the footsteps of a major daughter house of Cîteaux, Clairvaux, which gathered together about 300 manuscripts of the early Fathers of the Church. A monastic library was the focus of the lectio divina, 'the meditated reading', beginning with Scripture, that formed the third ingredient in the Benedictine Rule, the *Opus Intellectus* (alongside the *Opus Manus*, or manual work on the farm and so on). This 'work of the mind' was assigned to the end of the day's other work and to Sundays. From a core in the Bible, the range of literary material in these collections expanded over the course of time to take in saints' lives, accounts of miracles and history.[119]

Furness's east Lancashire sister house, Whalley, provided a leading example of this widening range of study:

> the Abbey mounted a programme of readings for delivery throughout the year in the refectory and infirmary, including the New Testament, Church fathers and leading medieval monastic writers, the whole making up a learned, diverse and

uplifting syllabus.[120]

Furness Abbey's best-known author was the monk Jocelyn of Furness, whose material was anchored in pre-Conquest saints' lives, coming from a Celtic cultural circuit which took in Cumbria, Scotland and Ireland, while Jocelyn also adapted his content for a new Anglo-Norman readership. Jocelin (d. 1199), Bishop of Glasgow and Abbot of the Cistercian house of Melrose, commissioned from Jocelyn a *vita* - a spiritualised biography - of Kentigern. John de Courci (d. 1219), conqueror of Ulster, and Thomas, or Tommaltach, Archbishop of Armagh, were his patrons for a biography of the evangelist of Ireland, Patrick (d. 461): it is in this *vita* that the legend of Patrick's expulsion of the snakes from the island originates. Jocelyn's links with Melrose were confirmed in his life of the Abbey's saintly head, Waltheof (or Waldef, d. 1159). Jocelyn's biography of the Romano-British Empress Helen (c. 255-c.330) may have been requested by a community of nuns, and a calendar of British bishops is attributed to him.[121]

Beyond Jocelyn, however, two books that are confirmed as survivors from the Abbey library indicate some switch in reading tastes away from the spirituality of *lectio divina*.

One of this pair is the *Polychronicon*, by Ralph, or Ranulph, Higden (c.1280-1364), a Benedictine monk of St Werburgh's, Chester. The *Polychronicon* offers the reader a world history and encyclopedia of science and geography, based on about 40 sources, serialised into seven volumes, on the basis of the seven days of the Creation, extending eventually down to c. 1352, during the reign of Edward III, and expanded by continuators to the date of the king's death.[122]

Higden's work was unsurprisingly popular: 100 manuscripts still survive, including those from Furness's Cistercian northern sisters, Fountains and Whalley. Part of its regional appeal lay in the fact that the author, based on Chester, travelled around the north, including Lancashire, and loyally described Crosthwaite's great church as a 'basilica'. Reaching out to a vernacular readership, Higden's Latin original was translated into English in 1387 by John of Trevisa (1326-1402), and the compilation continued to attract readers well into the 15th century, being printed in 1480 by William Caxton (c. 1422-c. 1491) and other early printers - further confirmations of the book's status, as 'the best seller of the age', embellished 'with considerable style and taste', a 'pleasant, easy-going Universal History'.[123]

Yet, though having the appearance of a 'universal' chronicle, *Polychronicon* centres on a narrative, in four final books, of *English* history, from the Saxons to the ruling Plantagenet dynasty. Crucially, Higden, brings the whole symphony towards a close in the era of the imperial triumphs of Edward III in the Hundred Years' War, 1377-1453, a reign culminating in France's catastrophic defeat at Crécy in 1346 and the decisive defeat of France's ally, Scotland at Neville's Cross in the same year. If the presence of this book is anything to go by, the secular-minded royalism and patriotism of an age of increasing English nationalism, focused on the dynasty, had found a place in the Furness Abbey library alongside *lectio divina*.[124]

Furness Abbey's other indisputably authentic medieval literary survivor is a copy, dating from the late 14th century of the *Historia regum Britanniae* - the 'History of the Kings of Britain' by the Welsh Oxford scholar Geoffrey of Monmouth (c. 1100-1154/5).[125]

Monmouth's work begins with the destruction of Troy, as depicted in Homer's *Iliad* (c. 850-800 BC). Great-grandson of the defeated Trojan hero Aeneas, Brutus, forefather and founder of the British people, settles in Britain, where he establishes a 'New

Troy'. King follows king in a cycle down to Caesar's invasion in 55 BC and the later Roman occupation, following which the barbarian invaders are repelled by the successive champions Ambrosius, Uther and Arthur, both curbing the Saxons and keeping the Romans at bay. Betrayed by an ambitious nephew, Arthur meets his end, only to rise again to the rescue of the Britons, *rex quondam et rex futurus* - 'the once and future king', the great exemplar of knightly kingship, since even Edward I, the chivalric 'flower of Christendom', took the palm only 'after king Arthur'.[126]

Grounded in Welsh literary sources such as the 7th-century *Gododdin* and the complex verse epics of the bardic *cyfarwyddon*, Monmouth's masterpiece catapulted the Celtic tales into an international literary success, 'a brilliant, picturesque and tragic fresco of a people destined for destruction'[127] - the source of endless continuing creativity in European art, literature, music and poetry. Among the hundreds of manuscript copies of the Monmouth original is the Furness edition. Too much of a case should not be made of the no doubt fortuitous survival of this work in the Abbey's library holdings, even though, along with that of the *Polychronicon*, it surely points towards some appetite among the Abbey's readers for works of non-religious interest and entertainment.

To the best of our knowledge, the Augustinian Canons of Lanercost did not possess any secular literary treasure on the lines of the Higden and Monmouth classics, but developed their own history, the *Chronicon de Lanercost*, as well as a remarkable version of a cartulary - a monastery's register book. Recently published and superbly edited, the *Lanercost Cartulary (Cumbria Record Office MS DZ/1*, ed., John M. Todd) provides the cartulary itself, along with accounts of the Priory, its patrons and coats of arms, the economy of the area and the history of the

Lanercost Abbey: Samuel and Nathaniel Buck, 1739

text.[128]

Lanercost probably never accommodated more than 12 Canons and was certainly never endowed sufficiently to became a north Cumberland Furness: compare the sheer scale of territorial awards to Furness in the 12th and 13th centuries with the sum of 12d. pa. that was settled on the Priory in c. 1236 out of the rent of a house in Carlisle's Finkle Street.[129] The 13th century was, even so, a period of steady expansion of the Lanercost fabric, when the nave of the church was completed, probably in c. 1220. Though the Statute of Mortmain of 1279, restricting the make-over of land into the 'dead hand' of the Church, staunched the already meagre flow of such donations to canonries of the likes of Lanercost, in c.1280 three bays towards the west end were completed and the magnificent west front was added. A visit by Edward I, Queen Eleanor (1241-90) and the court, en route to Newcastle at that time, would have cost the Canons dear.[130]

A 13th century of mixed fortunes for the house moved towards its close in 1296 with a new outbreak of war with Scotland. After burning Hexham Priory, the Scots army made

camp at Lanercost and, as the chronicler of Bridlington recorded:
> Tuo hous of religioun, Leynercoste and Hexham.
> They chaced the chanons out, ther godes bare away.
> And robbed alle about. [131]

In 1311 Robert (Bruce), king of Scots (r. 1306-29), caused 'endless damage' at Lanercost and in 1346 David II (r. 1324-71) 'ransacked' the church. In 1291 Lanercost's income had been rated at £74, but in 1318 stood at 'nil'.[132]

This region was indirectly touched by the vogue for religio-military orders that arose in Europe in the era of the successive Crusades in the Holy Land, from 1096 onwards. Of these organisations, the wealthy Knights Templar, founded in 1118, held a manor at Acorn Bank in Temple Sowerby from 1228, from which they drew income, without their having an actual presence at the site. In 1297 a local couple, Ingram de Dynes and his wife, owed 50 shillings to the master the Templars. Following the suppression of these Knights in 1312, their local property was transferred to another military Order, the Knights Hospitallers of St John - hence Spital Farm in Temple Sowerby.[133]

2: The Friars

In terms of the mission of the Church to the laity at large, a highly important development in the 13th-century diocese of Carlisle was the arrival of the orders of preaching friars. These were non-monastic and non-parochial clerics, trained preachers, vowed to voluntary poverty and mendicancy and reliant on donations from the laity. They targeted the growing populations of Europe's rising towns and cities, both as places for the reception of their teaching and as bases from which to reach out to country districts, where sermons might have been scarce.

Of the various orders of friars, 13-century Cumbria first received the Franciscans, the 'Friars Minor' or Grey Friars (founded in 1223 by Francis of Assisi, 1181/2-1226), in Carlisle in August 1233, and in September of the same year a party of the Dominican Order, the Order of Preachers, or Black Friars (founded in 1216 by Domingo de Guzmán, 1170-1221), arrived in the city. The Carmelites, or White Friars (formally established in 1247), came to Appleby in 1281, and the Augustinian, or Austin, Friars (formally established in 1256), were settled in Penrith by 1291.[134]

The Franciscans obtained a house to the south of Carlisle, safely within the walls, on a piece of land lying between today's Devonshire Street and Bank Street. In 1235 Henry III donated timber for a church and convent, while in the following year the Franciscans were presented with five marks for their church. This building was 'damaged or destroyed' by fire in 1251 and King Henry awarded 40 oaks and £20 towards the rebuilding. It was again destroyed in the city fire of 1292 and 'probably' in 1296 and 1391, until, at long last, it was replaced by a stone structure. Royal patronage at various levels of generosity continued into Edward I's gift of 22s 8d in c. 1300, offered in order to provide the friars with an allowance of food for three days.[135]

A hallmark of the Franciscan Order was voluntary poverty, rejecting all ownership of property, in imitation of that of Christ and the Apostles, as restored in the Rule of Francis of Assisi. However, from the time of the initial approval of the Franciscans by Pope Innocent III (r. 1198-1216), the papacy had tried to reconcile the practicalities of Franciscan life - for example, in the ownership of books - with Francis's rule of absolute poverty, giving rise to two schools of thought in the order, the 'Conventuals', who accepted some papal relaxations over possessions, and the 'Spirituals' who declined them.

The Carlisle convent became involved in these discords. In 1317 Pope John XXII (r. 1316-34) denounced the Spirituals as heretics, dissolved the party and condemned the belief that Christ and the Apostles adhered to absolute poverty. A work by the Spiritual Walter de Chatton, who was ordained in Carlisle, *Tractatus de Paupertate evangelica* - 'Booklet Concerning Evangelical Poverty' - took issue with Pope John's Bull *Ad conditorem* of 1322 and he was summoned to Avignon, the papacy's residence at that time, where he was consulted by John XXII's successor Benedict XII (r. 1334-42). Another Carlisle Franciscan, Thomas de Elmeden, took part in debates at Cambridge on the question of poverty.[136]

Twenty-three Franciscans were ordained priests by John de Halton (d. 1324) as Bishop of Carlisle, from 1292 to 1324, but a low point in local Franciscan numbers is evident in the post-Black Death Poll Tax of 1377, when only three of the *Fratres minores* - 'Friars Minor', a title signalling their humility, were returned, compared with the 13 of the Dominican *Fratres Praedicatores* - 'Friars Preachers'. However, an overall number of 82 Franciscans associated with Carlisle has been counted, 27 of whom were definitely Carlisle brethren, but 'only a small proportion of the friars belonged to the convent during the three centuries of its existence', the average falling to about 20 'towards the end', with the Dissolution under Henry VIII.[137]

Royal patronage benefitted the Carlisle Dominicans, who in March 1234 petitioned the king for a piece of ground in the *strata publica*, the public highway, and the sheriff of Cumberland was ordered to grant them possession. The choice of location of the medieval friaries was partly dictated by the friars' missionary strategies, often choosing 'to live in the suburbs, so as to be near the poorest and most recently arrived townsfolk who could be presumed to need their services'. In the case of the Carlisle Dominicans, this was a plot of land outside the walls, marked by today's Blackfriars Street. In 1237 the Dominicans were ordered to remove a building that they had put up in the *strata publica, extra civitatem* - 'outside the city' - a structure that was criticised as a nuisance - but in 1238 they moved to a place within the walls, perhaps with the support of their Order's long- standing patron, Bishop Walter Mauclerk (d. 1248, Bishop from 1223). The friary narrowly escaped destruction in the city fire of 1292, although after it Edward I ordered that the members be given amounts of grain worth nearly £10.[138]

The two Carlisle friaries formed a northern terminus to a string of houses of friars stationed on the 'junction towns', which were spread out on the western great north road, stretching from Warrington in Cheshire, via Preston and Lancaster in Lancashire to Carlisle. Appleby, on the west-east route, was one of these stations, and there, in 1281, the house of the Carmelite White Friars, in the northern, Battlebarrow, district of the town, was founded by the barons Vesey, Percy and Clifford. The complex 'would likely have consisted of a church with a belfry, surrounded by individual cells, a gatehouse (probably on Battlebarrow) and a cemetery on the south side of the church'. Edward I lodged in the friary on his border campaign in 1300, when it housed 12 members.[139]

In 1291 a royal licence was issued to the donor John de Capella (or de la Chapele), steward to the Bishop of Carlisle in 1292, to permit him to proceed with his award to the Augustinian friary of Newcastle upon Tyne in its move to set up a daughter house in Penrith. The property comprised a dwelling, with a little land attached, in what is today Friargate, below the present houses of Abbot Bank and the Friarage, in what was a medieval manufacturing area. In June 1290 Edward I passed through the town, making a donation of 2s 8d to the 'Brothers of St Augustine of Penrith' and on his return visit via the town in November paid 5s 8d to the friars: some of the brethren 'appear to have been in attendance on Edward during his journey south'.[140]

The establishment of the convents of friars in Cumberland's and Westmorland's urban settlements thus completed a process of effective religious settlement in the 13th-century Lakes region.

Chapter 6:
Faith and Religion in the Late Medieval Lake Counties

Between the late 13th and early 14th centuries, Cumbria's exposure to destruction during the Anglo-Scottish wars became acute. A survey of 1301 revealed that invasion after invasion had led to burning and desolation across the diocese, monasteries laid waste, their inmates scattered. Various churches had been razed to the ground, their parsons reduced to begging.[141]

Local churches had been turned into defensive citadels. At Newton Arlosh St John's, from c. 1303, ' a formidably tough-looking ... [small fort], tunnel-vaulted on the ground floor, with thick walls, no external door, slit windows, functional battlements ... the walls thick, the windows tiny' was constructed. A door led to the tower, from which boiling matter could be poured over the assailants. At nearby Burgh-by-Sands each of the two towers is a small castle, with walls up to seven feet thick, and at Bowness-on-Solway St Michael's the rectory was built as a small fort. Great Salkeld St Cuthbert's has its 'Powerful W tower of *c.* 1380, unmistakeably defensive ... and business-like battlements'.[142]

Such localised fortifications could not, however do much to impede the effects of warfare carried out by sack and burn. A survey of 1319:

> showed that twelve churches in the deanery of Carlisle, roughly the northern third of the county, had been entirely destroyed, and none of the churches in the deanery, numbering in all twenty-three, had sufficient resources left to maintain an incumbent.

*Newton Arlosh, an anonymous drawing from 1816.
The building was restored by Sarah Losh in 1843*

Several 'parishes [were] so comprehensively ravaged that there was deemed to be no point in assessing them at all': Burgh-by-Sands, for example, had been valued at £50 in 1291 but had fallen to £2 10s in 1318, while Wetheral church had fallen in value from £32 to only £1. It was not even considered worth bothering to assess Lanercost Priory or Armathwaite Nunnery, whereas Wetheral Priory's former value of over £52 had tumbled to £4. Wealthy Holm Cultram had been estimated at more than £206 in 1291, but by 1318 had dropped to £40. Lanercost's cloister was burned down by the earl of Buchan in 1296, followed by a raid led by King David II in 1346, from which the house 'never recovered'. Attacked again in 1384, the house was the subject of an appeal by the Archbishop of York in 1409 on account of its destitution. The income of the Bishops of Carlisle, always inadequate, was of course not immune, falling from over £126 to £20 between 1291 and 1318.[143]

The Bishops'residence, Rose Castle, near the village of Dalston, was in the forefront both of strategic operations and wartime damage: in 1314 Edward, earl of Carrick, brother of King Robert I, burned the building down. In 1336 John de Kirkby (d. 1352), Bishop from 1332 to 1352, received a royal licence to fortify it with battlements - as did Gilbert de Welton , Bishop between 1352 and 1362, while between 1400 and 1419, William Strickland (c. 1340- 1419), Bishop from 1400 to 1419, added a tower.[144]

Aside from attention to Rose itself, direct responsibility for the border defences was incumbent on the Bishops of Carlisle. Following the arrival in the city of the Scots military leader William Wallace (1272?-1305), in 1297 Bishop John de Halton took over from a Scot as garrison commander and was ordered by the king to pay £13 13 4d to Sir Henry Percy ('Hotspur', 1364-1403) in order to defend Carlisle.[145]

Because of the instability of the border, the long years of Halton's episcopate:

> were perhaps the most turbulent in the history of the diocese,when the upheaval and destruction of the Anglo-Scottish war added to the considerable difficulties of ruling one of the poorest and most remote of English sees.[146]

Trained in the royal administration and diplomatic service,Halton served as ambassador to Scotland in 1295, was custodian of the castle from 1297 and envoy to Scotland in 1320: 'a long and varied ... record of service to the Crown, pursued loyally despite its encroachments on Halton's primary responsibility, the administration and pastoral care of his diocese'. Such military and diplomatic duties continued to go with the role of Bishop of Carlisle, as in 1359, when Bishop Kirkby served as one of the two wardens of the Western March, and in 1362, when he was appointed to a commission to negotiate peace with the Scots.[147]

One of Carlisle's leading 'military' Bishops was William Strickland, a protégé of Thomas Appleby, Bishop from 1363 to 1395, who appointed him his representative in parliament in 1381. On Bishop Appleby's death, Strickland was chosen as his successor, and he was consecrated in August 1400, replacing Thomas Merke (d. 1419).[148]

Even before his consecration, Strickland had shown his military prowess, having been granted a licence in 1397 to fortify his 'chamber' in Penrith to defend the town, and after 1400 his combination of diplomatic and military acumen was activated as he became a commissioner to negotiate peace with the Scots in 1401; when this treaty failed and the Scots invaded with 2,000 men, he recruited an army to repel them.[149]

Beyond his active military and political life, William Strickland, an essentially practical-minded man, and, ranked among Carlisle's outstanding Bishops, was a devoted pastor who gave the cathedral a tower and six bells, rebuilt the north transept and added 46 choir stalls and misericords: for Penrith he endowed a grammar school and, it is believed, a water supply. Bishop Marmaduke Lumley (d. 1450), Bishop from 1429 to 1450, continued in the Carlisle tradition of military service on the part of Bishops, taking on the defence of the Western March for payment of the sum of £1,050 a year, 'in peace and war'.[150]

Strickland's career proved that military duties need not impinge on a major responsibility of Bishops of Carlisle, care for the upkeep of the Cathedral. The restoration of the 13th-century choir after the fire of 1292, taken in hand before 1300, and carried out in the first half of the 14th century, was taken forward, expensively, in the fashionable 'luxurious, spendthrift' architectural style known as Decorated, forming what has been termed 'a piece of poetry in stone'. The pillars were re-shaped and new capitals introduced, with a new roof, ceiling and east end window.[151]

After 1314 and Bruce's sweeping victory over the English at Bannockburn, the devastated condition of the border would have made money hard to raise, and construction work may have become spasmodic. Among the consequences of the outbreaks of the Black Death in 1348-9, 1361-2, 1369 and 1379 was a labour shortage. Even so, not only did Carlisle's Bishops continue to issue pleas for building funds, in 1354, 1356 and 1363, but these appeals were likely to be met with favourable responses from the laity: in 1359 John de Salkeld, of Little Salkeld and Corby, contributed £5 to the fabric fund and £2 'to make a window anew in the chancel there'.[152]

A key feature of the 14th-century restoration of Carlisle Cathedral was the design of the great east window, of 1340, 'unsurpassed by any other in the kingdom, perhaps there is not a window equal to it in the whole world ... a gorgeous display of flowering tracery, 51 ft. ... high, of nine lights ... with internal tracery and the side parts developing tracery of the type with leaves off a stem'.[153]

While the Cathedral construction was thus continuing, attention was being paid to the condition of the parish churches of the diocese. Founded in 1150 as a daughter of Kirkby Stephen, St Michael's in Brough-under-Stainmore underwent extensive enlargement between the 14th and 16th centuries, creating the very large interior, with additional Mass altars - 'a big church hugging the ground' - with a 67 foot south wall and a 14th-century nave arcade of seven bays and stylish windows from the later 14th century onwards.[154]

At Uldale, the parish church of St James the Apostle, whitewashed, 'Low and simple, just a nave with a double bellcote', was, even so, furnished with a Decorated east window. A grave slab in the churchyard bore the priestly symbols of a chalice and missal. From the early 14th century onwards there was a hermit's house at St Mary's chapel, with two acres of land, 'well equipped and in good order'.[155]

By 1240 St Mary's Abbey, York, had acquired Kirkby Lonsdale church, appropriating the parsonage and tithe. Following the destruction by King William the Lion of Scotland in 1173-4, the re-built church was probably again destroyed in 1314, but was re-constructed at the behest of the York Abbey. Brampton's St Martin's, appropriated to Lanercost in 1169, went through a 'relatively prosperous' period in the 12th and 13th centuries, when it was extended eastward, but was laid waste in 1314. St Martin's was granted a remission of dues in 1346, following the 'destruction by the Scots after Michaelmas last' and was again ravaged in 1384.[156]

In south Cumberland the most successful church restoration was at Greystoke's St Andrew's, with a plan for a collegiate church - a non-monastic resident clerical fraternity of 'secular Canons'.

This project was taken up by William, 14th Baron Greystoke, in 1358, and a crown permit and episcopal licence were issued, though Lord Greystoke's death in c.1359 halted progress. His cousin, Lord Ralph (d. 1374/5), however, procured a renewed licence in 1374. Set up in 1382, the college was staffed by a master, seven or eight chaplains, and six priests to celebrate Masses on behalf of the souls of the departed. It was, however, primarily 'not a monastic body, with the duty of praying for the souls of the founder and his kin as its primary obligation, but a college of clergy created for the express purpose of saving those of his tenants'.[157]

Building work was also required, for by 1382, the 'walls

St Andrew's, Greystoke: drawing by Sam Bough, 1840

[were] crazy, the belfry fallen, and the wooden shingles on the roof mostly scattered', so that the parishioners were commanded, under penalty of the Bishop's excommunication, to contribute to the restoration, as well to an enlargement of the interior, with a nave of five arches. This, though, was a slow task, extending into the following century, and probably beyond: its evolving architectural styling is that of the 'Perpendicular', the final form of the medieval Gothic in vogue in England down to about 1530. What magnificently survives - 'one of the largest medieval churches in Cumbria'[158] - sometimes even seems almost out of place, like a huge Somerset or Norfolk 'wool church', somehow transported to a lovely Cumberland estate village.

At Castle Sowerby St Kentigern's - 'White, low, vernacular, but surprisingly spacious' - a local devotion to the Blessed Virgin Mary arose: in 1362 Nicholas de Motherby left two shillings for roof repairs, plus one shilling 'to the vault of the Blessed Mary', suggesting a Lady Chapel, which included an image of Mary, with a 'light' - an expensive beeswax candle - 'for the maintenance of which he left an ox' [available to hire for ploughing]; de Motherby also bequeathed a shilling 'for the upkeep of the Holy Cross' - probably the rood screen representing the Crucifixion erected at the meeting point of the chancel with the nave.[159]

The increasing artistic professionalisation of the later middle ages in England made it possible to create a highly wrought iconography of parish priests, beyond the simpler chalice-and-missal grave slabs of the past. Thus Crosthwaite acquired an elaborate figure on its font, 'a splendid structure ... a memorial to an incumbent ... a remarkable piece of 14th-century work, almost certainly the memorial to a former vicar Sir Thomas de Eskead', parish priest from 1374 to 1390. Some damage to the figure may have been done during an official visitation in 1571, when Protestant officials were hunting down 'reliques [remnants] of superstition and idolatry'.[160]

At St Michael's in Bowness-on-Solway there is a 'rather enigmatic carving of an ecclesiastical figure' with a head-dress or 'mitred cap' - 'a pre-Reformation priest dressed in a chasuble and carrying a religious work'. In Musgrave's St Theobald's a statue of just over a foot in height was fashioned in memory of the parish priest, Thomas Ouds, who died in c. 1502: he is shown fully vested for Mass, with an inscription drawn across his chasuble - the outer vestment worn by a priest celebrating Mass.[161]

Further pious embellishments continued to be carried out in local churches, including the provision of the bells tolled to summon parishioners to worship: Westmorland has 21 medieval bells, spread over 15 churches, the three oldest being Appleby's St Michael's (13th century), Crosby Garrett's St Andrew's, with its small 'C13 tower, really an enclosed belfry', and Mallerstang chapel.[162]

Inscriptions on church bells provide insights into local

devotional inclinations and parochial dedications, as well as into saints' cults. Appleby's St Michael's is inscribed *Campana Sancti Michaelis* - 'the bells of St Michael'- and Crosby Garrett *Campana Sancti Andree* - 'the bells of St Andrew'. Devotion to the martyr Thomas Becket (1118-70), the most popular of native English saints, was echoed, in c. 1400, in Long Marton's St Margaret's, with the invocation *Sancte Thoma Ora Pro Nobis* - 'St Thomas, pray for us' - while at Burneside's St Oswald's, probably from the 15th century, a bell appealed *Sancte Gregori Ora Pro Nobis* - 'St Gregory, pray for us'. At Musgrave St Theobald's matched invocations were inscribed on the two 15th-century bells, one *Petre Ora Pro Nobis* - 'St Peter, pray for us' - and the other an abbreviation of the 'Angelic Salutation' in Luke, 1: 28: *Ave Gra.Plena Dns. Tecu* - 'Hail, full of Grace, the Lord is with thee', the opening of the popular prayer, the *Ave Maria* or 'Hail Mary'. At Ormside St James's one of three 15th-century bells is inscribed, laconically, *Paulus* - '[St] Paul' - and the other *Ave Maria Gracia Plena* - 'Hail Mary, full of grace'. In the 14th century the chapel of ease at Crook adopted an excerpt from the second instalment of the *Ave Maria* - *Sancta Maria Ora Pro Nobis* - 'Holy Mary, pray for us', with the same petition at Loweswater's St Bartholomew's, as also in Eskdale, probably from the 14th century, and at Muncaster, probably from the 15th century, and again also at Whicham, probably of the 15th century, with an additional invocation to the Archangel Michael. An unusual inscription, to St Christopher, at Distington may be attributable to the influence of the High Sheriff Sir Christopher Curwen (c. 1382-1453). At Beckermet's St Bridget's 'Jesus, Mary' were invoked, at Distington Cuthbert, at Ennerdale Bega, at Eskdale Catherine, at Muncaster the Blessed Virgin Mary and at Waberthwaite the Apostle James.[163]

A marked feature of late medieval popular piety was a

passion for pilgrimage, one feature of which was that those travelling to various shrines frequently returned home with pious mementoes which had been dispensed at the holy places in question. A pilgrim's badge discovered at Shap, probably 15th century in date, belongs to a 'well-known class of object which was sold at various religious shrines ... as a visible token of pilgrimage'. Perhaps linked with Shap Abbey, the medallion may have originated at the Blessed Virgin Mary's sanctuary of Walsingham in Norfolk, which, by the time of the Reformation, was England's most celebrated place of pilgrimage.[164]

Another frequent form of the pilgrim memento was the ampulla, a small vessel of holy water or oil, acquired at a pilgrimage venue. These lead, tin or tin alloy objects, carrying designs identifying the shrines and the saints in question, began appearing in western Europe in the late 12th century and rose in popularity to a high point in the 13th and early 14th centuries. Pinned to the individual's hat or worn around his or her neck, the device - as with the one located at Great Orton in 1995 - would have confirmed the bearer's status as a pilgrim.[165]

The presence of these artefacts, such as the 'cast lead ampulla in the form of a two-handled bottle', disinterred near Kendal, or an ampulla found in excavations in Carlisle in 1972, plus a 'fragmentary St Michael' unearthed in 1984,[166] establishes the fact that medieval Cumbrians were fully involved with powerful currents in European popular piety and the cult of pilgrimage of that period.

A further form of piety, originating in Continental Europe, was also taken up in Cumbria. In the 15th century, devotion to representations of the 'Holy Name' of Jesus, in the form of the monogram IHS, held to stand for *Iesu Hominum Salvator*, or 'Jesus, Saviour of Mankind', the letters being set out in a disc, was promoted in Italy by a leading Franciscan preacher,

Bernardino of Siena (1380-1444); the cult spread rapidly throughout late medieval Europe. Kendal Holy Trinity displayed this symbol for veneration, and a copper alloy disc, of late 15th to early 16th-century dating, with the object in outline, has come from Nether Denton, on the Scottish border. At Warcop church in Westmorland the antiquarian Thomas Machell (1647-98) observed 'over the doore of the right side is IHS, i. e. Jhesus hom Salvator'.[167]

A coin, double folded and dated 1280, has been found in the bed of the river Caldew, south of Cummersdale. The medieval practice of folding silver coins is recorded in accounts of saints' miracles, the custom being to bend a coin over the victim of an illness or other misfortune and invoke the help of the saint in effecting a cure. Once a cure had been accomplished, the bent coin became the rightful property of the saint who had assisted the cure and should be presented to the saint on a pilgrimage. In this case, however, the object might have had more of a local than a national significance, linked with the local cults of Cuthbert, Kentigern and Ninian and with the many holy wells of this region.[168]

The enrichment of religious belief and practice in later medieval Cumbria that has been reviewed in this chapter was manifested *inter alia* in the ongoing improvements to the Cathedral, the enlargement and improvement of parish churches, devotion to the Virgin Mary and to favoured saints inscribed on church bells, involvement in cultic practice adopted from the Continent and a familiarity with artefacts associated with pilgrimage.

Chapter 7:
Faith and Religion in the Late Medieval Lake Counties: An Essay in Iconography and Instruction

Over the course of the 14th and 15th centuries, the interior of Carlisle Cathedral became a theatre for the display of a varied range of religious representations, some of them purely visual, others twinning words with images. All of these works were executed within a comprehensive artistic repertoire which ranged in subjects from misericord carvings, to coded political persuasion, illustrations of the 'labours of the months', selected saints' lives and catechetical guidance on the Apostles' Creed. Such representation - in supposedly 'remote' Cumberland - were continuously drawing on intellectual, artistic and doctrinal influences that were present throughout late medieval western European life and thought.

(1) The Misericords
Forty-six new Canons' choir stalls were constructed in Carlisle Cathedral in c. 1410, probably inspired by Bishop William Strickland. They were furnished with misericords, the small hinged seats in choir stalls which are said to have been designed to provide support for those members of choirs who were unable to stand throughout the entire service of the 'office'. Traditionally, and because the undersides of these small benches were not normally seen in public, considerable freedom was given to their lay carvers to introduce secular images into their creations - scenes from lowlife, of wild men of the woods, and of a world-turned-upside-down, populated by comic bullied

The Pelican in her Piety misericord in Carlisle Cathedral

husbands, and so forth. The Carlisle series encapsulates much of this fantasy - a 'Splendid laughing wyvern', a lion and wyvern fighting, a wild man and dragon, a mermaid with her glass in her hand, and so on.[169]

Yet the inclusion in this set of the pious motif of the Pelican in her Piety, based on the notion that, just as the mother pelican feeds her chicks with her blood, so Christ at holy communion nourishes us with His, provides a reminder that the Cathedral misericords have a deeper devotional content and a more profound intellectual sophistication, going beyond popular culture and comedy. The group in fact forms:

> a unique and important collection of scholarly developed intellectual ideas, ranging from conceptions of the devil to the Virgin and her angelic throng ... topics from hand-written Bestiary Books [allegorical zoological works] which contained tales about mythic men, women and birds.

The view that this extraordinary repertoire 'has nothing to do with the Carlisle area ... [and] could have come straight for Normandy'[170] only confirms 14th-century Carlisle's firm place within a common late medieval international European culture, much of it based on northern France and the Low Countries.

(2) A Cult of a King
'On the north side of the stalls on the pulpitium screen boss - a raised ornamentation - appears, often taken to be a representation of the Coronation of the Blessed Virgin Mary as queen of heaven, with her musician angels'. [171] If this image were in fact that of the Virgin's celestial crowning, it would not have given rise to any surprise in a church dedicated to Mary, and at a time of ever-rising devotion to her in Christendom, as evidenced in the version of her heavenly coronation executed in 1432 by Giovanni da Fiesole - 'Fra Angelico'(1387-1445) - (Uffizi, Florence).

What, however, if this depiction is not of Mary's queenship at all, but carries a differently weighted and indeed a political agenda?

King Richard II (r. 1377-1399) had a strong following in Cumberland, as witnessed by the stained glass portrait of the king, rendered, to the life, crowned, with a sceptre - 'a softly handsome young man, unbearded and with a full head of very blond hair'. The portrait was a thank-offering, in expertly executed stained-glass, in a window in St Andrew's, Penrith, dedicated to Richard, in gratitude for his award in 1396 of the lucrative Penrith manors to Ralph (1364-1425), 6th Baron Neville of Raby and 1st earl of Westmorland, and his wife, Countess Joan.[172]

During the episcopate, from 1396 to 1399, of the Oxford scholar and former Westminster Benedictine monk Thomas Merke (d. 1409), Carlisle would also have become a centre of Ricardian allegiance, a fund of loyalty that may well have outlasted the deposition of the king in 1399:

The ceiling boss which may show King Richard II

the last Bishop appointed in the reign of Richard II, the celebrated Thomas Merke, was that king's personal friend ... a personal friend of Richard II, and though he was formally provided to the see by the pope, there can be no doubt that the choice was essentially the king's ... appointed for personal or political reasons ... thrust upon the chapter of Carlisle by the pope at the king's request.[173]

While it is true that because of the strategic and political centrality and military vulnerability of the diocese, all medieval Bishops of Carlisle had to be trusted and favoured by the sovereign and directly appointed by him, in the case of Merke and Richard there was an additional bond of personal fealty and friendship that was to prove crucial after the king was deposed in 1399 by Henry Bolingbroke, duke of Hereford, son of John of Gaunt (1340-99), duke of Lancaster, Bolingbroke succeeding to the throne as King Henry IV (r. 1399-1413).

That the king and the Oxford Doctor of Divinity and author, 'friend of Richard II', developed a personal bond is clear, perhaps one grounded in religious empathy between the devout king and the Benedictine monk, or in literary tastes, or those of a 'connoisseur'. Whatever the case, any personal relationship between the Bishop and the ruler would also have had to be translated into terms of unflinching political allegiance and service from the former to the latter, and so it was: one of the 'courtier bishops', Merke was on Richard's side in the faction fighting with Gaunt and his party in the 1390s, and he accompanied the king on his two expeditions to Ireland, in 1394 and 1399. When Richard returned from the second Irish campaign and was taken prisoner by Bolingbroke in North Wales, Merke was 'one of the few who remained with him to the last', 'a loyalist to the end'.[174]

The supreme test of Merke's continuing allegiance to Richard came in the autumn of 1399, in parliament, on 6 October, after the deposed king's renunciation of the throne to Henry had been read out on 30 September.[175] Did Merke make a speech on that occasion decrying the mistreatment of his former master? *Richard II* (1595) is Shakespeare's most 'political' play, in the sense of setting out the sanctity of monarchy by divine right and the great sin of deposing an anointed sovereign, issues that were very much to the fore in the playwright's Elizabethan and Jacobean world. In this great drama's Act IV, Sc. I, Merke is granted a prophetic rhetoric predicting the horrors that lay in wait for England and the House of Lancaster over the century to come, as divine retribution for the atrocity of 1399:

> My lord of Hereford here, whom you [parliament] call king,
>   is a foul traitor to proud Hereford's king:
>   And if you crown him, let me prophesy:

The blood of English shall manure the ground,
And future generations groan for this foul act.

It is true that there 'is no evidence that [Merke] raised his voice in Henry's behalf or uttered anywhere in public the fine sentiments which Shakespeare put into his mouth'.[176]

It is not, however, necessarily the case that, because Merke did not make a *Shakespearean* speech in parliament, he did not put forward some arguments in favour of the quality of mercy, words to be expected from a churchman who was closely associated with the deposed monarch. The 'probability that Merke had the great courage and loyalty to make such a speech is enhanced by the fact that he alone of the courtier Bishops was singled out for punishment' - on account of the 'bold protest' on 6 October against Henry's treatment of Richard, when all his other friends kept silence.[177] Merke thus gained a reputation as the country's leading clerical Ricardian.

Merke's most dangerous time as an unreconciled Richard II loyalist fell between October 1399 and November 1400. On 29 October, he was delivered from custody and brought before parliament and on the following 27 January was tried by a London jury and imprisoned in the Tower. 'Henry IV informed the pope in 1400 that he had deprived [Merke] of his bishopric for high treason and treachery to his royal person' and the king 'wrote to the pope on 15 March asking that 'he should be degraded and handed over to the secular arm' - the royal authorities.[178]

At a trial on 28 November 1400 Merke swore his innocence of treasonable conspiracy - a capital offence - and 'put himself on an inquisition by which he was found guilty'. However, a conditional 'pardon was granted to Thomas Merke, late Bishop of Carlisle, who was indicted, with others condemned to death, with having conspired at London and elsewhere to destroy the king'. At a hearing on 29 January 1401, Merke cited his royal pardon of the previous November, gave pledges for future good conduct - and was 'dismissed'.[179]

Thereafter, Merke made his peace with the Lancastrian status quo. In June 1401 Rome awarded him the rich prebend of Masham in the North Riding, in November Henry permitted him to accept further papal gifts and in the same month installed him in a vicarage in Dorset. In 1406 Merke became a proctor in the Church's parliament, Convocation, preaching the inaugural sermon as commissary of the Archbishop. In 1408 he may have been present in Lucca in disputes between Pope Gregory XIII (r. 1406-15) and dissident Cardinals. Thomas Merke died in 1409.[180]

What light might this extraordinary life shed on the subject of the Carlisle Cathedral boss? Before his return to royal, papal and ecclesiastical favour after 1401, between November 1400 and January 1401, in a succession of legal trials and imprisonments Merke was publicised as a focus of pro-Richard II resistance, and it would not have been surprising - given his high-level trials - if the survival of the last of Richard II's clerical loyalists did not create a suspicion that there existed in his former diocese a constituency in favour of the restoration of the ousted king. His close personal bond with Richard was well-known and there were months when he was close to a death sentence on account of his allegiance.

For a while, then, Merke might have been identified as a rallying for Richard's recovery of his crown, if such a reversal were at all possible. The most obvious condition for such an outcome was the former king's survival beyond 1400. All the evidence is that Richard died, probably of self-starvation, in Pontefract Castle in the West Riding in that year. At some point, his body was brought to London and openly displayed through the city's streets, an exhibition, however, that did not dispel the rumour that he had escaped from Pontefract and found refuge in Scotland [181] - perhaps a gateway for a restoration, and even with Merke's former base of Carlisle as a possible entry point.

Hopes for Richard's return to power were likely to have been at their height in both clerical and lay circles in Carlisle:

> The inhabitants of the diocese of Carlisle seem to have long retained somewhat of the spirit of their late Bishop in adhering to the interests of king Richard the second, in opposition to those of his successor Henry the fourth ... divers persons as well ecclesiastical as secular had given out that Richard the second was living in the parts of Scotland.[182]

The options for Richard's remaining partisans, in Carlisle if not elsewhere, appeared to be either that of facing the brutal fact that Richard was dead - with Henry IV directly or indirectly responsible - and of abandoning all hopes of putting him back on the throne, or of clinging to the belief that he lived as a once-and-future king in exile. There was, however, a third route, and one that offered a kind of quietus for any of Richard's remaining adherents. The solution lay in a technique - a highly ingenious iconographical one, as analysed by June Barnes - for gently undermining plans to bring back Richard, by apportioning him pictorially to a special category among the departed, that of the immortal and glorified.

Apotheosis was a form of deification originally applied to Roman emperors, and in Renaissance Europe could be applied to kings as a form of transfigured exaltation in their quasi-divine capacities: the best-known artistic rendition is the *Apotheosis of James I* by Peter Paul Rubens (1577-1640), commissioned for the Banqueting Hall in Whitehall. And it may be that the Carlisle apotheosis of Richard II was intended to sooth away all hopes of a legitimist counter-revolution against Henry IV, for in this epiphany, as June Barnes showed, the king enjoys celestial glorification beyond the range of mundane political recall.[183] During his reign, Richard had already figured artistically, in a beautiful rendition of his numinous rank, in the Wilton Diptych of c. 1395-9 (National Gallery), in which various saints present the monarch to the Virgin and Child. The Carlisle apotheosis safely restores him to that empyrean sphere, to a kingdom not of this world, wearing an eternal crown.

(3) The Labours of the Months

'To every thing there is a season, and a time to every purpose under the heaven.' (Ecclesiastes 3:1): the widespread late medieval European artistic calendar-based theme of the 'Labours of the Months' showed the mainly agricultural activities appropriate to each of the 12 months of the year and may have been linked with the agricultural improvements of the period across Europe, which required collective time management and a planned and methodical approach to farming tasks.[184]

The 'Labours of the Months' were frequently entered as illuminations in the devotional productions known as 'Books of Hours', the best-known set being the *Très riches heures du Duc de Berry* of 1412-16 by Hermann Pol and Johan de Limburg. Sculptured series of the Labours were particularly popular in Italy and France. Outstanding English examples are to be found in Canterbury Cathedral and St Augustine's church, Brookland, in Kent.[185]

The Carlisle 'Labours'- made up of 12 months, plus two addition on the north and south sides - and probably mid-14th century in date, are of 'quite exceptional importance and interest',[186] further confirming the ways in which Carlisle in particular and Cumbria in general were fully open to cultural

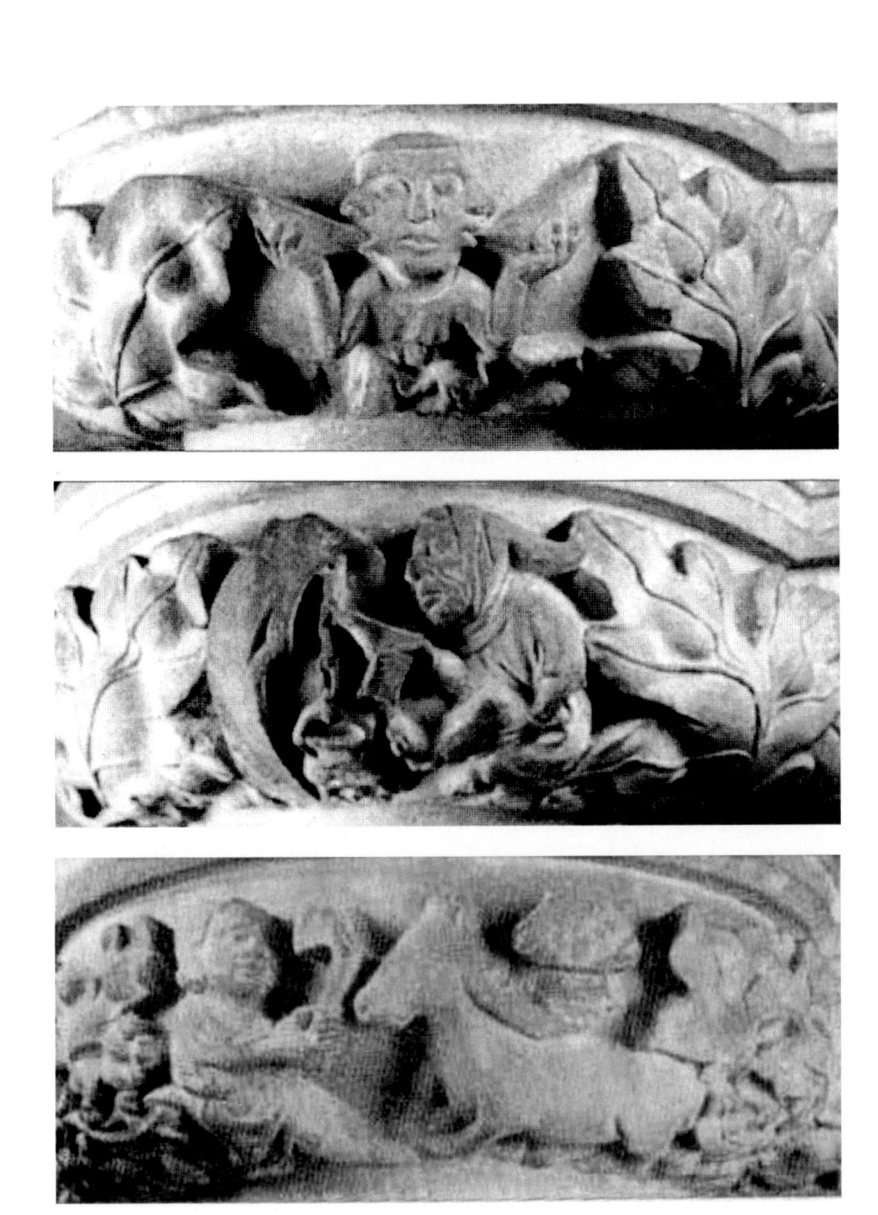

Labours of the Months: January, February and December

influences flowing into England from Continental points of origin.

The repertoire in the 'Labours' series tended to vary somewhat across Europe, according to climate and crops - for instance, the preoccupation with viticulture in French and Italian designs. Among the 'nobbly foliage' of the Carlisle series and the 'fox and goose, harpies, musician and tumbler, owl and mouse', the sequence of the months opens with January. In this instalment, as in the common European genre, the pagan deity Janus gives out wine. February in the Carlisle rendition has a standard international stock-type, the man warming his chilblained feet at his log fire and emptying his boot of the midwinter rain and melted snow. The working year wakes up in March for digging, in April for pruning, and in May for the coming of new spring growth. June offers a hawking holiday, but the summer months of July, August and September are dedicated to the hard effort of mowing, weeding and reaping. October borrows from the Continental genre in the form of a *vendage*. November prepares for the following year with early sowing, but December repays the year's toil with the feeding of pigs and the slaughter of an ox for Christmas.[187]

On the face of it, the Carlisle 'Labours' present us with an abrupt intrusion of comedy and secularity injected into the 'sacred space' of the Cathedral: we can still find wry humour in the sad man with the sodden boot. And these mundane knockabout scenes may appear to be as unspiritual as were the most bucolic of misericord renditions. Nor is there even any reference in the Carlisle monthly calendar to the Church's own cycle of feasts and fasts - no mention, for instance, of Lent. The inclusion of the deity Janus to introduce the cycle may confirm a suggestion of incipient paganism. The only allusions to Christmas lie in illustrations on how it is prepared for as a feast.

There had, however, to be a more than a merely decorative or entertaining purpose to these creations, installed as they were in the heart of the main place of worship of a diocese, and indeed there was a deep-laid, yet entirely intelligible, Christian significance to the genre of the 'Labours of the Months', entered as they were in the devotional 'Books of Hours', for the underlying meaning of all these portrayals, as they were fashioned across western Europe was orderly labour, and its sanctity.

Adam's and Eve's 'original sin' against God's majesty was to be punished by a long and laborious penitential servitude for them and their descendants, a millennia-long act of penance: 'In the sweat of thy face shalt thou eat thy bread, till thou return to the ground' (Genesis 3:19): it was through manual work that humanity's contribution to satisfaction for Adam's and Eve's offence was made, 'work becoming a way of redeeming [one]self'. By contrast, sloth was one of the Seven Deadly (or 'Capital') Sins, the sources of sinful actions, as defined by Pope Gregory I (r. 590-604).[188]

Manual labour, then, was expiatory and holy: reverence for it was central to the monastic Rule of St Benedict, in which, as the *Opus Manus* - the 'work of the hand' - it was the 'most normal' form of monastic asceticism, six hours a day in summer being devoted to it - three times more than to prayer, since, as Benedict wrote, 'If the monks live by the work of their hands, like our fathers and the Apostles, then they will truly be monks'. In the 12th century 'the Cistercians rehabilitated manual labour as a work of God'.[189]

Thus the Carlisle 'Labours' exalt mankind's partnership with the Creator, in hard manual labour, as a great act of reparation: in March a hooded man digs, and in April another, bare-legged, prunes a tree; July shows a mower, August a patient weeder; a man harvests grapes in October, and in November a sower goes forth to sow, while December brings on the pig herder and the ox slaughterer.[190]

These much more than purely decorative scenes in honour of manual work epitomise, in a profound 'spiritual allegory', an ecological unison with God's orderly plan for nature and humanity and, above all, the use of precious time, with the working country folk - the *laboratores*, the *rustici* - as His primary stewards, and the reminder of the 'necessity of using [mankind's] time as God has ordained'.[191]

Thus the 'Labour of the Months' at Carlisle may be analysed for what they tell us, on the deepest-rooted strata, about the medieval Church's understanding of the nature and status of human work and its place in the divine plan: they form a further vital element in a five-part programme of instruction, through which, over the course of the later middle ages, Carlisle Cathedral emerged as a religious teaching centre for its diocese.

(4) Lives of the Saints

Next, then, by closely interpreting pictorial and literary depictions of the lives of three saints conserved in the Cathedral, it will be possible to study in further detail the extension of the functions of the buildings in the later middle ages into that of a media teaching centre of the city, the diocese and the region.

A group of three late 15th-century paintings on the reverses of the choir stalls were designed with a view to vivid, popularised instruction on the lives of three selected saints. The set, consisting of Augustine of Hippo, Antony of Egypt and Cuthbert of Lindisfarne, opens with an account, painted, and with an accompanying text, in rhymed blackletter Middle English, with Cumbrian dialect intrusions, of the *vita* of Augustine of Hippo (354-430), the reputed founder of the Augustinian Order.

Detail of the painted panel of St Cuthbert

Neither the 22 Augustine portraits nor their partners, those of Antony of Egypt (c. 251-356) and Cuthbert of Lindisfarne, can claim great artistic merit in their own right: 'all bad', declared Pevsner, though 'they are bold and lively, and this is one of the most complete survivals in the country'.[192] Stylistically, they may be compared with a set in another northern house of Augustinian Canons, Hexham Priory in Northumberland, and it might even be surmised that such commissions were carried out by itinerant painters belonging to the Order. The aesthetic quality of these works is, however, somewhat beside the point, since they were intended, not as artistic adornments, or as foci of prayer and piety, but as visual teaching aids for explanatory oral deliveries.

The Augustine of the Carlisle panels is not the same as the St Augustine of Hippo, the relentless campaigner against heresy, founder, in his 'Confessions' (c. 400), of the tradition of Christian spiritual biography, and fountainhead of medieval Catholic theology. But the literary roots of the Carlisle Augustine portrayals lie not in the saint's massive literary legacy but rather in a hugely popular medieval hagiographic classic, the *Legenda Aurea*, or 'Golden Legend', also known as the *Lombard Historia*, by the Italian Dominican Giacomo, or Jacopus, de Voragine (c.1230-c.98). In 177 (or 182) chapters, an 'engagingly written narrative, full of anecdote and curious etymologies', designed to 'foster piety', the 'Golden Legend' is replete with human and family interest (in the case of Augustine, the hero's saintly mother Monica (c. 332-87), along with fantasy, improbability and, above all, miracles associated with the subject of the *vita*.[193]

The Carlisle Augustine sets out as a young and promising scholar, encouraged by his loving parents. The captions for the panels open with 'Her' - 'Here' - for an instructor to explain, perhaps with some kind of pointer, the contents of the art work:

The twenty-two pictures showing the Life of St Augustine in Carlisle Cathedral in copies made by Lady Frances Harcourt

99

[panel 1]   Her Fader and Mdr of Sanct Austyne
            First put hym to lerne doctryne
[panel 2]   Her taught he gramor and rethorike
            emongys all doctors non was hys lyke
[panel 3]   Her promised he with hys moder to abide
            bot he left hyr to wepyng & stal y Tide [*by the shore?*]

 In Italy Augustine studies a life of Antony of Egypt (panel 6) and is baptised by one of the great leaders of the early Church, Ambrose (c. 339-97), Bishop of Milan - (panel 10) 'Her of Sainct Ambrose chrysteyned was' - and (panel 15) 'Consecrate Byshop was this doctour'.

 Characteristic of Voragine's approach was his personalisation of encounters between his subjects and their rivals, turning these collisions into dramatic and conclusive face-to-face victories on the part of the author's heroes, as with the effortless confuting of 40 pagan philosophers by the 4th-century martyr Catherine of Alexandria. This *ad hominem* dialectical technique is to the fore in Voragine's treatment of Augustine's offensive against the Manichaean movement, which stressed the prevalence of evil in the material world, and to which he had been drawn earlier in life.

 Yet of Augustine's erudite and abstract Latin classics writings against the Manichaean doctrinal system, 'On Genesis Against the Manichees' and 'On the Catholic and Manichaean Ways of Life' (388-9),[194] there is no mention in the Carlisle *vita* series. Instead, in line with a determinedly concrete approach, the great theologian encounters not Manichaeism but a Manichaean missionary, teaching the sect's doctrine on the basis of a written text:

[panel14]   Her fortunate the heretyk concludit he
            [*Fortunately, he encountered the heretic directly.*]

The seventeen pictures showing the Life of St Antony in Carlisle Cathedral in copies made by Lady Frances Harcourt

informing *[spreading]* the laws of Maneche

The defeat of the dissident, however, comes about through the disappearance of his text in an abstruse miracle, involving a vision of the Trinity, and a woman of Augustine's household who:

[panels 15-17]

    As ys woman come to hym for consolacion

    She saw hym with the Trinite in meditacion *[She witnessed him contemplating the Trinity.]*

    When he Complyn *[the concluding prayer in the daily liturgical cycle]* had said and come to luke *[investigate]*

    He was full cleyn olkt *[completely rid]* of yis knafys *[this villain's]* buke *[He apologises to the lady]*

    Penitet me tibi ostendisse librum - *['I am deeply sorry for having shown you this book'.]*

The rest of the Augustine *vita* is posthumous in content, including a hint of faraway places:

[panel 18] They beried hys body wyth deligence

    Her in hys aurn kirk *[own church]* of Yp'onese *[Hippo in North Africa]*

    As for what might have been urgent audience questions at the time of these allocutions, amidst a religious culture that was preoccupied with relics - where was the saint buried? what journeys, or 'translations', had his relics undergone? and where might pilgrims travel to honour them ? - very detailed answers are given:

[panel 19] Her Liedbrand the kyng of Luberdy *[the Pavia-born nobleman, Liutprand or Luitbrand, c. 922-72, Bishop of Cremona in Lombardy]*

    hym translate from Sardyne *[Sardinia]* to Pavye *[Pavia]*.

    Thei shryned hys banes solemnly *[They solemnly made a shrine of his bones]*

In sanct Peter kyrk thus at Pavye

(In the 14th-century the 12th-century church of S. Pietro in Cielo in Pavia eventually acquired a magnificent shrine of Augustine.) [195]

[panel 21] Miracles followed the saint's death, including the cure of a cleric, following three years of illness, whom Augustine commands to sing compline:

>Thys prior he bad soon do evynsang her
>And helyd hym that was sek thre yer.

[panel 22]. Some missing text obscures the meaning of a final apparition:

>Her he apperyd un to these men tre
>and bad yam go to ... yt hale [that hall]. [196]

Next, following the Augustine series, a 17-panel narrative suite is dedicated to Antony, or Anthony, of Egypt, the hermit whose hagiography, *Vita Antonii* by Athanasius of Alexandria (d. 373), transformed him into a founder of monasticism, the 'father of monks', anachronistically styled in English 'Antony Abbot'. Coming from 'prosperous peasant stock', or the son of 'a prosperous Coptic family',[197] in the Carlisle version Antony is upgraded to the status of 'great lands and renttes to hym [which] do fawl ... to leve in poverty is hys intent' (2, 4), an epitome of the medieval, and particularly Franciscan, cult of voluntary 'holy poverty'.

The somewhat routine verse biography of this holy man, involving minor miracles featuring water (panels 12 and 14), comes alive, in a rendition of *the Temptation of St Antony*. The best-known Continental iconographical versions of this central trauma in Antony's life are by Hieronymus Bosch (or van Aken, c. 1460-1516, the work, now in Lisbon, dated 1495), plus its inclusion in the 1516 Isenheim Altarpiece by Matthias Grünewald (or Mathis Nithardt, or Gothard, c.1480-1528), now in Colmar in Alsace. In these classic and horrific renditions of Antony's temptation, the tension between, on the one hand, the holy man's quest for monastic perfection and, on the other, the near-fatal pull of the world - riches, the flesh - meaning sex - and the devil - is imaged as a painful physical assault on him by diabolic and horrific monsters:

[panels 7-8] Here to the wyldernes as armet *[hermit]* geon he
And thus temptyth hym covytice *[covetousness tempts]* with oon gold dyshie.
The sprytt of fornycacon to hy *[him]* her doth apper
& thus he chastith *[punishes]* his body with thorn and brer *[briar]*

Since the spiritual combat is echoed as a physical encounter, Antony's victory over the underworld becomes a knightly triumph by force of arms:

[panel 9] The devil thus hat he wounded wt lance and staf
[panel 10] Christ comes to heal his wounds and bring him comfort, removing the evil spirit's corpse and leaving it up to the cave's mouth:

Here Crist haith hym heyled the devill he doth away
And comforted hys confessor deyd as he *[the vanquished demon]* lay
And levth hy' for deyd lyying at his cayf *[cave]*

Whereas in two - those of Augustine and Cuthbert - out of these three *vitae* the verse commentaries provide ample information about the bodily remnants of the subjects - their journeys, re-locations and states of preservation - there is an inescapable lacuna over Antony's body parts: as with Moses, of whom 'no man knoweth his sepulchre to this day' (Deuteronomy, 4:36), Antony's interment is a secret sealed by order of his own modesty:

[panel 16] here in wilderns they bery hym that no man shud him knaw

    For soo he commanded syne hom first tha draw *[He ordered someone who was present intending to sketch the site to return home.]* [198]

    The inclusion of a third set of these illustrated discourses - 17 panels, dedicated to Cuthbert of Lindisfarne - would have been mandatory, not only because the saint had visited Carlisle, in 685 and 686, but also because of his status as Cumberland's primary holy man.

    Thirteen of the Cuthbert depictions are derived from manuscript miniatures of a 12th-century life, once housed in Durham's monastery library and now in the British Library.[199]

    A particular emphasis in the Carlisle Cuthbert series is an impulse to anchor and validate him within a communion of saints belonging to the first millennium. Thus the source for his straitlaced boyhood - 'no layks [*games*] and plays' - is (panel 1) 'S. Bede i' hys story says': St Bede, known as 'The Venerable' (c. 673-735), the Northumbrian monk and author of the *Historia Ecclesiastica Gentis Anglorum*, 'Ecclesiastical History of the English People' (731), wrote the metrical verse composition *De Miraculis Sancti Cuthberti* - 'Concerning St Cuthbert's Miracles' - and the prose work *De Vita et Miraculis S. Cuthberti, Episcopi Lindisfarnensis* - 'Concerning the Life and Miracles of St Cuthbert, Bishop of Lindisfarne'. [200]

    Born probably near Melrose, Cuthbert trained for the monastic life at the Scottish abbey, which had been founded by Aidan of Lindisfarne (d. 651), whom Cuthbert was to succeed as Prior in 662. The Carlisle couplet draws particular attention to Cuthbert's connection with Aidan, in the form of a vision:
[panel 3] Her saw he Aydan's sawl go up
    To hevyn blys [*heavenly bliss*] wit angels two
[panel 7] His predecessor, 'Basel', as Bishop of Lindisfarne,

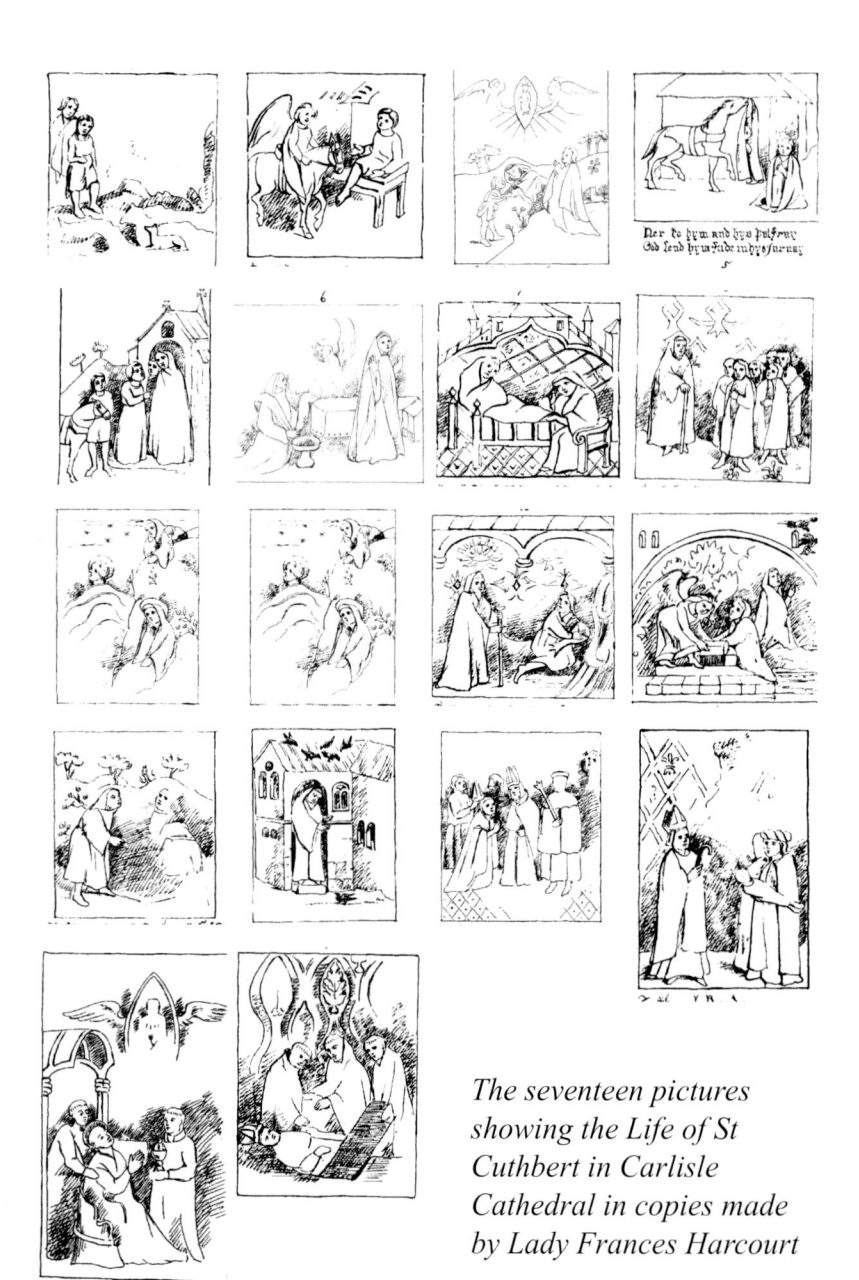

The seventeen pictures showing the Life of St Cuthbert in Carlisle Cathedral in copies made by Lady Frances Harcourt

106

predicting his own death, forecasts Cuthbert's succession.

The narration continues [panel 9] with a marvel of endurance, if not quite a miracle, in the form of Cuthbert's recitation of all 150 Psalms standing in the waters of the Northumbrian North Sea.[201]

In that religious culture that was preoccupied with the relics of saints, their various travels, whereabouts and state of preservation, Cuthbert's final vindication and achievement is the miraculous incorruption of his mortal remains:
[panel 17] vi yere after yt beryd was he
> Yai fand hym hole as red may ye
> [*Six year after his burial*
> *they discovered him intact, as you can read.*]

In devising this combination of words and images, their composers would have been sensitively aware of what their hearers wanted and expected of their *vitae* - including family background where available, the abandonment of great wealth association with other famous figures, episodes, incidents, miracles, wonders and feats. Because of the rapid growth of the relic cult in the later middle ages, demands for data about partial or complete bodies, objects associated with Christ, Mary and the saints - from the international treasures of the Crown of Thorns, the True Cross, Christ's 'Holy Coat', and the Virgin's milk to physical remains of revered regional figures and objects associated with them - were insatiable.

In the category of focal figures of regional piety few could compete with the northern Cuthbert cult, beginning, as his *vita* recounts, with his body's miraculous wholeness after death:
[panel 17] *xi yere after yt beryd was he*
> *Yai fand hym hole as red may ye*

[Six years after he was buried, they found his body intact, as you may read.] [202]

This couplet, marking the point in time at which Cuthbert's body was found to be miraculously undecayed, opens up the celebration of Cuthbert as primarily the subject of a largely autonomous regional religious observance. Regional faith in the therapeutic power of Cuthbert's fragment grew steadily, including the cure in 728 of a Dacre young man's eye infection by the application of one of the saint's hairs.[203]

In c. 875 Eadred, one of Cuthbert's successors as Bishop of Lindisfarne, led a party of his monks westwards, carrying Cuthbert's remains to safety, away from Viking raiders. The chronicler Simeon of Durham (c. 1060- 1130) related that the party arrived at the mouth of the Derwent, near modern Workington, intending to cross over to Ireland, until Cuthbert's spirit arose to oppose the plan. The ship was turned back, great waves washing over it, which were 'changed into blood', until, as popular tradition had it, the group arrived at Ninian's former base, Whithorn.[204]

Cuthbert's reburial at Lindisfarne in 698 in an elaborate oak coffin is a further instalment in the much-retold adventures of the preserved corpse. The head of the martyr and king of Northumbria Oswald (r. 616-42) was placed in Cuthbert's coffin in 875. In 995 the 'community of Cuthbert', 'guided by what they thought was the will of the saint', brought the coffin to Chester-le-Street, Co. Durham.[205]

The miraculously imperishable cadaver, then, became Cuthbert's cachet, towed from place to place by devoted disciples until the unresting assemblage found peace with interment in Durham. As has been seen, a whole literature - 'as red may ye' - and a vast oral tradition arose around these adventures, in which Cuthbert was hallowed into his own preserved and miracle-working corpse. It was he and his relic cult that became the focus of the veneration: as Simeon of Durham recorded, he defended his worshippers - 'the people of St Cuthbert', the 'people of the saint' - from invasion 'by the mediation of holy St Cuthbert and the presence of the said holy Relic'.[206]

Yet in the form of Cumbrian religion assembled around Cuthbert and his relic a whole doctrinal balance was lost, and popular and lay piety overcame doctrinal orthodoxy. Medieval theologians:

> distinguished the *cultus absolutus* (reverence paid to God and to God through saints) from the *cultus relativus* (honor paid to things related through the holy person). These distinctions were often inoperative in the Church at large, however, where relics were thought to possess an inherent power parallel to Christ's redemptive act.[207]

For orthodox theologians, the miracles of the saints were performed not *ex opere operato* - 'of their own power' - but by God working through the saints and their relics.

> The veneration paid to these saints was secondary to the adoration reserved for God, although *the niceties of such distinctions were not always significant for the popular devotees of saints' cults*.[208] [my emphasis]

In fact, apart from Cuthbert's preaching 'godys word myld and mek' [panel 8], the Deity makes no appearance in his *vita*, though [panel 10] 'Christ haith hym helyd' after Cuthbert's agony.[209]

Thus in the regional cult of Cuthbert as an avatar, as it was set out in the Carlisle Cathedral wood panels, the Church's theocentric and Christocentric concerns were swept aside - 'such distinctions were not always significant' - in an urgency to cater for the lay - and heterodox - veneration of a superhuman hero, wielding his own wonder-working bodily remnants. The Cumbrian Cuthbert relic cult, as a free-standing corpus of public veneration, had abandoned Catholicism's insistence on the primacy of the Trinity, in a classic example of the subordination of the Church's doctrinal guidelines to popular customer demand. As will be seen in chapter 10 (Volume II), the doctrinal imbalances present in the popular regional cult of Cuthbert as an autonomously potent super-saint and wonder-worker were rectified in the new, internationally current piety of the Catholic Reformation from the 16th century onwards.

(5) The Apostles' Creed
Carlisle Cathedral's didactic function was completed in a set of paintings, on the reverses of the choir stalls, dating from the period c. 1465-c. 1500. These depictions feature the 12 Apostles, each one surmounted by two lines of Latin blackletter script setting out an article of the Apostles' Creed. [210]

A 'concise, formal and authorized statement of important points of Christian doctrine', in the early Christian Church a creed (*'credo'* - 'I believe') was a form of words requiring assent on the part of candidates for baptism. By c. 390 the specific title 'Apostles' Creed' had come into use for the variant being considered here, along with the legend that this creed, which was used only in the Western ('Latin') Church, was composed jointly by the 12 Apostles. This 12-part formulary sets out the basics of a consensual and intelligible core Christian doctrinal grammar.[211]

The term Apostle (Greek *apostolos* - 'a messenger', 'one sent out') was current in the early Church to indicate individuals concerned with evangelism. The Carlisle 'Paintings of the Apostles', as these were copied by the artist Matthew Ellis Nutter (1795-1862) after they came to light in 1810, was based on the standard list originating in Matthew 10:1-4.[212]

Following the sequence in Matthew's gospel, Peter, 'Prince of the Apostles', believed by Catholics to have been Bishop of

Matthew Nutter's copies of The Apostles' Creed made in 1810
St Peter; St Andrew; St James; St John; / St Thomas; St James; St Philip;
St Bartholomew; / St Matthew; St Simon; St Thaddeus; St Matthias

Rome and hence the first pope, opens the agenda, portrayed wearing a full dark beard, with what appears to be a monastic tonsure. He carries the crossed keys of his authority granted him by Christ (Matthew 16:18-19) and the New Testament containing his two attributed Epistles; there is a suggestion of a priest's chasuble. His emblem of the crossed keys can also be seen in depictions in Darmstadt, Vienna, Munich and the Vatican City.[213]

Like all the other Apostles, Peter puts his name to a two-line form of words, the head of the dozen being apportioned the first article of the 12, translated as: 'I believe in God the Father Creator of heaven and earth'.[214]

To Peter's right stands the Apostle Andrew, displaying an X-shaped 'saltire' cross, the emblem of his humble refusal to be crucified on a cross of the same shape as Jesus's. The saltire, featuring on Scotland's flag in honour of the country's patron Andrew, appears on the Continent, for example, in a work of c. 1460 in Freising and, locally, on the historic seal of the town of Penrith, whose parish church is dedicated to the saint. A ring, probably of 13th-century provenance, found at Penton, near Carlisle, in 1991, has the St Andrew saltire cross in relief on its mount.[215]

The Carlisle image shows Andrew haloed and richly dressed, proclaiming the second article of the Creed, 'And in Jesus Christ his only Son our Lord'.[216]

The third figure to the right in the top row is that of James, known as 'the Great', whose caption proclaims the doctrine of Christ's Nativity and the Virgin Birth: 'Who was conceived by the Holy Spirit, born of the Virgin Mary'.[217]

The book James holds, bound by a double clasp, would be the New Testament Epistle of James. His clothing and accoutrements can be explained in terms of the complex evolution of medieval beliefs about him.

From the 7th century onwards, the conviction circulated that, before his martyrdom in c.44, James had preached in Spain: a Spanish tradition arose that his body had been translated from Jerusalem to Compostela - (Santiago [St James] de Compostela) in Galicia, north-west Spain. Among the legends around this transfer was that of the passage of James's relics from Jerusalem to Compostela in a marble ship. When a knight saw the vessel coming into port, his horse bolted, throwing him into the water, though he was able to scramble on to the ship, finding that his body was covered with scallop shells.[218]

The scallops shell eventually became the badge of pilgrims - the 'cockle hat' - of those travelling to the internationally acclaimed shrine of Compostela, and that of pilgrims in general. James, the patron saint of pilgrims, is shown in the Carlisle set as himself a pilgrim, with a scallop hat badge, the pilgrim device that became an iconographic standard for him, as may be seen for example in Munich, Erfurt and Pamplona.[219] In the Carlisle rendition he also carries a long and sturdy staff to aid his peregrinations and he grasps a finely wrought white vessel.

On the far right of the top row of the portraits stands John the Evangelist, who proclaims the fourth article of the Apostles' Creed - 'Suffered under Pontius Pilate, was crucified, died, and was buried'.[220]

This is a highly significant phrase of the Creed, because, from the time of the gospels onwards (e.g. Matthew 27:1, 20:25) and during the centuries of persecution, Christian spokesmen, afraid of alienating the Romans by attributing the execution of their founder to the Roman Empire, placed responsibility for the Crucifixion instead on the Jewish people. The end of persecution under the Emperor Constantine (r. 312-337) made it possible to address the facts of the matter, which were that Christ was put to death by a Roman provincial governor, as in Matthew 26: 26-27.

The Nicene creed compiled by the General Council convened by Constantine at Nicea in 325, like the Apostles' Creed, declared 'He was crucified also for us, suffered under Pontius Pilate, and was buried'.

Despite an enduring belief that he was long-lived, surviving into the reign of Trajan, John is represented in his Carlisle portrait as a young man, beardless, with light-coloured hair and wearing a kind of turban. He is shown without an emblem - for example, his recurrent motif of a chalice containing a pair of serpents, but is holding together the folds of his rich garments.[221]

The first figure to the left of the next line down is that of the Apostle Thomas, who announces the next article of the Apostles' Creed, 'He descended into hell; the third day he rose again from the dead'.[222]

While this article, which is not included in the Nicene Creed, affirms the literal truth of Christ's Resurrection, the first words of the phrase allude to the belief known in medieval England as the 'Harrowing of Hell', a familiar subject of religious art and drama: in this episode, Christ, after the Crucifixion, enters a domain, sometimes known as 'Limbo', or the *limbus patrum*, where the righteous who lived before His coming awaited the gospel message.

A New Testament source is in 1 Peter 3: 18-19: 'in the spirit he was raised to life, and, in the spirit, he went to preach to the spirits in prison' - along with Old Testament prophecies, including Psalm 16:10. The 'Harrowing' was a favourite subject of medieval Mystery Plays, featuring a fight between Jesus and Satan for possession of the imprisoned souls. One of the invocations in the medieval prayer *Adoro te Domine Jesu Christe* ... ran 'I adore you, Lord Jesus Christ, liberating the captives: I beseech you, never let me enter there'. The theme is depicted in the work by Jan Brueghel the Elder (1568-1625), with Hans Rottenhammer, *Christ Descending into Limbo* (1597).[223]

The Descent may also be read as Christ's victory over the power of evil but can also be understood as a view of the Cross as Jesus's spiritual nadir, acute dejection and sense of abandonment - of 'the full bearing by Christ of the fruits of sin in our stead': as John Calvin (1509-64) put it, the Descent was an element in the 'fearful agonies by which [Christ's] soul was pierced'. 'Calvin believed that Christ endured the torment of the damned in descending into hell'. [224]

Thomas, who is hooded in a sort of cowl, holds a book: no New Testament Epistles are credited to him, but works adopting his name include the 'Acts of Thomas', and the 'Gospel of Thomas', a collection of sayings of Jesus said to have been recorded by him. Thomas is displayed here with one of his emblems, a tall lance, which features in depictions of him conserved in various places in Europe - for example, Esslingen and Vienna: these portrayals show him being stabbed by such a weapon by two servants, or being attacked with the lance at the altar or of his being stabbed in the back.[225]

To the right of Thomas appears James, sometimes known as 'the Less', who affixes his name to the article 'He ascended into heaven, sits the right hand of God the Father almighty'. With a full blond beard, this James is richly clothed and appears to be holding a small text or a plaque, plus a staff which may be the fuller's stick with which he was beaten to death, as shown in a portrayal in Aachen Cathedral.[226]

To James's right stands Philip, whose article from the Apostles' Creed summarises the Last Judgement: 'From thence he shall come to judge the living and the dead'. Like the other Apostles, Philip is richly clothed; he wears a halo, has blond hair and a beard and carries a plain cross, the symbol which accepts the tradition that he suffered martyrdom by crucifixion, as portrayed in designs of him with the cross present in Prague, Tübingen, Munich and Brussels.[227]

To the far right of the second row of portraits going downwards, Bartholomew is depicted. In the Carlisle image, the tradition that he was martyred by being flayed alive is upheld in the sharp pointed knife he holds up. His emblems of flaying and flayed skin have been identified in eight European venues.[228]

Bartholomew wears opulent clothes and has a fair beard and hair. His attestation, 'I believe in the Holy Spirit', is also inscribed in Latin around in a 15th-century mural of him by Pietro Matteo d'Amelia in the Vatican's Borgia Apartment.[229]

To the far left of the bottom line of the paintings, Matthew is displayed. He is asserting the article of the Creed 'the holy Catholic Church, the communion of saints', and shown with a white halo, rich costume, and light-coloured beard and hair. He is holding the gospel credited to him and, in his other hand, a saw-toothed axe, the axe being the reputed instrument of his martyrdom, as identified in Munich in a figure of c. 1500.[230]

To Matthew's right, Simon affirms 'the forgiveness of sins'. Balding, with a light brown beard, Simon wears layers of fine clothing. His emblem, a long wooden staff surmounted by a halberd - one of the attributed weapons of his martyrdom - is shown in a 15th-century painting in the Vatican City Museums.[231]

In the figures and verses in the final panels, Matthias, who replaced the traitor Judas Iscariot to make up the number of the Apostles (Acts 1:15-26), affirms the last article of the Creed, 'and life everlasting Amen', and Thaddaeus acclaims 'the resurrection of the body'. Drawn, quite roughly, in profile Matthias has a dark halo, hair and beard and carries no emblem but only a rugged wooden staff. Handsome, haloed and fair-bearded, in a fold of his ample clothing Thaddaeus displays three loaves: over the course of time, he came to be 'much invoked in circumstances of special difficulty', care for feeding the desperately poor and starving being evoked in this image.[232]

It has been seen that the figures in the Carlisle Apostles portrayals draw on a rich accumulation of medieval European hagiographical literature and legend, in an international cultural thesaurus in which Carlisle was fully involved. As has also been seen, recognition symbols associated with these figures are to be viewed in venues across Europe, from Belgium, the Czech Republic, Germany, Spain, Austria and Italy.

There were at the same time also certain recognised stylistic conventions that governed the way that these portraits were to be executed. As has been seen, with the exception of the black-bearded Peter, and possibly Matthias, all these individuals are portrayed as tall, lightly coloured northern Europeans, rather than as people of the eastern Mediterranean.

The reason for this artistic requirement was a marked revival in Christian anti-Judaism in medieval Europe, fuelled by the renewed conviction that the Jewish people were guilty of Christ's torment and death, with associated destructive fantasies such as that Jews abused the Catholic eucharist and tortured Christian children to death for ritual purposes.

Just as there existed a working artistic convention that debarred the representation of the Blessed Virgin Mary as a Jewish woman, and because 'the idea prevailed that Judas was the emblematic figure of the Jewish people whom the Christians never ceased to accuse of having killed the Messiah', the responsibility of Judas (replaced by Matthias) for the betrayal of Christ made it imperative to dissociate the Apostles from any Jewish identity.[233]

Especially on account of the Judas link, then, the Apostles were programmed to lose anything but a northern European appearance, as, for example, in the case of 'St John on Patmos' and his flowing mane of golden yellow hair, by Hans Burgkmair the Elder (1473-1531) (Munich).[234] The Caucasian figures in the Carlisle panels obey these dictates.

There were other ways in which certain widely accepted stylistic rulings guided the steps of the Carlisle panellist, for example in their stereotypically lavish dress, in conformity with the what was understood to have been 'traditional dress of the Apostles'. This intentionally archaic and stylised costume was assigned to the Apostles as if to mark out their role as the historic architects of the Christian Church in the 1st century, wearing what was taken to have been the male dress of that period. Likewise, their beards posited them back in time, to a period, before in the 5th century, which was when clerics in the western Church were ordered to be clean shaven, sanctions reinforced by ecclesiastical councils from the 12th century onwards.[235] Thus in such details as dress and beards the historicity of the Apostles as figures belonging to the early 1st century was affirmed in this remarkable set of didactic illustrations, which brought to a local and lay Cumbrian consciousness a complex set of religious and cultural assumptions that were current across late medieval western Europe.

The evidence from the broadly educational material on display in the medieval Carlisle Cathedral interior raises further questions about the nature of religious experience offered there in the pre-Reformation period. What is known, for instance, about the quality of the priestly ministry that was supposed to provide the religious instruction and spiritual guidance of the laity? Certain long-held historiographical views of the 16th-century English Reformation have assumed its popularity and indeed its inevitability on account of the alleged moral and ministerial defects of the late medieval Catholic clergy, including notorious avarice. So, given that it was the Augustinian Canons who were in control of the worship, preaching and sacramental provisions of Carlisle Cathedral, were these clerics to be accounted a corporation of self-interested (and numerically declining?) sinecurists, 'an expensive parasite on the body of the Church'? Or did they - as was the case, for instance, with the clergy of Exeter Cathedral - provide 'the major religious power house in the diocese', harmonised 'with 15th-century lay spirituality'? [236]

In part-answer to the question, the number of Canons, intended never to exceed 26, was holding up remarkably well over the course of the period: 13 in 1366: 12 in 1379; 16 in 1396; 19 in 1521- five of them novices - and a high point of 23 at the time of the surrender of the Cathedral as a house of Canons in 1540. In order to fulfil the demanding requirements of the Cathedral liturgy and music, the Canons had the services of lay choristers, while they supplemented parochial ministry in the city. Though as a community they were not as wealthy or as numerous as, for example, the Cistercian monks at Holm Cultram, the absence of conflict between them and the populace (as was the case in some cathedral cities in the south of England) assured them a steady collective income of least £400. The ample (now beautifully restored) Tithe Barn, traditionally dated to the period 1484 to 1507, and used to store wool, hemp, hay and straw coming in from the Priory's granges and farms in the neighbourhood, suggests the moderate, agriculturally derived, financial sufficiency of the Canons, forming in the city 'an establishment easy to live with'.[237]

It was also under the direction of the Canons that Carlisle Cathedral emerged in the 15th century as a major centre of popular piety in the north, with people 'flocking there on pilgrimage', the focus being Mary, the original dedicatee of the priory. The Virgin had already functioned as protector of Carlisle: in 1385 an invading Scots army, camped at Carlisle, encountered a woman who warned them that the king and his army were on their way to the rescue, and the invaders scattered. The word went out, however, that the woman was 'thought to have been the glorious Virgin Mary, *patrona de Carleyl*, who often appears to the inhabitants of that city'.[238]

To Mary's capacity of protector of Carlisle was added that of the focus of a shrine, said to rival that of Cuthbert at Durham. In 1451 the Canons acquired an 'image of the Blessed Virgin covered with plates of silver and with gold, gems and precious stones' in order to satisfy 'the devotion of Christ's faithful'. This Marian shrine became a powerful magnet for pilgrims, and 'it was a special veneration for the Blessed Virgin which was the chief cause of making Carlisle a place of pilgrimage' - as, for example in 1518, when a butcher of York left a request for his wife, after his death, to 'goo pilgrimage for me' to four locations, including 'Our Lady of Kerlell'.[239]

Such devotional initiatives may be understood in the light of 'an astonishing revival of ecclesiastical activity in the diocese of Carlisle between the close of the fifteenth century and the early years of the sixteenth century', a development also evident, for example at York, and assisted throughout England by the descent of peace following the accession in 1485 of the Tudor dynasty with the end of the violent conflict over the succession to the throne, the Wars of the Roses of 1455-85. The Cathedral was at the heart of this religious renewal in the diocese, guided by Prior Thomas Gondicourt, who served from 1465 to about 1500: it is 'scarcely possible to exaggerate the value and amount of the work done by him and his two successors within the priory precincts'. Gondicourt's building and decoration work reveal his religious aims.[240]

This legacy may be seen at its finest in the screen in St Catherine's chapel within the Cathedral, including 'intricate Flamboyant [the final phase of medieval French architecture, with graceful tracery]... [and] forms of Scottish or Flemish type'. Here Carlisle Cathedral can be seen at the centre of a regional, Anglo-Scottish and cosmopolitan cultural and devotional nexus, linking Melrose and Holm Cultram with influences from the Low Countries, via Scotland: there are similarities with work in King's College Chapel, Aberdeen.[241]

(6) The Chantries
Gondibour's screen adorns a chantry chapel, on the eastern side of the cathedral's south transept, dedicated to the early 4th-century martyr St Catherine of Alexandria: the institution was said to have been established by the Carlisle citizen John de Capella in 1342, and, if so, it belongs to the great age of the chantry foundations in the Europe of the 14th and 15th centuries and in an age of recurrent lethal epidemic: over half of the Cumberland and Westmorland chantries set up between 1252 and 1523 fell within the period 1340-1400, during which, in 1362, there was an estimated 20% plague death rate in the Eden valley.[242]

A chantry (from the Latin *cantare*, 'to sing') was a clerical 'office or ... benefice maintained to sing or say mass for the souls of the founder and his friends and also to the little chapel in which masses were usually said'.[243] The doctrinal key was the offering of Masses so as to expedite the release of the deceased from Purgatory, the punitive state of preparation through the elimination of the remaining guilt for earthly sins in preparation for reception into heaven. Chantries, located within parish churches and cathedrals, were dedicated to saints or to particular devotions.

The key economic difference between these later medieval foundations and the great cashless land grants of the earlier middle ages was that the chantry, in an age of a rising cash economy in Europe, 'required a monetary endowment for its erection', usually drawn on rents from properties, and transmuted into a stipend for the priest, known as a chantrist, who was often appointed to other services, especially teaching at a school. The example in Carlisle Cathedral was a classic of the type, providing for a chantrist to celebrate Mass daily in the chapel, with an annual income from two households, six shops, a garden and 30s 6d in Carlisle.[244]

Other examples of Cumbrian foundations include a second chantry of St Lawrence in Appleby, endowed at the sum £3 14 7d by Robert Threlkeld, of the town, in 1334; the site of the St Nicholas chantry in St Lawrence's is now occupied by Lady Anne Clifford's tomb (1657). Also in 1334 Sir William L'Engleys, of Highhead, MP for Cumberland in 1319-38 and Chief Forester of Inglewood from 1328, set up a chantry dedicated to the Blessed Virgin Mary in St Michael's, Appleby. In Kirkby Lonsdale a chantry was set up by Dr William Middleton in 1482, with an endowment of £4 13 4d: the chapel stood in the north-east aisle and was demolished in the 18th century.[245]

Extra religious duties were required in the foundation chantry statutes at Brigham, which 'envisaged a quasi-monastic existence' on the part of the incumbent and required him to sing a solemn Mass on Sundays, another in honour of the angels on Mondays, on Tuesdays one for St Thomas Becket, on Wednesdays, Thursdays and Saturdays in tribute to Mary - and on Fridays the main requiem Mass for the benefactor: the chantrist was also to help the parish priest with his general duties. At Hutton-in-the- Forest the chantrist was required to assist the

St Lawrence, Appleby by Thomas Allom, 1832

rector with his daily priest's 'office' of prayer.[246]

It was probably Thomas de Roos (d. 1390) who set up the first Thomas Becket chantry in Kendal Holy Trinity, which the family's heirs, the Parr family, inherited. The courtier Sir William Parr (1434-83) lived in Kendal between 1475 and his death and 'almost certainly commissioned the new Becket chantry'. Holy Trinity eventually accommodated no fewer than six chantries. One 'exceptionally rich' Kendal chantry chaplain was paid £6 13 4d pa. - while the chantry of St Anthony drew on 12 rents totalling £6 18 10d.[247]

In a significant number of cases, to the chantrist's liturgical duties there were added those of schoolmaster. As Nicolson and Burn recorded, William Strickland, later Bishop of Carlisle, required his chantry priest in Penrith St Andrew's 'to teach music and grammar for the salary of 6l [£6] a year'. In Cockermouth the chantrist taught 'a grammar scole'. Brough-under-Stainmore, where the chantry was financed by 16 rents, totalling £12 11 4d, from as far afield as Barnard Castle, had the extra service of a 'side master', teaching Latin grammar. A new chantry established at Brough-under-Stainmore by John Brunskill in 1506 was served by two priests. The teaching of Latin in the town was salaried at a high £7 19 6d pa., and there was a separate teaching entry of £5 for 'song'.[248]

In Appleby in 1479 the mayor, bailiff and 'commonalty' amalgamated three long- standing chantries in the two parish churches for a priest in order to keep a school and in 1516 awarded a teacher salary of £4 13 4d, the corporation being closely involved in the transaction, since it may be that town governments were as interested in the educational side-effects of the chantries as they were in their spiritual concerns, as this rationalising of the originally triple foundation indicates. Indeed, a sense of altered, if not inverted, priorities, as between the spiritual and the educational advantages of chantries, may have been incipient, perhaps being more marked in the region's market towns.[249]

Thus in early 16th-century Kendal, a different concept of what was being required from a chantry foundation was unveiled when the trustees of the lands of Adam Pennington (d. 1526) in Lincolnshire were instructed to pay £10 pa. to a master 'to teche a free schole to all that commyn ... in Kendal', and 'to sing [at Mass] and pray for the souls of the founder, his wife & parents'. Almost insistently, the reversed and utilitarian priorities are set out: for 24 years the chantrist was:

> to kepe a fre grammar schole in Kendal *and* [my emphasis] to celebrate [Mass] and praye for the soulle of the founder.[250]

One testamentary case is not sufficient to document any more widespread shift in the collective mind-set in this area.

However, whereas in an earlier period a school might have been attached to a chantry as a kind of add-on, or to give the chantrist something useful to do with his day once his morning Mass was celebrated, a heightening awareness of the importance of schooling may have been coming to mean that, at least in this instance, the obituary Masses were viewed as a secondary supplement to the primacy of the school. Thus, perhaps a glimpse of a secularising, even a modernising, imperative may have been beginning to infiltrate religious life and assumptions in early modern urban Cumbria. Yet, and despite this evident prioritising of the 'this worldly' potential social, and specifically the educational, spin-offs arising from the amounts of capital locked away in the chantry economy, as will be seen in the next chapter, early Tudor Cumbrians remained closely attached to the chantry cult as a primarily spiritual phenomenon, focused on the afterlife and on anxieties over the welfare of the person's soul.

Chapter 7:
Reformation and Resistance in the Tudor Lake Counties, 1485-1603

As was observed in the previous chapter, an 'astonishing revival of ecclesiastical activity in the diocese of Carlisle' was under way before the close of the 15th century. As that 15th-century Cumbrian religious renewal ran on vigorously into the 16th century, it would put up a barrier to Protestantisation in the region, not because 'traditional religion' was inert, static and reactionary, but because it was both dynamic and firmly rooted in regional life and culture.[251]

It may well be, as a school of 'revisionist' Reformation historians now argue, that, a few pockets of dissidence apart, the English were in c. 1500 an orthodox Catholic nation - and that it would take decades of official pressure to convert them into a Protestant people. It may, however, also become apparent that the vitality of the late medieval and early Tudor Cumbrian religious renewal lent additional force to 'traditional' beliefs and practices in Cumberland and Westmorland, fostering exceptionally strong opposition to innovations imposed by the crown in doctrine, worship and institutions. In terms of emphasis, rather than its being the case that 'Nothing in late medieval Cumbria predisposed the region to religious reformation', the religious culture of the 15th and early 16th centuries strongly inclined the region to retain the vigorous rhythms of traditional faith and action and, in particular, to manifest the 'healthy condition of the Church in these parts in the years just before the Reformation'.[252]

Cumbria's religious traditionalism was epitomised in its immunity to the late medieval heretical Lollard movement which was was initiated by the Oxford clerical academic John Wyclif (d. 1384) and which is sometimes portrayed as an anticipation of the Protestant Reformation of the 16th century: it has been claimed that the 'fact that the canons of Carlisle consistently failed to send the inmates of their house to Oxford or Cambridge would at least have served to insulate them from heretical opinions when these began to get a foothold in the universities'.[253]

It was not, however, as if the Lake Counties had no connection with Oxford: because of the 'waste, desolate and illiterate condition of those [Cumbrian] counties', in 1341 Robert Eaglesfield (or d'Eaglesfield), of Eaglesfield in Cumberland, confessor and chaplain to Queen Philippa (1311-69), founded, in honour of the queen, The Queen's College, Oxford, giving preference to entrants from Cumberland and Westmorland who were of 'distinguished character, poor in means', 'apt for the study of theology'.[254] This Oxford link, however, had no identifiable effect in introducing Wycliffian or Lollard beliefs into Cumbria.

Originating among academics in Wyclif's Oxford and some supportive gentry, Lollardy quickly became a minority dissident faith which found adherents, especially among artisans and in the textile industries, in London and the south-east, in commercial and industrial centres such as Leicester, Coventry, Northampton and Bristol and in the west Midlands, though 'no evidence of their activity in this [Cumbrian] part of England has been discovered'.[255]

One possible exception to Canon Bouch's generalisation of 'no evidence' of a Lollard presence may illustrate some attitudes towards conformity or nonconformity present within the

Cumbrian community. The case concerns a woman whose dereliction of religious duties had given rise to a legal action, in the manor court of Derwentfells, in May 1508:

> Also they (the jury) say that Issabil Kendal, late of Pardishow [Pardshaw] in the county of Cumberland spinster, lives in a suspicious manner in that she has received no sacraments of the church in her parish church of Brighame nor elsewhere as they believe for the space of one year last past.[256]

Isabel Kendal's offence was an ecclesiastical one, a sin, not a crime in common law: in 1215 the Church's Fourth Lateran Council ordained that Catholics were obliged to receive holy communion annually, at some point during the Easter season, as well as to confess their sins to their parish priests in the Sacrament of Penance during Lent: the dual 'Easter duties'. When Kendal's case came before the manor court in May, the Easter season would have been over, but the lady had not received communion, and the omission was taken into account by a secular manorial jury of laymen, albeit assuming for themselves the enforcement of ecclesiastical legislation.[257]

Further, the jury traced Kendal's lapse not to simple negligence but to a doctrinal error - 'a perverse opinion as to belief'. The Lollards derived from Wyclif a disbelief in a 'Real Presence' of Christ in the eucharist, and many, if not all, of them, abstained from parish communion. Perhaps, then, the Derenwentfells manor court had detected a Cumberland Lollard, maybe one influenced by notions introduced by southern merchants trading in nearby Cockermouth.[258]

Observance of the 'Easter duties', and on a massive and indeed demonstrative public scale, was, by way of contrast, the hallmark of traditional Catholic behaviour in Carlisle in 1540, with a self- awareness that such communal conduct was ancestral

- 'customary' - 'creating a great labour for the parish priests to hear confessions'. Two priests were paid 6s 8d 'in reward given them in time of Lent for hearing the confessions of Christ's faithful, as has been customary from time immemorial'.[259]

The continuity of the late medieval Catholic revival into the Tudor century in Cumbria is additionally evident in an ongoing programme of church building and embellishment, there being 'a good deal of church building on either side of 1500'. At St Michael's, Brough-under-Stainmore, perhaps in 1513, a second reconstruction, 'even more radical' than the large-scale enlargement that had been carried out in the 14th century, was implemented, with the north aisle housing a chantry dedicated to the Virgin Mary. Fragments of 16th-century stained glass featured John the Baptist and Mary and also exhibited the *Arma Christi*, depictions of a chivalric-based analogy of Christ as a victorious knight, a fashionable iconology, maintaining 'arms' in the sense of heraldry, and also the weapons Christ used to achieve His conquest over Satan - the 'Instruments of the Passion'.[260]

Even the 80 amateur carvings in a prison cell in Carlisle Castle, dated to between 1450 and 1550, express key features of late-medieval piety. As well as a patriotic St George in armour, they represent (no. 48) Christ on the cross, with the two Marys in prayer, and, probably (no. 49) the Virgin Mary and St Mary Magdalene. The easily reproduced motif of initials of Jesus's name, 'IHS', an international devotion originating in late medieval Italy, and also present in Holy Trinity, Kendal, and on a disc discovered at Nether Denton, appears in number 53 in the sequence.[261]

In 1504 a local yeoman, Robert Briggs, of 'the well-to-do and pious ... family' of Cowmire Hall, left a bequest to build a chapel-of-ease on Cartmel Fell for the people of the Cartmel area - 'one of the gems among the pre-Reformation churches of northern England'. The chapel was dedicated to Antony of Egypt, of whom, as was seen in the previous chapter, a 17-panel illustrated *vita* was created in Carlisle Cathedral.[262]

Exquisitely executed stained-glass, restored in 1911, features a depiction of Antony with a bell and 'T-shaped staff'- 'the Tau-cross, a cross in the form of the [Greek letter] T ... a staff with a cross- piece at the top like a crutch'. The inclusion of the Tau-cross in the representation of Antony links this iconography with other European realisations of the same motif - in Colmar, Zoschau in Saxony and in Gallmannsweil, near Stockach in Baden-Württemberg. Antony's other symbol in the window is a pig or boar, 'with its own bell 'possibly representing the Deadly Sin of gluttony which he had overcome'.[263]

The twinned images of pig and bells in the east widow on Cartmel Fell chapel join a Continental artistic production of these themes - piglets in Altenbeken in Westphalia, in Fehmarn Castle in Germany, and in Beisigheim in Baden-Württemberg, while the bells appear in Lübeck, Münster, Rostock, and in Reisbach in Lower Bavaria. In an English rendition - a 15th-century alabaster carving, probably from a workshop in Nottinghamshire, 'the bearded saint is depicted with a pig at his feet, his trademark "attribute" or symbol in art.'[264] This artistry, in this lonely upland chapel, aligns Cartmel Fell with an iconographic theme encountered deep into Central Europe.

On the right hand side of the window is the hermit saint Leonard and, at the feet of the saint, donors. Then, in the centre of the glass, is a depiction of the Crucifixion, 'half Flemish, half English' in style. In a vivid red 'pigmentation to represent the blood from the crown of thorns ... an outflowing of ruby-red blood' is shown: [265]

Christ crucified with red rays from His seven wounds leading

East Window, St Anthony's, Cartmel Fell

to adjacent panels depicting the Seven Sacraments of the Church ... the crucified Christ, with dark arrows proceeding from His wounds directing the eye to a number of panels on each side, small pictures ... representing the seven sacraments of the Church. [266]

A complex theology of the wounded, crucified Christ as the source of sacramental grace - the 'image of the Wounds as wells of grace' [267] - is thus encapsulated in a window of this fellside chapel.

As was seen towards the close of the previous chapter, it is possible to detect traces, from arrangements being made in late 15th- and early 16th-century Kendal of an emergent social and utilitarian approach to the resources that were stored up in the chantry system. Even so, just as in the later middle ages, an inherently non-materialistic care for the welfare of individuals' souls after death, continuing to motivate considerable financial investment in the chantry apparatus, still preoccupied the early Tudor Cumbrian laity. Thus, if between the late 15th and early 16th centuries Kendalians were beginning to apportion educational priorities to established spiritual provisions, in 1522 the will of the Kendal chapman Richard Andrew retained the traditional understanding of a chantry as a vehicle for endowing Masses to be celebrated in the interests of the individual donor's *soul*, with no commitment to financing social or educational welfare: Andrew set aside £8 3 4d for 'two preests to minister of my soule in the church & in the Kendal chapel of All Hallows' - one 'to sing [Mass] for me for one year in St George's loft' and the other 'to sing for me for a year in the said chapel of All Hallows'.[268]

Preoccupation with the situation of the individual's soul in purgatory also characterised the specifications that testators wrote into the instructions that they left for their executors, including the discharge of debts, and above all those to the Church, especially unpaid tithes, which left 'the soul longer in purgatory': Richard Andrew shared that anxiety, with his demand that 'the church to have what it ought to have, according to the manner of the country'.[269]

The passage of the decades saw no diminution in Cumbrians' commitment to the routines and the finances of the chantries as insurance packages for the spirit's existence after death. In 1531, for instance, Thomas Wilkinson of Kendal made provision, on an exceptionally lavish scale, for Masses to be celebrated for the welfare of his soul: donations were made to four neighbouring houses of friars, which would have been the two in Carlisle and those in Appleby and Penrith, plus trentals - each trental being 30 Masses, celebrated on 30 consecutive days - at Cartmel and Conishead priories, Furness Abbey and the

Carthusian Abbey of Mount Grace in Yorkshire.[270]

In 1533 the chantry 'Chapel of our Lady within this church of Kendal' was set up by Sir Roger Bellingham in a 'confident assertion of Catholic faith'. In 1542 in Ulverston Leonard Fell left £2 for a priest to celebrate Masses for a year for the benefit of his soul, commending it to 'the faithful company of saints', and leaving 'six pence to as many priests to pray for me on the day of my death as may be gotten'.[271]

In so far as the chantries were the tangible - and expensive - expression of Catholic faith anchored in the doctrine of Purgatory and the means that might be adopted to alleviate its rigours, early Tudor Cumbrians were continuing to buy into them.

Into the earlier Tudor period the continuing iconographic elaboration of Carlisle Cathedral was extended into an ambitious synthesis between the religious symbols of traditional piety and the political ideology of dynastic loyalism.

Lancelot Salkeld (d. 1560) was the last prior of the Augustinian Priory before its dissolution under Henry VIII, when he made the surrender in 1540 and became the first Dean, heading the newly instituted Chapter, of the new, non-monastic Cathedral following its creation in 1541, which may have been when he commissioned the screen, in the north aisle, initialled 'L.S., D. K'. Identified as cooperative with the crown's religious policies in the period before a full range of Protestant measures was adopted, Salkeld 'was made prior of the house for the purpose of its surrender'.[272]

Salkeld's screen represents a 'complete example of English early Renaissance decoration, a world away from the Gothic stalls', 'unique in its developed Renaissance detail'. Within the tradition of Carlisle Cathedral's long-standing receptivity to motifs and designs of Continental European provenance, the

Salkeld Screen, Carlisle Cathedral

screen's workmanship may have been by a 'Flemish firm which executed the Gondibour screen a few decades previously', or it may be 'that one of the Italian artists imported into England ... was asked to design the new work, the various motifs, badges and heraldry being suggested by ... the priory, the whole contract being carried out in London'.[273]

The retention of control of this composition by the Priory meant that, although features of the ensemble were, in artistic terms, of fashionable Renaissance styling - 'Profile heads in lozenges and medallions, stylized dolphins'- the basic spiritual content of the screen was 'entirely given over to ecclesiastical and devotional devices' and was redolent of the medieval devout tradition, focused on Christ, His Passion and wounds. Salkeld was himself an upholder of conservative piety, rejecting the radical religious reforms of the reign of Edward VI (r. 1547-53) and resigning as dean in 1548, but being restored during the Catholic reign of Mary I (r. 1553-8).[274]

Thus the devotional foci of the screen, as commissioned by Dean Salkeld, are: to the left the Crown of Thorns, with the crossed nails used to impale Christ's hands and feet and, below, the spear with which the Roman soldier pierced His side (John 19: 34); in the centre, as in Holy Trinity, Kendal, is the IHS monogram of the 'Holy Name', here surrounded by a garter ring; and on the right, the Five Wounds of Jesus's pierced hands, feet and heart, or side, are displayed - 'a most unusual device and very boldly and magnificently carved in high relief'. So central was the image of the Wounds to traditional religion in England that 'It is hardly surprising that the symbol of the Five Wounds should have been chosen by the Pilgrims of Grace as the emblem of their loyalty to the whole medieval Catholic system'. The motif was emblazoned, along with the IHS device, on the banners carried by Yorkshire participants in the northern rising in support of traditional religion, the Pilgrimage of Grace of 1536-7.[275]

Yet this pious traditionalism is combined in the Salkeld screen with allegiance to the Tudor dynasty, which is announced in the initials 'G. S. P. E', standing for 'God Save Prince Edward', a prayer for the welfare of Edward, Prince of Wales, born in 1537, 'the long-awaited Tudor heir'. Besides the invocation for Prince Edward, the screen extends its 'celebration of the Tudor lineage' with images of Henry VIII's mother Elizabeth of York (1466-1503); of Owen Tudor, the grandfather of Henry VIII's father, Henry VII (r. 1485-1509); of Prince Edward's mother, Jane Seymour (c. 1505-37); of King Henry VII's mother, Lady Margaret Beaufort, (1443-1509), countess of Richmond and Derby; and of Catherine de Valois (1401-37), the grandmother of Henry VII.[276]

The synthesis in the Salkeld screen between loyalty to the dynasty and retention of the icons of traditional worship calls for comment, inasmuch as by 1541 the dynasty, headed by Henry VIII, had dismantled so much of the faith, practices and institutions of the past: by the Act of Supremacy of 1534 papal headship was replaced by the king's supremacy over the Church in England; the divorce from Queen Catherine of Aragon (1485-1536) had been completed by 1533; the king had been excommunicated by Pope Paul III (r. 1534- 49); the suppression of the monasteries and friaries was finished by 1540; and the iconoclastic campaign by radicals against the visual accoutrements of customary piety as 'idolatry' was carried forward under the leadership of Thomas Cromwell (c. 1485-1540), as the king's leading minister in ecclesiastical affairs.[277]

Yet Salkeld was able to reconcile his attachment to the features of customary piety that are emblematised in the screen with ardent allegiance to the Tudor line. It is true that English religious reformism had not yet proceeded as far as it was to do, under Continental influences, in the reign of Edward VI, and the Six Articles of Religion of 1539 were part of a conservative retreat, underscored by the fall of the radicals' patron, Cromwell, in 1540. Salkeld's Cumberland contemporary John Hoton of Penrith, whose will was drawn up in 1542, was also able to bring together 'political loyalty to the king as both sovereign in the realm *and* head of the Church of England with firm attachment to … Catholic belief' - that of Purgatory (a doctrine not yet officially proscribed).[278]

Salkeld and Hoton both moved in circles which reverenced the Tudor monarchy that had brought peace to England, and allowed its clerical and lay elites to flourish, after the murderous chaos of the 15th-century civil wars for the succession to the crown, the Wars of the Roses. What mattered to Salkeld and his like was the safety of a peaceful succession in the person of an uncontested Tudor male heir who, by 1541, had survived the contemporaneous health risks of infancy: 'God Save Prince Edward'.

The force of the Tudor ideology in Henrician England and the emphasis on Henry VIII's monarchy by divine right meant that acceptance of the royal supremacy was widespread, certainly on upper class levels, including the landed gentry membership of the 'Reformation Parliament' which legislated the Acts of Parliament that brought in extensive religious change in the 1530s. On the senior clerical front, the influential *De Vera Obedientia* ('Concerning True Obedience') of 1535 by the doctrinally Catholic Bishop of Winchester Stephen Gardiner (1497-1555) vindicated the royal supremacy in the Church, as in the state. Thomas Howard, (1473-1554), earl of Surrey and 3rd duke of Norfolk , President of Henry VIII's Privy Council , the 'greatest magnate of the land', who was responsibile for crushing the northern Catholic rebellion, the Pilgrimage of Grace, was Gardiner's religiously conservative 'kindred spirit' and struggled in 1532 to save a Norfolk shrine from the iconoclasts.[279] Few indeed of those in positions of power and influence in the Tudor Church and society were prepared to follow Thomas More (1478-1535) in his defence of the papal headship - and to his execution.

Perhaps, however, the upholders of the pope's primacy - and of at least implicit consequent denial of the king's - were to be found further down the social scale - and in Cumbria, where in Kendal in 1537 'sundry persons of no consequence' plunged the parson into the water for obeying the government's ban on reciting the Rosary and on praying for the pope; in Brough-under-Stainmore locals ordered the vicar to pray for the pontiff.[280]

Defence of the papal supremacy over the Church was voiced

by the rank-and-file monk, John Broughton, probably of Furness, who stated that 'the Bishop of Rome was unjustly put down, and shud be restored again in three yeres'. It was a short step from upholding the papal headship to denying the royal version, and Henry Salley, probably of the Lancashire Abbey of Sawley, took that step when he 'said that no secular knave shud be head of the church'. It was an even more advanced step when the monk Christopher Rodde, at the height of the northern rising against government-imposed religious change, the Pilgrimage of Grace, called into question Henry VIII's very title, as well as the whole basis of the Tudor succession: 'that the king was not right heeir to the crowne, for his father cam in by no true lyne, but by the sworde'.[281]

Even so, neither the institutional issue of the royal supremacy nor that of the papal primacy was the central concern of the great northern rising of 1536-7, for the 1534 Act of Supremacy, legislating away the pope's primacy and installing in its place the royal headship over the English Church, did not provoke religious rebellion. Rather, it was mass exasperation with the latest instalment of state-directed reform, in the form of the Dissolution of the Monasteries, that awoke violent resistance in the north in 1536-7. It was because the Pilgrimage of Grace was a people's crusade in defence of traditional religion, and lacking committed support from the titled baronage of the north, that it was bound to fail.

For at the heart of the matter in the Pilgrimage of Grace was defence of Catholic worship, institutions and belief, against the royal reforms that culminated, and were seen as at their most intolerable, in the Dissolution. It is true that in the causation of this rebellion some socio-economic complaints were at work, at least in the background of discontent: enclosure of common land was on the increase, and admission charges to tenancies had been raised sharply by landlords, but agrarian grievances were not sufficient to inspire 30,000 northerners to take up arms against a militarily formidable monarchy, in a matter of life or death.[282] Again, somewhere in the background of the rebellion there would have been unease on the part of a great English region - the northern shires - at the accelerating centralisation of the Tudor state.

The motives put forward by the ideologue of the Pilgrimage, the Yorkshire lawyer Robert Aske (c. 1500-37), to justify the great revolt of 1536-7 included praise for the role of the monks in maintaining sea defences, in building bridges and roads, lending money to the gentry, bringing up gentlemen's daughters 'in virtue' and providing accommodation for travellers in wild country.[283]

These social goals were important, but they were secondary. The Pilgrims' 'Oath of the Honourable Men', whether or not it was composed by Aske, was much more germane to the ethos and purpose of the rising than any list of social and economic by-products of the monks' presence. Apart from the 'preservation of the King's person and his issue' and the elimination from the government of 'all villein [lower class] blood' - meaning Cromwell, a Putney brewer's son - the insurrection was not to be politically motivated - not 'for the Commonwealth' - but to be mounted 'only for the love that ye do bear unto Almighty God his faith, and to Holy Church militant [the Church on earth] ... [and] in your hearts put away all fear and dread, and take afore you the Cross of Christ, and in your hearts His faith, the Restitution of the Church'. While this high-flown crusading rhetoric perfectly suited the fervent aims of this 'Pilgrimage', there was a tone of menace only in the promise of 'the suppression of these Heritics and their opinions'.[284]

Thus 'Religious grievances ... remained at the forefront of

the minds of the Cumbrian Pilgrims, dominating the agenda in a manner not demonstrable elsewhere' and 'The immediate causes of the Pilgrimage of Grace were the changes in religion introduced by Henry's government and the dissolution of the smaller monasteries' (exempting, for the time being, Furness, whose annual income was above the £200 cut-off point below which the less wealthy houses fell).[285]

As, by October 1536, the rising spread from its original Lincolnshire and Yorkshire heartlands, the question of the 'abbeys' moved increasingly to the fore, since it was 'the destruction of the religious houses [that] became a subject of agitation', amidst what has been described as 'the religious revival which preceded the dissolution of the monasteries':[286]

> [An] acute sense of deprivation caused by the Dissolution of the Monasteries ignited support in the [Furness] district for ... 'The Pilgrimage of Grace'. The major grievance raised by the Pilgrims was the suppression of the religious houses, which they sought to have reinstated ... within a month of the outbreak of the rising, the armed commons around Conishead had restored the canons to their priory, soon followed, at the request of the canons themselves, of the Augustinians to Cartmel. ... Thus the people of Furness joined the Pilgrimage because they feared for the survival of Furness Abbey and for their parish worship.[287]

In these ways, local direct action over-turned the royal policy of Dissolution by putting the monks, friars and canons back into their houses.

The primacy of spiritual motivation in the Cumbrian Pilgrimage of Grace - 'the love that ye do bear unto Almighty God his faith ... take before you the cross of Christ ... His faith, the Restitution of the Church'- received graphic confirmation in

Penrith, which, from October 1536, 'became established as a mustering point for the insurgents of east Cumberland', described by the king's commander, the duke of Norfolk, as 'the worst town in the county at the ... rebellion'. A message sent from Richmondshire in Yorkshire by the vicar of Brough-under-Stainmore, Robert Thompson, made the point that the 'cause of insurrection' was entirely spiritual:

> Well beloved brethren in God, we greet you well, signifying to you that we your brethren in Christ have assembled us together and put us in readiness for the maintenance of the faith of God, His laws and His Church and where abbeys were suppressed we have restored them again and put the religious men [back] into their houses: where we exhort you to do the same.

A direct link was forged between the command centre at Penrith and the resistance to closure on the part of the monks themselves, through the gift of £2 by the Abbot of Holm Cultram - an institution which 'showed no abhorrence of violence during the 1536 rising' and 'resisted the changes' - to allow Penrithian activists to travel to Pilgrimage locations in Yorkshire.[288]

The way in which the movement's operations were conducted in Penrith's St Andrew's parish church further confirms the essence of the Pilgrimage as a protest in the cause of piety. The military drilling took its inspiration from the Church's liturgy, as when the four local men who were chosen as captains in October were preceded in their processing together by a priest carrying the church's processional crucifix. The captains, each of whom had a chaplain recruited from local clergy, ordered their followers to live in peace and to recite regularly the *Ave Maria*, the Creed and the 'Our Father'. Each of the captains had a code-name summing up virtues proclaimed by the Church - 'charity', 'faith', 'pity' [piety] - while one of the officers, Gilbert Whelpdale, of a local gentry family, espoused 'poverty'- conceivably an allusion to the merits of 'holy poverty', which was the hallmark of the Mendicant Augustinian Friars, who were soon to be suppressed in Penrith. Whelpdale's brother-in-law, the charismatic Robert Thompson, 'a popular preacher and regarded by the people as a prophet', maintained the moral momentum of the rising locally by delivering sermons on each the Ten Commandments, showing that it was protest against disobedience of them that had provoked the insurrection.[289]

After the duke of Norfolk made a pretence of negotiation with the rebels, the Pilgrimage broke up in December, though further outbreaks in January 1537 led to its rapid suppression, amidst harsh repression. The Pilgrimage of Grace was the most serious of all the various regional rebellions that successive Tudor monarchs faced, and exemplary recrimination was bound to be severe, with 66 hangings in Cumberland and Westmorland, 45 in the latter county, 21 in the former, eight of them in Penrith. The monasteries were also punished with a comprehensive closure, culminating with Furness, that 'troublesome house in a rebellious region'.[290]

The Dissolution of the Monasteries amounted to the gravest blow to the institutional apparatus of 'traditional religion' in Tudor England. As was seen in chapter 7, the chantries made up a further essential ingredient in lay religion in late medieval and earlier 16th-century Cumbria, 'one of the last' being set up in the will of 1543 of Sir Thomas Curwen (1494-1543) of Workington.[291]

An Act of Parliament of 1545 prepared the way for the closure of the chantries, while its successor, the Act of 1547, under the Protestant Edward VI, indicated the extent to which the measure amounted to a conscious and vehement offensive against a core element of customary piety:

> superstition and errors in the Christian religion, brought into the minds of men by devising and phantasying vain opinions of purgatory and masses satisfactory to be done for them which be departed, the which doctrine and vain opinion by nothing more is maintained and upholden than by abuse of trentals, chantries and other provisions made for the continuance of the said blindness and ignorance.[292]

The suppression of the chantries confronted the 29 of them in the Lake Counties, besides those that had been linked to monasteries before the Dissolution. In the region they possessed a total income of £155 and an average stipend of £5 5 0d for each chantrist, ranging from £7 6 8d at St Michael's in Brigham to £11 9 8d in Wharton.[293]

The losses of these institutions included the Hutton family chantry, dedicated to the Virgin Mary in Hutton-in-the-Forest, near Penrith, and, in Penrith itself, the royal-sponsored chantry in the castle, along with Bishop Strickland's foundation, that also supported the town's grammar school. The chantries of the Virgin Mary in Skelton church, of St Leonard in Bromfield, St Katherine in Wigton church, of St Mary Magdalene in Crosthwaite, as well as those of Torpenhow, Egremont, Brigham, Edenhall, Great Salkeld and Mosser were among those closed, while Carlisle lost its six chantries, including the four in the Cathedral. In terms of staffing, the huge parish of Greystoke, with its 3,000 parishioners, was a severe loser from the closures, its number of clergy being cut from seven to three.[294]

In parish churches around the diocese of Carlisle, then, parishioners could witness for themselves, in the sudden loss of the chantries, a massive defeat for the entire apparatus of 'traditional religion' - the Latin chantry Masses recited to allay peoples' anxieties over Purgatory; the generational links embedded in praying for the souls of ones'parents, relatives and benefactors; the ardent devotion to Mary and the saints; the pilgrimage shrines suppressed in Cromwell's campaigns; the attacks on images and relics; the offensive against the cult of the Rosary; the drastic reduction in the number of holy days in honour of the saints: these were the main battle fronts in a war against the medieval Catholic legacy, its performative colour and theatre, in England.[295]

If government actions thus had the effect of creating a vacuum, where there had earlier been a plethora of communal piety, was there a new content of religious action and belief to fill that lacuna? The answer is that, in the course of the 16th century, the British Isles, along with the other reformed areas of northern and central Europe, underwent a media revolution that placed the written, printed and spoken word - the book, the sermon, and above all, the vernacular Scripture - at the heart of religious observance. A new, reflective, individualised and literate religious culture was being unfolded.

While medieval Europe was familiar with translations of the Bible into the languages of the people, the early 16th century saw a Scriptural renaissance in Europe, led by the Dutch scholar Desiderius Erasmus (1466/9-1536). Adopting the techniques of literary research developed in Renaissance Italy by humanist scholars, in 1516 Erasmus first published one of the most important of his many writings, an edition of the New Testament in its original Greek text, with a parallel Latin translation. Printed in over 200 editions in the 16th century, Erasmus's New Testament, with its vivid realisation of the mindset of the early Christian Church, became the basis of vernacular versions, such as that by the German Protestant reformer Martin Luther (1483-1546).[296]

Because of official suspicion of the manuscript English-language Bible that had been produced by the Lollards in the 14th century, the Bible was not legally available in medieval England. Then, in 1526, in Germany, William Tyndale (c. 1494-1536) published the New Testament in plain and intelligible English, based on Erasmus's text, delivering the 'four Gospels, complete and accurate to the Greek original', along with the Epistles of St Paul, which embody the essence of Reformation theology, and the rest of the Testament. The Tyndale version subsequently fed into the English-language 'Matthew Bible', which was issued under royal licence in 1537, followed by the appearance of the crown-authorised 'Great Bible', in seven editions, between 1539 and 1541.[297]

Erasmus's considerable influence in Tudor England extended to Robert Aldrich (or Aldridge, d. 1556), Provost of Eton, who was made Bishop of Carlisle in 1537: he was a correspondent and collaborator with Erasmus, who addressed him in one letter as 'my Robert, dearly beloved in Christ'. However, Henrician England's leading Erasmian figure after the death of Thomas More was of Westmerian extraction, the king's last wife, married in 1543, Catherine Parr (c. 1512-48), daughter of Sir Thomas Parr of Kendal.[298]

With her 'very real place' in the group around Erasmus and his scholarly and devotional legacy, the queen belonged to an English and Continental 'tradition of erudite ladies who both patronized scholars and divines and contributed her own writings'. Among those writings, Scriptural material figured prominently, including paraphrases of the Psalms of the Old Testament, and the queen promoted an English-language edition of Erasmus's own 'Paraphrases' of the Bible. In her 'greatest spiritual tract', *the Lamentations, or complaints of a Sinner, made by the most vertuous and right gratious Ladie, Quene Catherine* she cited about 100 Scriptural sources.[299]

Coming as she did from a learned 'humanist-educated' background, Queen Catherine upheld a 'total commitment' to the vernacular Bible, 'concerned in making available to the English populace cheap and readily available English language Bibles'. In the year of her death, she would surely have approved of the purchase by the churchwardens of Great Salkeld of a 'bybell buke'.[300]

In the following year, Edward VI's Protestant government commanded the exclusive use in all the nation's parish churches of the English-language *Book of the Common Prayer and Administration of the Sacraments ... after the Use of the Church of England*, doctrinally a relatively conservative text whose innovative essence lay in its apperace in the vernacular rather than the Catholic Church's Latin Mass: the parish of Great Salkeld authorised the purchase of a 'commynion buke'.[301]

These purchases, albeit commanded by the central government, open up the possibility that central aspects of the Edwardine Reformation had an appeal to significant numbers of individuals, in Cumbria as well as elsewhere in the country. For one thing, the Prayer Book, bought by Great Salkeld, was directly connected with the release of the English-language Bible stemming from Tyndale, as obtained by the same parish. These two texts provided the indispensable foundations for the vernacularisation of religious faith and practice, worship and belief, being both now in the language of the people:

> nothyng to be read, but the very pure worde of God, the holy scriptures, or that whiche is euidently grounded upon the same; and that in such a language and ordre, as is moste easy and plaine for the understanding bothe of the readers and hearers ... al thinges shalbe read and [sung] in the churche, in the

Englishe tongue, to thende yt the congregacion maie be therby edified.[302]

'Maie be therby edified': these instructions envisaged congregational hearing of the Scripture but they also pointed towards an individually-oriented consciousness, in which the Christian was introduced to a directly personal relationship with Christ as Redeemer, without the intervention of intercessory Masses or 'vain opinions of purgatory or masses satisfactory'. Queen Catherine's *Lamentations* - her 'conversion narrative'- put forward the Protestant reformist view, set out by Luther from his understanding of St Paul, that 'faith in the righteousness of Christ is the sinner's only hope'. It may, however, come as more of a surprise that it was the former chantrist Richard Robinson who, in 1549, drew up 'the first Protestant-oriented will in Cumberland':

> I commend my soule to Almighty Jhesu my maker and redemer, in whome and by the merites of whose blessed passion is all my hole trust of the remission and forgeveness of my synnes.[303]

If such wills are anything to go by in charting confessional shifts in Tudor Cumbria, the notary Bernard Aglionby 'left a good Protestant will', as did the lawyer Thomas Tallentire.[304]

In Kendal, which had links with Protestant influences from Bristol, Cambridge and Southampton, preaching by the vicar James Pilkington (1520-76, Bishop of Durham, 1561-76) and Nicholas Assheton encouraged members of the important Wilson family to introduce Reformation doctrines into their wills. Pilkington was one of the many clerical and lay 'Marian exiles' who found safety in Reformed areas on the Continent and was later to become a leading architect in Queen Elizabeth I's Protestant Church of England, but his departure in 1554 obviously brought to a close his Protestant influence in Kendal.[305]

While, however, there were conversions to Reformation beliefs among Cumbrian individuals, including clerics and schoolmasters, the absence of Protestant penetration on any large or popular scale in Edwardine Cumberland and Westmorland meant that there was no basis for resistance in the region to Mary's re-Catholicisation programme, and indeed 'it seems likely that her restoration of Catholic ways was welcomed in Cumberland in general'. A conservative outlook certainly appears to have prevailed over the retention of the liturgical equipment of the 'old religion': an inventory of 1552 disclosed that Penrith's St Andrew's still possessed two chalices, a rich white silk chasuble, another set of vestments, four altar cloths, and the two 'gret belles' that were sounded when the consecrated eucharistic Host was elevated at the high point of the Mass, plus other valuables surviving from the dissolved chantry.[306] The retention of equipment for the Mass in one of Cumberland's most important urban parish churches may be revealing a readiness to welcome Queen Mary's Counter-Reformation that was to be enacted between 1553 and 1558.

Following the death of Bishop Aldridge in 1556, Mary's appointee to Carlisle was the firmly Catholic Dean of Windsor, Owen Oglethorpe (d. 1559), but his brief tenure of the diocese from 1557 to 1559 gave him little opportunity to bring in a Catholic renewal and he 'left little mark on the diocese', though the standing down of the Protestant layman Sir Thomas Smith (1513-77) made way in 1554 for the return as Dean of Lancelot Salkeld. Two of the Cathedral Canons were ejected by Mary's officials on the grounds that they were married, thereby violating Catholic priestly celibacy. The married parsons of Ormside and Bridekirk were also ousted. [307]

Mary ordered the executions, by burning, of nearly 300

Protestants. The geography of these executions, with a concentration on south-east England, also provides us with a map of Protestant uptake in mid-Tudor England: there were none in the diocese of Carlisle - an absence of martyrdoms that Thomas Fuller (1608-66) in *Church History of Britain* (1665) attributed to the fact that Cumbrians were 'nuzzled in ignorance and superstition'.[308]

In such circumstances, the prospects for a speedy renewal of Protestant initiatives in Cumbria following the accession of Elizabeth I in 1558, with the issue of a new Protestant Book of Common Prayer in the Act of Uniformity in 1559 and the restoration of the royal supremacy in the Act of Supremacy of same year, were not promising. The conservative-minded Oglethorpe was the only one of the bishops who was both qualified and willing to crown the queen, but in the coronation service he antagonised Elizabeth by elevating the eucharistic Host in the Catholic fashion, while he voted in the House of Lords against the Act of Uniformity, refused the oath contained in the Act of Supremacy and was deprived and imprisoned before his death, in December 1559.[309]

While efforts were made to get leading Protestant clerics to accept Carlisle, nearly two years were lost until John Best (d. 1570) was appointed in March 1561. With 'an abrasive and single-minded evangelical approach', the extent to which Best was able 'to set his stamp on a reluctant clergy and resistant laity' would be debateable.[310]

As for the 'reluctant clergy' of the diocese, Best found that these 'priestes, wicked ympes [sons] of antichrist' were 'for the most parte very ignorante and stubborne, past measure false and sotle [sly]; onlie feare maketh them obedient'. Part of the problem was the numerical shortage of clergy in the area: in the Kendal Deanery, for instance, the numbers were reduced from

47 to 24 between 1524 and 1554, in Heversham from nine to three and in Cockermouth from five to one. The staffing shortage meant that only the most overt opponents of reform were proceeded against. During Best's episcopate selective sanctions were applied against opponents of change: Hugh Hodgson, rector of Skelton, and Robert Thomson, rector of Beaumont, were deprived of their parishes and in 1562 Henry Brown, rector of St Cuthbert's, Carlisle, and Thomas Ellerton, vicar of Penrith, were disciplined in York by the ecclesiastical tribunal known as the High Commission.[311]

As for the Cathedral clergy, they were, to say the least, of little assistance in putting the Reformation into effect, for there was 'a want of preaching in [Best's] diocese, having no help at all in his Cathedral,' while the Cumbrian-born Bishop of London and Best's strong supporter, Edmund Grindal (1515/20-83), described the members of the Cathedral Chapter as 'ignorante preists or olde unlearned monkes'- 'distressingly conservative' from the viewpoint of the reformers. The restored Dean, Sir Thomas Smith, was a particular problem: though 'continuously absent', he still clung on to his authority, while the whole Chapter was embroiled in 'shady financial dealings' over leases on property that were 'so scandalous' as to lead to a government enquiry: Carlisle, Best complained, 'is decaid by theym, and Godes truth sclanderyled'.[312]

Most of the Cumbrian laity were also regarded by reformists as incorrigibly resistant to religious innovations, the local folk being reported to be 'more superstitious than virtuous, long accustomed to frantic fantasies and ceremonies, which they regard more than either God or their prince, right far alienate from true religion'. Grindal, born into a farming family in St Bees parish, described his homeland as 'my lawless country' and 'that little angle where I was born ... the ignorantest part in religion ...

of any one part of the realm': his death-bed decision to found St Bees School was intended to put an end to the religious ignorance in the region.[313]

Grindal linked the religious backwardness of his native country to its being 'most oppressed of covetous landlords', and indeed the landed gentry of the region were regarded by the authorities as obstructing ecclesiastical reform: in 1564 only five out of 12 of the Cumberland JPs - the echelon that was especially expected to assist the Protestant clergy in forwarding the state's religious measures - and only three out of nine in Westmorland - were described as 'satisfactory'.[314]

Some members of the Cumbrian landed elite may also have continued to cultivate pre-Reformation faith and practice, albeit in some cases in a relatively un-provocative way. The inscription, dated 1562, within the period of Ellerton's Penrith ministry, on the tomb in St Andrew's of a Plumpton gentleman invited prayers 'for the soul of Richard Coledale ... on whose soul may God have mercy', an explicit invocation of the Catholic custom of prayers 'for the souls of the faithful departed' and the concept of Purgatory. The wording on a memorial brass in Morland church dated 1562-3 closes with the traditional Catholic formula 'on whose soule Jhu have mcy. am'. The funeral of William, 3rd Lord Dacre (1500-63) in Carlisle Cathedral 'retained as much of the ceremonial of the Catholic requiem as was possible without actually breaking the law'.[315]

Others may have been more demonstrative in their rejection of reform: John Aglionby (b. c. 1520), for example, was described by Best's successor Richard Barnes (1532-87, Bishop, 1570-77) as 'a vain man, a blasphemous papist, having no fear of God'. Higher ranking pro-Catholic patronage came from the powerful baronial Dacres, who in in 1561 were protecting Hugh Hodgson, the rector of Skelton who had refused to swear the Oath of Supremacy, while the 'nearest thing to active opposition' came from this dynasty, headed by Thomas (c. 1524-66), 4th Baron Dacre, and his strongly Catholic wife Elizabeth: Best was aware that Lord Dacre and his officials would 'wynke' at Mass said openly, while conservative clergy in his north Cumberland domain of Gilsland, based on Naworth Castle, as well as in the Greystoke area, were used to 'bearying themselves' on his protection.[316]

The problem for the government of the situation in Cumbria in the 1560s was political as well as religious, or, rather, it was the case that religious conservatism was the concomitant of opposition to alterations taking place on the political and social fronts - the centralisation of power to London and the ongoing challenge to the status of the old feudal nobility of the region, with their ancestral networks of patronage, clientage and border military service. Dacre and his ally, Henry Clifford (d. 1570), 2nd earl of Cumberland, were Best's most troublesome opponents, and in the Bishop's view a pernicious influence on their dependents, while Grindal insisted that 'If [these] two noblemen of which [Best had] complained were touched by the authority of the Privy Council it would be a terror to the rest'.[317]

In the absence of these noblemen, Best, albeit somewhat ingenuously, protested that reform would thrive, for:

> Before the great men came into these parts I could do more in a day concerning Christ's gospel ... such men ... are not only supported and borne withall ... and ... those of evil religion are encouraged to be stubborn ... so long as the high authority is in his hands that now hath it God's glorious gospel cannot take place here.[318]

Yet the Bishop himself was so much in thrall to the power of the two northern magnates that, when he wrote in 1563 to the

Secretary of State, William Cecil (1520-98), to complain of their misdeeds, he did so in a coded format.[319]

By the 1560s, the authoritarian and centralising policies of the Tudor state, which had been introduced in the 1530s by Thomas Cromwell, had still not destroyed 'the feudal power of the great Border families', an ascendancy which was grounded in the deference and 'olde good-wyll' of their tenants. Dacre was viewed by Best as 'something too mighty in this country and as it were a prince', and it has been said of the border barons of whom he was the archetype that 'their vast possessions and the power which they wielded as almost independent rulers made them also a possible menace to royal authority'. The Dacres' own 'resistance to Protestantism was probably given an additional urgency by their determination to fend off encroachments by the central government on their control of their border fastnesses'.[320]

As has been seen, Grindal and Best pleaded with the central government to intervene in order to suppress the autonomous regional power of the likes of the Dacres, but in the event it was the northern magnates themselves who brought down the Cumbrian social and political order that had largely survived the middle ages and, with it, the edifice of 'Cumbrian bastard feudal Catholicism'.[321]

Following the death of Thomas, 4th baron, in 1566, the claim to the title of his would-be heir Leonard Dacre (d. 1573) was set aside, and the deeply aggrieved Dacre joined with Sir Thomas Percy (1528-72), 7th earl of Northumberland, and Charles Neville (1543-1601), 6th earl of Westmorland, in the rebellion known as the Revolt of the Northern Earls, in support of the claim to the throne of Elizabeth I's Catholic rival, Mary Queen of Scots (1542-87). The revolt was dispersed by royal forces in December 1569 and the leaders fled to Scotland, while an attempted renewal of the rising's momentum led by Leonard

Dacre early in 1570 was defeated, followed by 800 executions.

The Revolt of the Northern Earls was an act of political suicide by the border barons, and its defeat by the crown's forces a watershed in the social, political and religious history of Elizabethan Cumbria, inasmuch as it dismantled the neo-feudal social apparatus and governmental quasi-independence that had acted as barriers to religious reform. The Dacre lordships were re-assigned, and the 'Marches of the North were no longer to be governed by their ancient rulers, but by royal officials'.[322]

The crown's victory over the Revolt of the Earls also had the effect of altering influential hearts and minds in favour of the Tudor queen. Until the defeat of the 1569-70 insurrection, for a natural gambler and risk-taker such as Gerard Lowther (1537-97) of Lowther, an option that was centred on the prospects of Mary Queen of Scots was as good a wager as any. An illegal 'recusant', absenting himself from official parish worship, in 1569 Lowther was 'up to the very hilt of treason', carrying messages to the earl of Northumberland. Then, however, in 1570, facing extreme danger, his arrest and imprisonment in the Tower had a conversionary effect, and, after a short escape to Scotland but, assisted by Cecil, Lowther made a comeback as an Elizabethan Protestant. Eventually, as a skilled Lincoln's Inn lawyer, he won for Queen Elizabeth the former Dacre estates in Cumberland and Westmorland and made a fortune: his surviving Penrith mansion, the 'Two Lions', is the memorial to the successful outcome of Lowther's change of heart.[323]

Gerard Lowther also epitomised a societal change in Elizabethan Cumbria following the collapse of the Revolt of the Northern Earls. This was an evolutionary transformation in which the ascendancy of the baronage made way for the ascent of the next stratum below the titled peers: the landed gentry, made up of families whose fortunes depended on their certified loyalty to the Tudor queen and on their Protestantism, gaining commendations that would be transmitted from Rose Castle to London, as was the case when Walter Strickland of Sizergh was described by Bishop Best in 1564 as being 'of good Religion'.[324]

In Penrith the new gentry elite was typified by Nicholas Bost (or Boste), Thomas Carleton, Anthony Hutton and John Whelpdale, a closely allied group of 'most discreet persons of the town and parish' whose religious conformity and social prominence were attested in their appointment in 1564 as governors of the new Queen Elizabeth Grammar School. Such individuals could be relied upon as JPs to lend legal and political support to the work of making the community Protestant. Bost's Protestant convictions were set out in his will of 1570, with its bequest of his 'sowle to God Almyghte, trystyng in the mercye of Chryst and throwgh his Passyone tht yt shall be partyner wt. the holye company of Hevyne'.[325]

Evidence from wills, including some in Carlisle, indicates that 'Protestant doctrine had begun to establish itself'. Even so, the process of change was to be slower and more impeded than is suggested by reports from Bishop Barnes, at the beginning of his episcopate:

> I find these Cumberland and Westmorland commonality far more comfortable, pliable, and tractable in all matters of religion ... not so far from God's religion as they have been thought. Praised be the Lord, who, even in this utmost corner, amongst these savage people, has mightily prospered his gospel and my simple ministry.

In October 1570 Barnes reported to Cecil that, with government help, he could guarantee:

> as faythfull, paynefull [painstaking] and (if God will) effectuall travell [work] as ever poore Bishoppe did performe within his

cure.

This over-optimism - later reports would be less sanguine - may be variously explained, either by the Bishop's awareness of the government's ignorance of the actual situation in Cumbria, plus, perhaps, his desire to take the credit for the success of his 'simple ministry', or of the wish forming the thought, but, whatever the case, Barnes's sunny picture was distorted because, as he admitted, 'Some indeed are not reclaimed in all things' - ('but are in a good way').[326]

For the religious situation in the Elizabethan Lake Counties remained too complex, and too chequered by questions of social class, education and culture, for any broad generalisations over Protestant success or Catholic survival to be safe, since there were simultaneously both Catholic persistence and Protestant progress in this region. It is no doubt true that 'It was in Kendal, the sole Cumbrian specimen of a standard English town, that the Reformation took root', but the town also had a tradition of lower class religious conservatism going back to the time of the Pilgrimage of Grace. The corporation's puritan-inspired campaign against popular pleasures and festivals and, in particular, the drive to suppress the still surviving medieval annual Corpus Christi play, encountered opposition from 'Very many and divers of the common inhabitants of this incorporation'.[327]

As well as social class, geography, especially as between the urban and the rural, the market towns and the villages, were determinants of variable response to reform. Penrith and Kendal may well have been making steady strides in the direction of reform, but after Barnes had submitted his reports on Protestant progress in his diocese, in 1571 he conducted a visitation which revealed, in deeply rural Crosthwaite, an extraordinary surviving treasury, of high financial value, of 'relics and monuments of superstition and idolatry' - silver eucharistic vessels, a vestment embroidered with cloth of gold, two silver chalices, censers for incense used to reverence the consecrated Host at High Mass, a brass holy water tankard for sprinkling the congregation at the beginning of High Mass, five priests' chasubles, and other vestment for deacons - a complete repertoire of clothing and 'ornaments' for carrying out Catholicism's most solemn rites. The Crosthwaite churchwardens were ordered to sell all these items and, in their place, to buy the wherewithal for the Anglican congregational reception of holy communion - 'two fayre potts or flaggons of tyne [tin] for the wyne'.[328]

The question remains, though, of why the parish authorities were clinging on to this liturgical treasury, which could have been used for no other ritual but the Mass - and not just the Mass but the Mass in its most elaborate and solemn form: 'High' or 'Solemn' sung Mass. Was this storage, for instance, an insurance policy against a time when - perhaps with a change of dynasty - the equipment and vestments might be called on again and the Mass brought back into favour?

In addition, in 1573 'popish' books and 'ornaments' came to light in Carlisle, Wigton, Bolton and in 1578 even in Kendal, as well as in Skelsmergh, Selside and Kirkby Lonsdale. Yet while Catholic liturgical and literary materials were thus surviving, provision was not always forthcoming for the introduction of the wherewithal for the services of the Church of England. As late as 1584, payment was being made in Great Salkeld church for the very belated installation of two indispensable essentials of Anglican worship, the pulpit and the communion table - 'the Lord's table'.[329]

The inception of Barnes's episcopate at the opening of the 1570s, however, marked a metamorphosis in the character of Cumbrian religious traditionalism, as a widespread, if somewhat inert, amorphous and negative rejection of Protestant innovation gave way to a more defined, positive and denominational profession on the part of a minority which could now defined as a Cumbrian Catholic community.

Three factors gave rise to this clearer profiling. First, the publication in 1570 of the Bull of Pope Pius V (r. 1566-72) *Regnans in Excelsis* which excommunicated, and called for the deposition of, Queen Elizabeth had the effect of identifying 'Catholicism with disaffection and treason [and] induced many traditionalists to draw back from the more crystallised minority Catholicism that emerged ... in the 1570s'. Secondly, under the Acts of Uniformity of 1552 and 1559, those who refused to attend parish worship were subject to the appreciable fine of a shilling a week, raised in 1581 to the astronomic sum of £20 per month, and increased in 1587 to the forfeiture of two-thirds of an offender's property. Those who, in compliance with a papal ban of 1566 on attending Church of England services, absented themselves from them acquired a categorical and legal label - 'recusants' or 'popish recusants' (from the Latin *recusare*, to refuse) - 'a very small but definite and well instructed group ... quite distinct from the amorphous and fading mass of more or less conservative conformists and "mislikers of religion"'. The lay Catholics belonged to what has been called 'a new and alien institution, half religious and half political, glowing with enthusiasm and tainted with treason, bringing disastrous consequences for those who came under its spell'.[330] Their absenteeism also put them in the legal category of criminal offenders, for which they were liable to pay fines.

The third factor in the emergence of a clearly defined Catholic element within the Cumbrian population was reaction to the evolving pronounced Protestantism of the Church of England as it moved away from the more inclusive *via media*, or 'middle way', atmosphere of the first years of Elizabeth's reign. Around the time that Barnes became Bishop of Carlisle, his ally Grindal, who was on the more reformist, if not the puritan, wing of the Church, became Archbishop of York, and gave his support to Henry Hastings (1535-95), 3rd earl of Huntingdon, the pro-puritan Lord President from 1572 of the York-based regional executive, the Council of the North, in a drive to make the northern counties Protestant. The 'unambiguously Protestant' programme envisaged by Grindal and his group of like-minded fellow diocesan bishops involved the propagation of Reformation principle through preaching on the part of properly trained 'godly' ministers of 'God's Word'. These clerics were required to be in conformity with the doctrines of the Church of England, as set out in the Thirty-Nine Articles of Religion of 1563, teachings which were 'essentially those of the Reformation' and to which during the period 1571-6 the Cumbrian clergy were required to subscribe as tests of their conformity.[331]

On the assumption that deprivations of clergy came about because of their refusals to give their assent to the Articles, the ministers of Dacre (1571), Melmerby, Crosby Ravensworth, and Asby (1572), Brougham and Isel (1575) and Kirklinton (1576) were ejected for their non-compliance and there were 'two or three' other ejections in 1575. Three of these dissidents, those of Melmerby, Asby and Kirklinton, had been appointed since 1558 and others presumably earlier, perhaps in Mary's Catholic reign.[332] However, the Thirty-Nine Articles had been authorised in 1563 so that it was taking eight years for the ejections that they called for to be enforced in Dacre and later in the other parishes, in a belated purge of Cumbrian conservative clerics which was a necessary measure in the unfolding Protestantisation agenda under the leadership of the Cumbrian Grindal.

The reason for leaving traditionally minded clerics in place in Cumbria until the 1570s was that the dearth of parish clergy - only two deacons and one priest were ordained between 1561 and 1568 - made it necessary to retain such individuals rather than leave parishes completely without any ministry. However, from the turn of the 1560s and 1570s the supply of officially acceptable new clergy began to improve, at first appreciably, then sensationally: from the ordination of seven deacons and four priests in 1569, numbers went up, during Barnes's Protestantising drive between 1571 and 1576, to 56 priests and 70 deacons. Local young men who had grown up knowing only an officially Protestant England and who had been educated chiefly in the area's schools were now being confidently appointed to parishes within the diocese.[333]

In so far as Barnes's success in erecting a Reformation system in Cumbria repelled adherents of religious tradition into adopting an outright recusant posture, this was a minority option, weighted towards the landed gentry, and their wives, daughters and widows who did not face all the legal sanctions of outright non-conformism. It was a numerically small party, though characterised increasingly, as will be seen in the next chapter, by a fervent Catholic piety, reflecting the ascending movement of renewal in Continental Europe known as the Counter-Reformation or Catholic Reformation - albeit a faith that was in essential continuity with the pre-Reformation Catholic past. Even if it is true that 'during the reign of Elizabeth I there were about 400 or 500 practising Roman Catholics in Cumbria', out of an overall Cumberland population of about 30,000, that makes a very small percentage, though now marked by serious commitment to Catholic belief and practice.[334]

Figures coming from legal presentments for recusancy show lower totals: in 1581 four recusants were indicted at Carlisle; in 1592-3 five were identified in Cumberland and 34 in

Westmorland; in 1595-6 53 were listed in the Carlisle diocese, 31 of them in Cumberland, 22 in Westmorland, plus 16 in the Kendal Deanery, three in Furness and 24 in Lonsdale. Recusant clusters have been traced at Wetheral (nine) and Grayrigg (13), with others at Dalston, Sebergham, Hesket, Newbiggin, Castle Carrock, Askham, Lowther, Morland, Kirkby Thore, Dufton, Appleby, Crosby Ravensworth, Brough-under-Stainmore and Warcop; a Catholic lady dwelt at Hartsop, Ullswater, and the Radcliffe family maintained a Catholic presence on Derwentwater Island, Sir Francis Radcliffe, who was to be involved in the 1605 Gunpowder Plot, being described as 'an obstinate, dangerous and not unlearned recusant'.[335]

Recusancy under Elizabeth was also now acquiring what was to be the predominant social profile that it was would largely retain until the 19th century: a pattern of rural and seigneurial protection of priests, based on country houses, and affording opportunities for Catholic worship to tenants and employees: 35 out of 53 recusants in Cumberland and Westmorland were gentry and ten their servants.[336]

Towns such as Penrith and Kendal were closely supervised by their Protestant elites, but the prosperous farming country in Penrith's vicinity supported a number of estates where the recusant patronal model prevailed. At Greystoke and Gilsland Lord William Howard (1563-1640) was converted in 1584 and his Catholic influence would have been considerable in those localities. At Johnby Hall, near Greystoke, Leonard Musgrave may have been a 'church papist' - a Catholic who attended parish worship (without communicating) so as to avoid paying the fines - but he gave his assent to the use of his house for the celebration of Mass. At Askham, near Lowther, the Sandfords (or Sandforths), with their inherited household chantry chapel, typified the continuity between late medieval piety and early modern recusancy. Thomas Sandford (1538-74) was another church papist, whose wife Anne stayed away from the parish church.[337]

The affection of leading Cumberland gentry for 'traditional' faith was dramatically typified in the will of October 1595 of Sir Henry Curwen (d. 1597), MP for Cumberland in Queen Mary's parliament in 1554-6, sheriff in 1562, 1570, 1580 and 1589 and host in Workington to Mary Queen of Scots in her flight from her kingdom in 1568:

> my bodie shall be buried in the Chantrie of the church side of the Church of Workington ... [and] that my sonne Nicholas Curwen [1550-1605] with one whole yeare rent after my death shall cause the same Chanterie to be mayde and buylded with one leanto roof covered with lead with two glasse windows the stones thereof to be hewen with masons worke.[338]

Lay Catholics in Cumbria, as elsewhere, needed the ministry of their own priests, of whom there were 21 in the diocese of Carlisle by 1593. One of them, George Spenser, served at Bewcastle in 1568, the proximity of the border giving him some freedom of movement. Otherwise, in Cumbria 'None of the old priests had anything to do with the [recusant] movement' and the supply of priests to the English mission began with the arrival, from 1574, of alumni from the seminaries that had been established in various locations on the Continent.[339] Their arrival was followed by that of priests of the newly formed Society of Jesus - Jesuits.

The commitment of these 'seminarian' priets was typified by John Bost (1543-94), the 'Catholic apostle of the North', born in Dufton, younger son of the Protestant Nicholas - but also of the latter's Catholic wife Janet, *née* Hutton, of Hutton Hall, Penrith. Trained and ordained in the seminary at Douai in the

Low Countries, Bost came on the English 'mission' in 1581, in the same year as a new Act of Parliament, implicitly recognising the effectiveness of the seminarians' work, made it high treason to be converted to the Catholic Church. The Act against Jesuits, Seminary Priests and such other like Disobedient Persons of 1585 made it high treason for a priest ordained abroad to be present in the realm at any point after 1559 and declared it a felony for anyone to give such a person assistance.[340]

Tightened security was implemented, coordinated from the centre by one of the Secretaries of State, Sir Francis Walsingham (c. 1530-90), operating a spy network which closely watched the two counties, where Walsingham's surveillance system was direccted by Henry le Scrope (1534-1592), 9th Baron Scrope of Bolton, governor of Carlisle and Warden of the West March between 1562 and 92. Scrope's partner in the drive against recusancy in the diocese was John May (or Meye, d. 1598), who became Bishop of Carlisle, following Barnes's transfer to Durham, in 1577.[341]

Scrope and May targeted Catholic laity such as John Bost's ally, the 'wicked piller of papistrie', Andrew Hilton, at Warcop, as well as Bost's elder brother, Lancelot, along with a Scottish seminary priest named Mountford.[342] May's most sensational coup against the Cumbrian recusant community involved the seminary priest Christopher Robinson.

Born in Woodside near Wigton, Robinson was ordained at the seminary at Reims in February 1592 and was sent to England in September. John Bost was arrested in September 1593 and Robinson was present at his trial and execution in Durham in July 1594, writing a powerful account of the event. Robinson himself was taken prisoner by May at Leonard Musgrave's home, Johnby Hall, in March 1597 and was put to death by being hung, drawn and quartered in Carlisle at some point before 7 April 1597.[343]

May's account of Robinson's capture, communicated in July to the Secretary of State, Robert Cecil (c. 1563-1612), reveals the mechanics and the limitations of the intelligence system. The Bishop had an agent, one Thomas Lancaster:

> the only man that I have trusted or can trust to discover such Jesuits and seminaries as do lurk within my diocese, to the corruption of many of her Majesty's subjects. He was the only man that gave me sure intelligence when and where I might apprehend, as I did, Christopher Robinson, our late condemned seminary.

The implication may be that others knew when and where Robinson might be arrested, but that it was Lancaster who broke through the wall of protective silence.

The Bishop was hopeful that his unusual action would have an intimidating effect, and that Robinson's execution 'hath terrified a great sort of our obstinate recusants'. He was, at the same time, aware that one exemplary execution would not solve his problems with the missionary priests, for even after Robinson's death in Carlisle, 'there still be harboured three or four more notable seminaries or Jesuits, who pass and repass within my diocese without controlment'.[344]

There were two reasons for the failure of 'controlment'. One had to do with both the inland and the coastal geography of the region, which delayed, if it did not prevent, the arrest of priests, giving Christopher Robinson 52 months of freedom between December 1592 and March 1597 before his eventual arrest. Inland, in the intractable Westmorland uplands - 'a fellish country in Westmerland' - in c. 1590 the seminarian John Middleton was 'kepte secret ... with an ould woman called Agnes Hodgson ... and so often as the saide Middleton repaires thither, she kepeth him very secretly, he is never sene abroad unless he walke into the woodes. (In Cartmel another woman was able 'att any tyme [to] fetch a papiste priste'.)[345]

The long and indented north-western maritime approaches also facilitated the concealment and swift movement of priests on the run, keeping them ahead of the law enforcers, since:

> Yf search be made for any of the ['Seminaryes and Papists'] in Lancashire upon an howers warning they wilbe in Westmerland and if searche be made there upon aother howers warning they wilbe in Cumberland etc.[346]

A smoothly run underground coastal network smuggled the fugitives around the Irish Sea littoral:

> there is one little fleebotte [a fly-boat, a fast sail-boat] kepte by a gentleman or two in that country nere unto the saide Pilafurther [the Pile of Foulney, near modern Barrow-in-Furness] which doth carry and convey out of Scotland Ireland England and other places, certain Semynaries Jesuwetts and Papists and so hath their severall passages to such places as they desire to be att.[347]

Geography apart, the second factor identified by May in accounting for the continuing freedom enjoyed by a group of Catholic priests in Cumbria was 'the careless or partial dealing of some our justices'. As proof of this negligence, the Bishop cited the ease of movement and action that were available to the seminarian Richard Dudley (b. 1563).[348]

Richard Dudley was the son of Edmund and Catherine Dudley, of the influential and well-connected Yanwath family, who were related to Queen Elizabeth's favourite Robert Dudley (1533-88), earl of Leicester. Richard Dudley was trained for the priesthood in the English College, Rome, ordained in April 1588, sent on the English mission, 'made his way to Lancs. and was not molested for several years': Christopher Robinson acclaimed him as 'the angel of that profession' of seminary priests. Dudley was eventually arrested in March 1599, imprisoned in London but escaped, being imprisoned again in London in 1602. In 1603 Dudley was in Paris, dealing with disputes within the English Catholic priesthood (the last recorded notification of him).[349]

Bishop May was convinced that Dudley's open immunity from arrest was attributable to deference, within his own gentry class, towards his rank:

> He is the only heir of Edmund Dudley, esquire … . It is known to many of our gentlemen that the said angelical … seminary is harboured in those parts, yet none of them will, though they see him, lay hands on him.

Unless May could employ his agent Thomas Lancaster, who had led him to Christopher Robinson, 'to apprehend Dudley and his associates, now lurking in this country, they will never be taken'.[350] Thus the nature of Cumbria's landscape and seascape, plus the social assumptions guiding the region's landed gentry, all conspired to make May's problem with the seminary priests acute.

Nor would the lay recusants disappear. A survey of January 1597 - 'Presentments of recusants in the diocese of Carlisle', which were intended to incriminate the offenders, in fact revealed how many of them there were - 42 - men and women (minus children but including servants), distributed throughout the area and belonging to old-established gentry families.[351]

Thus, just at the close of the 16th century - and following decades of legal pressure - Cumbria's recusant element was still extant, for Henry Robinson (1553?- 1616), Bishop of Carlisle from 1598 to his death, and a dedicated preacher and reformer, complained in December 1599 that he had encountered more of them than he had expected - but that there were many more in the Deaneries of Kendal and Coupland, both within the oversight of the diocese of Chester. Even so, the century's end may have seen developments in the Cumbrian recusant community that would lead to its continuing erosion over the course of the following century: Robinson enumerated eight or nine who had conformed over a recent two-month period and named eight adults, led by Lady Katherine Radcliffe and her son Francis, and including Thomas and Martha Sandford (probably temporary emigrants) who left the region [352] - perhaps for more strongly Catholic Lancashire.

As the 16th century drew to a close, an optimistic prospect for the Stuart future was summed up in the Anglo-Scottish Treaty of Carlisle of 1597 which:

> recognised the civilising and conforming influences of organized religion. Churches were to be repaired and 'good ministers planted at every border church to inform the lawless people of their duty,and to watch over their manners'.
> The formative role of religion and education in improving border society was by now beginning to be appreciated. Protestant ministers also would counter Romanist influences which were regarded as a source of border turbulence.

Even so, Robinson persisted in his dismal account of the Cumbrian, who, he found, remained 'pitifully ignorant of the foundations of Christianity ... many of them are without all fear of God, adulterers, thieves, murderers'.[353]

The Cumbrian plague outbreak of the late 1590s, from which Bishop May died in February 1598, presented clerics with knotty problems of interpretation.The contagion reached a surge in Penrith between October 1597 and January 1599, with 615 carefully recorded deaths, and high regional epidemic mortality, for example in Carlisle, Gosforth, Appleby, Keswick,

Kirkoswald, Kirkby Lonsdale and Gilsland. Even though the Penrith figure was accurate, compiled by the vicar of St Andrew's and carefully entered in the parish register on the basis of named individual deaths over the course of the months, a profoundly pessimistic and moralistic psychological approach to the infection as 'GOD PUNISMENT' warped the vicar's accurate arithmetic, to replace it, in a brass plate set up in St Andrew's church, with a grossly inflated Penrith death toll of 2060, with similar massive exaggerations for Kendal, Richmond and Carlisle.[354] This grotesque over-estimate was designed to supplant the vicar's meticulously collated data in order to draw a penitential message from the apocalyptic, but essentially misleading, head-count.

Richard Leake was vicar of Killington between 1597 and 1599. In the immediate aftermath of the cessation of the contagion - 'the cup of afflictions ... these fearful and afflicted times wherein we have lately been' - his four published plague sermons of 1599 explained the scourge as divine punishment for:

> the masse and multitude of our sins, in rebelling against the holie one of *Israel* filthy ... provokers of the Almightie ... those great and capitall sinnes, which rule and raigne amongst vs: as gross Poperie, and blinde superstition in very many places, in so much ... that the abhominable Idoll of indignation, the Masse, is vsed in diverse places about vs and that very boldly ... filthy drunkenness, abhominable whoredomes, open profanation of the Sabbath, vnlawfull pastimes.

Leake watched his parishioners closely as they:

> After the receiuing of this holy sacrament and seale of the true Christian saluation ... they then goe for good fellowship to the tauerne ... altogether, and thence they come not till they are

inflamed and made drunke with strong drinke.[355]

Preoccupation with epidemic as divine retribution for sin massively exaggerated, to more catastrophically dramatic levels, the numbers of plague deaths in Penrith in the late 1590s. In similar fashion, and in the absence of any scientific analysis of the causes of the contagion, the origin of the visitation in Cumberland was accounted for by Leake, in entirely moralistic terms, as God's vengeful punishment, provoked by sin: Leake 'attributed the causes of the plague exclusively to the sins of the people in the "North part"'.[356]

Sinfulness was highlighted by Leake as failing to observe Sunday religiously, drunkenness, promiscuity, superstition and omitting to suppress 'Poperie' and the Mass. In the Stuart century, England in general and Cumberland and Westmorland in particular, were to be the theatre of culture wars to make their people less sinful, more sober and chaste, to get them into church and away from 'vnlawful pastimes' on the 'Sabbath', to eliminate the Catholic faith - perhaps in part so as to ward off the lethal wrath of a vengeful, plague-delivering 'Almightie'.

Leake also found those who did 'counsel with witches and sorcerers' - like the three named men and four women who were presented for such offences in Cumberland between 1575 and 1590. Much of the popular necromantic culture of the period was apotropaic, in the sense of employing supposed magical devices and procedures for cures of ailments in people, especially in children, and in livestock. The scarcity, expense and general incompetenece of professional medical services encouraged the use of amateur cures, perhaps with homeopathic bases, though typically supplemented by the use of charms and spells. The withdrawal of such curative solutions as the religious houses had offered might have fostered a fall-back onto non-professional medication. Women were to the fore in prosecutions for witchcraft as a legal offence, as the widow Anna Harrison was presented on suspicion in the wave of general cases that came before the ecclesiastical Court of High Commision in Cumberland in the years between 1575 and 1590. In the same series, Jannet Huggen faced accusation as 'a sorcerer and medicioner of children'. Jannet Wyse was a 'medicioner for the waffe [waving away] of an ill winde' - perhaps Cumbria's notorious 'Helm Wind', with its 'formidably destructive force ... in a subsistence economy'- and 'for the fayryes'. Men too, faced court appearances for witchcraft, as with the blacksmith Anthony Huggen, presumably husband - and business partner - of Janet Huggen and presented to the High Commission 'for medicioning children'. Robert Sanderson's specialty was 'medicioning for the worme' - treatment of intestinal parasitic worms. Less benign, Mabell Browne faced an allegation commonly made against poor widows - 'a witche and taketh mylke from Kye'- cows. [357]

Chapter 8:
Faith and Religion in the Stuart Lake Counties, 1603-1689

The 17th century saw the decisive confirmation of the once Catholic English as overwhelmingly, though not entirely, one of Europe's Protestant peoples - in the formal and public sense of possessing a Protestant Established Church whose services all were obliged by law to attend and to maintain its finances; the royal head of state was Supreme Governor of the Church and 'Defender of the Faith'.

Further, and beyond those legal and constitutional provisions, between the 16th and 17th centuries uncounted numbers of English women and men were taking into their hearts and minds the doctrines of the Protestant Reformation. As set out by the 16th-century Reformers, beginning with Luther and Calvin, these themes were developed by the Church of England, in its Thirty-Nine Article of Religion of 1563, in the classics of its religious and devotional literature and in its massive output of sermons. Preached to many generations of English people by successive numbers of their parsons, Sunday after Sunday, in thousands of parish churches, lengthy, Scripture-based sermons laid down for many English people the lineaments of a new cognizance and spirituality.

In particular, the Protestant faith of the Church of England, which was centred on acceptance of Christ crucified as the Christian's sole Redeemer, became etched into the consciousness of numerous individuals, as recorded in the preambles to their wills, in which their deepest convictions were embedded, as death approached. Such testimonies drawn up in the Lake

Counties reveal that, like thousands of other English people, numbers of Cumbrian men and women of the Stuart age were absorbing, and voicing in their own words, the Reformation doctrines of the Atonement as set out in the Thirty-Nine Articles, according to which Christ was the only and all-sufficient ransom for sin, the Crucifixion rendering all other means redundant. As the Articles put it:

> Christ ... truly suffered, was crucified, dead, and buried, to reconcile his Father to us, and to be a sacrifice [Article II] ... We are accounted righteous before God, only for the merit of our Lord and Saviour Jesus Christ by faith [Article XI]. ... The Offering of Christ once made is that perfect redemption, propitiation, for all the sins of the whole world ... and there is none other satisfaction for sin, but that alone [Article XXXI].[358]

Following in such a direction, the declaration of faith by Rowland Vaux (d. 1586) is a straightforward setting out of standard Elizabethan Protestant beliefs about how humanity's redemption has been accomplished, solely by the sacrifice of the crucified Saviour:

> having a full faeth and belyeffe of remission of all my synnes onely by the bitter death and passion of my sweet saviour and redemer Jesus Christ.... .[359]

In 1604 Miles Philipson of Crook Hall near Kendal (who left land adjacent to Abbot Hall to provide 'Godly and virtuous instruction of the youth' of the town) commended his:

> soul into the hands of thallmightie god and to his well beloved sonne Jesus Christ by whose death and blood shedding upon the crosse I hope onelie to be saved and by noe other means or meritt of any one or others.[360]

The same kind of faith in a personal salvation secured for

the Christian by Christ alone was reiterated by another member of a family that led the puritan cause in Kendal, Hudleston Philipson, whose will of 1657 stated:

> first and principally I commend my soule into the mercifull hands of Almighty God my creator Jesus Christ my redeemer and the Holy Ghost my sanctifier stedfastly believing by and through the meritts and mediation of Jesus Christ my saviour to have full and free remission of all my sins and to be made a inheritor of the kingdom of heaven.[361]

In 1638 Anne Preston of Canon Winder placed herself:

> into the merciful hands of All mightie G[od] surely trusting in Jesus Christ my redeemer to obtaine full pardone and remission of all my sines & Fruition of eternall life.[362]

(The inscriptions on Westmorland church bells, which were likely in the middle ages to favour the Virgin Mary and the other saints, might now be focused on Christ, as with the inscription 'Jesus be our speed' [success], in a church bell at Troutbeck in 1631, with the same message on two bells in Orton dated 1637. One of the Orton bells also contains Calvin's motto *Soli Deo Gloria* - 'Glory to God alone'.)[363]

The simple, almost stark, existential force of individuals' declarations of faith and trust fixed on the crucified Saviour alone, as evident in the preambles to wills cited above, stands in even higher relief when contrasted with the confidence that a Cumbrian Catholic squire, John Vaux (1583-1652), of Catterlen, near Penrith, placed in a wider range of celestial supporters. Having lodged his hopes in God as his creator and Christ as his Redeemer, John Vaux went on to call on selected figures from Catholicism's heavenly hosts of the Deity's sainted assistants. Thus, alongside Reformation orthodoxy on the key issue of how humanity's redemption was brought about, a Catholic antithesis provided a nuanced alternative.[364] The introduction of the Protesant English Reformation, though without the extinction of the 'old faith', permitted, in the case of John Vaux, the survival of a Catholic culture in early modern Cumbria, albeit one adapted to the newer currents of the European Catholic renewal known as the Catholic Reformation or Counter-Reformation.

In 1623 a 'private declaration' by John Vaux treads the familiar path of Reformation soteriology –the doctrine of salvation, appealing to Christ alone for the achievement of our redemption, 'for I have none in Heaven without thee nor any in earth but thee only' It is, however, at this point that Vaux's piety departs from the Protestant norm, in this significantly entitled 'private' statement. The Reformation doctrine of salvation which was set out in the Thirty-Nine Articles envisaged redemption as forensic, in the sense ... Saviour Jesus Christ'.

Calvinist theologians 'added to the legalistic interpretation of the Atonement by speaking of a "covenant" between the Father and Christ for the redemption of the elect at large', and it was towards this kind of transactional model that the Thirty-Nine Articles inclined, seeing the saved elect as the passive beneficiaries of a pre-arranged contract which was sealed on their behalf, and without their involvement, between the Father and the obedient Son in order to restore peace between sinful humanity and the Godhead: according to Calvin,'an expiation must intervene in order that Christ ... may obtain God's favour for us and appease [God's] wrath ... God as retributive justice demanded the punishment ... [but] the motif which Calvin ... consistently sounds is that of Christ's total and willing obedience ... "the whole course of his obedience"'.[365]

Alongside this legal approach, a leading English Calvinist theologian, John Bunyan (1628-88), was capable of a conception of the Atonement that was personal and 'affective, almost reciprocal, in the way that it responded fervently to the sufferings that Christ underwent in order to bring about mankind's - and Bunyan's own - reconciliation with the Father: 'I saw how gently he gave himself to be hanged and nailed on [the cross] for sins'. Thus there may have been some surviving undertow of medieval devotionalism in Bunyan's consciousness that drew him towards a Christ-centred piety 'which was personalistic, devotional and emotive, rather than legal and forensic in its emphases' - a piety that resembles that of the great medieval English mystics Julian of Norwich (c. 1342-c. 1413) and Margery Kempe (c. 1373-c. 1433).[366]

Members of the stricty enclosed monastic Carthusian Order made their impact felt in the world beyond the cloister through their published devotional writings, none more so than Ludolph of Saxony (c. 1300-78), whose *Vita Christi*, first printed in 1477, achieved immense popularity throughout western Europe. Ludolph's impulse to see the suffering brother Christ as less of a terrifying judge but rather 'a man bearing every aspect of human nature to the end' found condensed expression in a reiterated use for Christ of the adjective 'sweet' - *dulcis*, in the sense of 'kind', 'dear', 'loving', 'beloved': 'O Good Jesus, how sweet you are in the heart of one who thinks upon you and loves you ... sweeter in that which is humble than in that which is exalted ...'. Ludolph's acclamation 'O Good Jesus' was repeated in the popular medieval English prayer known as *O bone Jesu*, which continued 'O good Jesu, o sweet Jesu ... This name of Jesus is a sweet name'.[367]

This medieval image of 'sweet Jesus' had indeed surfaced in the 1586 will of Rowland Vaux - 'my sweet saviour and redemer Jesus Christ' - but is strongly reiterated in his grandson John's 1623 'private declaration': '[I] Humbly beseech sweet Jesus ... Sweet Jesus, Amen'. In addition to these shared affective evocations of the beloved Christ, but missing from Rowland Vaux's doctrinally 'correct' Protestant testimonial, there is John Vaux's calling on a range of other assistance: he invoked the aid of a group of saints, beseeching the favour of 'sweet Jesus' 'for thy blessed mother's sake for thy dearly beloved disciple St. John's [Vaux's patronal saint from his baptism], and that Mary Magdalene who loved so fervently'. [368]

The inclusion of the Apostle John was an obvious choice for a man christened by that name. The saint that Vaux had in mind was John, known as the Evangelist, the figure who was generally aligned with the un-named disciple 'whom Jesus loved' and who leaned on His breast at the Last Supper. In a final act of love Jesus entrusts His mother to the disciple (John 13:23, 19:26). John's first Epistle announces that God Himself is love (1 John 4:16). One form of 'affectionate dependence' in a pre-Reformation English will preamble invoked John the Evangelist 'whom I have always worshipped and loved'. Mary's inclusion -'for thy blessed mother's sake' - in Vaux's group as the summation of maternal love was mandatory, while Mary Magdalene 'who loved so fervently' was traditionally aligned with the anonymous 'woman in the city, which was a sinner' who anointed Jesus with precious oil and of whom Jesus said 'Her sins ... are forgiven; for she loved much' (Luke, 7:38, 47). Vaux's selection of this trio from a myriad of heavenly patrons was thus shaped by their being identified with the primary 'affective' attribute, *caritas, agape* - love. In 1623 the appeal was to the loving and beloved Blessed Virgin Mary and the emblems of love John and Mary Magalene, and in his will preamble of 1650 John Vaux was 'believinge by the merits death and passion of my glorious Saviour Jesus my sinnes to be forgiven, in the Communion of the blessed Virgin Mary and all his Saintes and Elect'.[369]

What do the key words 'in the Communion of' mean here? The prayer 'Invocation of the Saints' at the Canon of the Mass in the 'Tridentine' Latin rite authorised by the Catholic Church's reforming Council of Trent (1545-63) opens with the memorial *Communicantes, et memoriam venerantes, in primis gloriosæ semper Virginis Mariæ* ... 'Communicating with, and honouring in the first place the memory of the glorious ever Virgin Mary, ...' and proceeds to enlist the Apostles and a group of saints and martyrs belonging to Rome. Vaux's phrase 'in the Communion with' echoes the Mass in seeing Mary and the saints of the Church as being in some not fully defined way in association with the Trinity in mankind's eternal rescue. Vaux's assemblage is, then, entirely 'Catholic' in inspiration and also specifically Tridentine in taking its cue from the Council's re-affirmation, in its decree *De Invocatione Sanctorum* - 'Concerning the Invocation of Saints' - of December 1563 - against the main Protestant Reformers' exclusive Christocentricity - of a traditional doctrine of veneration and supplication of the saints, primarily as channels of grace from God through Christ and of the value of the 'intercession and invocation of the saints'. [370]

However, just as significant as Vaux's *in*clusions in his declaration of certain saints were his *ex*clusions of others - in particular of regional figures such as Aidan, Kentigern and, above all, Cuthbert: these omissions from his list deserve as much explanation as do his inclusions in it. Sensitive to allegation of credulity and superstition, especially around the cult of relics such as were made in Calvin's bitter and brilliant *Avertissement tresutile* of 1543, Catholic Reformation doctrine drew back from popular excesses which bishops were urged to rein in. The early modern Jesuit scholars who made up the Bollandist movement aimed to purge Catholic hagiography of all 'legendary or apocryphal material' of the kind that was apparent in the

Cumbrian Cuthbert cultus, with its legendary fantasies and intense concentration on relics and their power - the feature of popular piety that was considered in chapter 7 above. Neither Cuthbert, Kentigern nor Aidan was included in Vaux's little canon and for this omission a tentative explanation is being suggested here.[371]

Some of the foci of Vaux's piety had their origins in late medieval and early Tudor Cumbrian devotions, though these drew on wells of pan-European religion: dedication to the human and suffering 'sweet Jesus' is traceable to the recurrent monogram of the 'IHS' found around the Lakes counties, for example in the figure of the Crucified as *Schmerzenmann* - the 'Man of Sorrows' and 'Suffering Servant' - in Cartmel Fell chapel; and in the adoption of the device of Christ's Five Wounds as a rallying symbol in the Pilgrimage of Grace. But as well as being rooted in the Catholic piety of the 14th, 15th and earlier 16th centuries, Vaux's religious life is typical of the post-Reformation English Catholic religious atmosphere in fusing late medieval themes with Tridentine emphases, in particular with the internationality (and in particular the centrality of Rome) in the Counter-Reformation Church, its saints having universal (rather than primarily regional) identities, as well as Scriptural credentials where these were present [372]

Vaux, then, selected his saintly schedule on the basis of criteria that would have been approved both by the Council of Trent and the Bollandists. Paradoxically the post-Reformation English Catholic community (like the Dutch) was exceptionally open to the clerical influences of the Catholic Reformation because all its priests were products of the new seminaries established under the influence of Trent. In John Vaux's case that influence may be traceable to a family source: as Hugh Vaux has shown, one of John Vaux's uncles, Leonard Musgrave of Johnby

Hall (c. 1565-1609), provided (illegal) accommodation to the Douai seminarian (and martyr of 1597), Christopher Robinson. [373]

Cumbria's Catholic life from the 16th and through the 17th and 18th centuries was sustained by the minor aristocrats of the landed gentry families, families which in such cases as the Dudleys, Leyburnes, Thornburghs and Stricklands also provided priestly leadership via the Contintental seminaries, above all Douai, with their Tridentine ethos. As John Vaux's testimony shows, this socially high-status faith provided no room for the now discredited fabulist popular religiosity of the demotic Cuthbert cultus. That said, this Catholicity of the manor house provided a minority strand in an unfolding pluralistic Cumbrian religious sociology which would never again, after the 17th century, support a form of Christianity with a single character.

Even so, as was seen at the beginning of this chapter, it was the Church of England that retained control of and responsibility for the region's religious life and it was upon the Established Church that the duty of care of the counties' places of worshp fell. This, in turn, required a programme of church building and repair which could be safely initiated with the arrival of peace between England and Scotland upon the accession to the English throne of the Scots king James I in 1603 (d. 1625). Because of their border location, the northernmost Cumberland parishes, Arthuret, near Longtown, Kirkandrews-on-Esk and Bewcastle's St Andrew's, had been vulnerable to damage and neglect. In 1604 the walls of Bewcastle St Andrew's were still standing, but all the slate and timber had disappeared. The church of St Andrew in Kirkandrews had been pulled down and the site was used only for burials. Arthuret's church of St Michael was 'in a very poor condition: a narrow building and covered with heather and ling [also heather]'.[374]

James I took a keen interest in the condition of the north of England, which he regarded as the midlands of his intended Anglo-Scottish kingdom of Great Britain. At Arthuret

> In 1607 James I passing this way took compassion on the church here which had been frequently laid waste by the Scotch and ordered a brief [a royal authorised appeal for funding] for rebuilding. Much money [£1,500] was raised and a handsome church built.[375]

Another royal intervention saved Kirkandrews church when, in 1631, a petition was submitted to Charles I (r. 1625-49) for funds to restore the building. A collection was taken around the diocese, the rebuilding being completed in 1637. (The present church dates from 1775.) [376]

These operations were part of a remarkable enterprise of renovation of churches in Cumbria in the reigns of the first two Stuart kings: Burneside in 1602; Colton in 1603; Ireleth, Stainmore and Swindle in 1608; Staveley-in-Cartmel in 1618; Rampside in 1621; Lindale in 1627; Middleton and Martindale in 1635; and Whitehaven in 1642 were all restored. By the last-named date, 'a notable advance had been made on the Cumberland Borders in church rebuilding'.[377]

If progress was being made with the restoration of the parish churches, what steps were being taken to improve the quality of the parochial clergy, to secure 'the appointment of well-qualified clergy to safe benefices', to improve their ability to unfold the doctrines of the Church of England and, perhaps, to provide a moral example to the mass of parishioners - who continued to be regarded as practitioners of 'lewd vices', arising from their ignorance of God and inclined to 'grow from ignorance to brutishness'.[378]

The first Stuart Bishop of Carlisle, Henry Robinson,

expressed a mixture of pessimism and optimism over the standards of his parish clergy, with the pessimism, however, winning through:

In the more peaceful parts of the diocese there are some clergymen of very commendable parts, both for knowledge and conscience, but their number is very small.

Overall, however, standards were low, exacerbated by exploitation of parochial incomes by lay patrons and consequent meagre clerical incomes, plus the great distances of many rural communities from their parish churches:

Others there were that might do much good if they had half that delight in discharging their function which they have in idleness, vain pleasures, and worldly cares. The far greater number is utterly unlearned, unable to read English truly and distinctly.[379]

One particular case of malpractice was, however, exceptional. By 1605 Richard Graham, who had been in possession of the parsonage of Stapleton, near Bewcastle, 'for eight years, did say service, minister the sacraments, baptize children, and do all other rites and ceremonies belonging to a clergyman to do, and … has been reputed and taken to be a full minister.'

That, however, he was not, being a product of a system that Bishop May had deployed to boost his own inadequate finances. This practice was what May's successor Robinson called 'the great facility of my predecessor' in ordaining five men to no higher order than that of deacon but not to the full priesthood, appropriating their clerical incomes for himself, paying the individual deacon a lower stipend and trusting that, whereas a 'curate in priestly orders could demand a living; a deacon with a parsonage was not likely to raise much noise'.[380]

existence???

Despite Robinson's negative view of the educational condition of his parish clergy and of their vocational commitment, his episcopate saw the tenures of two exemplars of the ministry in Cumbria, Leonard Lowther at Greystoke and Ralph Tyrer in Kendal. As for the former, 'Between 1597 and 1609, the rector of Greystoke, Leonard Lowther (c. 1553-1609), turned his parish into a model of Protestant reform, largely eliminating recusancy', preaching regularly and bringing up to 480 men and women to communion in the parish church. Following Lowther's death, Greystoke continued as a beacon of parochial reform when Bishop Robinson took over as rector: in 1610 there were sermons nearly every Sunday.[381]

The 1604 Hampton Court Conference, which was summoned by James I to heal the rift between the puritan and the more conservative wings of the Church, echoed Robinson's enthusiasm for preaching: the Conference, of which Robinson was a member, resolved to place preachers in the border areas.[382]

The most important contribution that Robinson made as a diocesan reformer came in the form of his pioneering 44 Visitation Articles of 1612, a set of interrogatories directed at churchwardens which provided the parishes with the norms of recommended practice.[383]

It was entirely in line with Robinson's priorities that his Articles would place the giving of sermons at the head of his enquiries:

I Imprimis whether yor Parson, Vicar, Curate, or Minister be a preacher of God's word and a maintainer and furtherer of Religion now Established by Publicke Authoritie within this Realme of England or no.

The anxious enquiry was repeated:

4. Item whether he [the parson] be painfull and diligent in

182

Henry Robinson, Bishop of Carlisle

preaching to all ... and how many sermons hath yor parson ... preached in his owne church within this year last.[384]

Given that under the 1559 Act of Uniformity the Church of England had the monarch as its Supreme Governor, it was to be expected that a further enquiry should ask:

2. Item whether he [the parson] doo in his sermons, lectures & other discourses move the people to joyne with him in prayer for the Kings Matie, our Gracious Queene Anne [of Denmark, 1574-1619], the Noble Prince Henrie [Henry Frederick, 1594-1612, Prince of Wales] and their Roiall Issue.[385]

The same note of loyalty to the crown and the dynasty was struck in the 12th Article. Following the 1605 Gunpowder Conspiracy, which was undertaken by Catholic extremists to slaughter the King, Lords and Commons, in January 1606 parliament passed An Act for Public Thanksgiving to Almighty God every Year on the Fifth day of November, offering the Almighty thanks for the nation's deliverance from 'an invention so inhumane, barbarous and cruel as the like was never before heard of'. On every 5 November each parish in the country was to conduct a service of thanksgiving, at which attendance was compulsory; the order of service remained in the Book of Common Prayer until 1859.[386]

Robinson took his cue from the statute:

12 Item whether doeth yor parson ... according to an Act of Parlamt in that behalve made call upon and require the people of his parish to solemnize the 5th day of November, and yt day doo come to the churche to joyne in prayers and thanksgiving for the happie deliverance of his Matie, the Quene, prince and states [estates] of Parlmt from the most traterous and bloody intended massacre by gunpowder.[387]

Although Robinson did not use this opportunity for an anti-

Catholic tirade, a further Article was to enquire:

> 24 Item whether are there any pson or persons ... within yor parish ... that be notorious recusants or who negligently or seldom come to yor church ... upon Sabaoth or festival dayes ... and what estate, condition, or degree are they of.

Vigilance had also to be exercised over those 'church papists' who attended parish worship, though without receiving communion and 'who doo not yearly communicate thrise'.[388]

Close observance of Robinson's Visitation Articles would have kept the worship of the parishes of his diocese within the orthodox Elizabethan Prayer Book tradition, above all with regard to the vestments of the minister conducting the service. The Hampton Court Conference had been summoned in response to the allegedly 1,000- strong Millenary Petition of puritan ministers to the king in 1603 proposing further ecclesiastical alterations in a more pronounced Protestant direction. High on the list of these submissions was a request to end the requirement that ministers adminstering communion wear the surplice, which puritan reformists regarded as a 'popish' remnant in the Church of England: they alleged that its use demonstrably encapsulated the half-way-house nature of the English Reformation, compared with those of Calvinist Scotland and the 'Best Reformed Churches' of the Continent.

Robinson's Articles insisted on the strict delivery of the authorised text of the Book of Common Prayer, with no allowance (6) for 'innovacon or omission', meaning the flexibility that puritans demanded, and asked:

> 7 Item whether dooth yor minister usually weare the surpless whyle he ys saying the publicke prayers & ministering the Sacrament.

A checklist of indispensable equipment to furnish the parish

185

church included the Book of Common Prayer, the 'largest volume' of the Bible, books of Psalms, 'a comely and decent pulpitt,' a 'comely communion table' and a 'faire and comely communion cup of silver' and 'a decent large surplice with sleyves'.[389]

While, over the issue of the surplice or freedom to improvise the service, Robinson was at odds with the 'godly' puritan party, he was at one with them over the strict observance of Sunday as a 'Sabbath' of religious observance, forbidding work, sport, games or trade. The legal sanctions around Sunday arose partly from an attempt to eliminate rival attractions to churchgoing. As Robinson's Articles expressed it:

> 30 Item whether any within yor parish … do suffer any to eat, drinke, play, jangle [brawl] or talke in their house or yard or any butcher or tradesman their shop windows to be kept open to sell meate [food], drinke or wares on Sondayes, in time of morning or evening prayers; sermons lectures or catechizing, or that worke on the Saboathe or other commanded festival dayes.

In addition to the prohibition of work, play or commerce on Sunday, Robinson also demanded a ban on social customs and recreations that interfered with the primacy of worship or the solemnity of the 'Lord's Day':

> 32 Item whether are their within yor parish... any rush bearing [celebrations accompanying the re-flooring of the church with rushes], boarbaytings, bullbaytings, may games, morrris dances, ales [originating in medieval drinking parties to raise church funds], or any such lyke prophane assemblies on the Sabboathe to the hinderance of prayers, sermons, or other godly exercises.[390]

The above clause represented a declaration of war by

Robinson, and clergy and laity of his persuasion, against the traditional use of Sunday - generally speaking the only work-free day of the week - as a period, after church-going, for games, dancing, drinking, folk rituals and the tormenting of animals. For 'Sunday stood at the point of collision between two cultures' and the struggle for the possession of that day focused the whole conflict between festive popular culture and puritan restraint. The 'strict, enforced public observance of the Sabbath ... was, for the godly, the badge of a covenant of the entire realm with God, as it had been with the Israel of old'. The leading mentor of early Stuart puritanism, William Perkins (1558-1602), ruled that 'as for ... recreations and pastimes, as bowling, and such like, they are not at this time [Sunday] to be used'.[391] Opposing this approach to the conduct of Sunday, in 1618 James I issued his Declaration (or Book) of Sports, commending healthful exercises on that day, once church attendance had been observed.

What reformers such as Bishop Robinson were undertaking, over the sacralisation of Sundays, was a key ingredient in an extensive radical overhaul of the nation's daily life and customs. Certain ancestral practices and rituals accompanying death which were no longer consciously 'Catholic' nevertheless had their distant origins in medieval 'traditional religion'. These surviving ceremonies, performed in families and neighbourhoods as the final instalments in the rites of passage which marked out a person's life, were now to be censured:

33 Item ... whether there be any superstitious ringing, superstitious burning of candles upon the corpes in the day tyme ... or praying for the dead at crosses that have bene in the way to the churche, or other superstitious use of the crosse, with towels, palmes, netwands or other memories of idolatrie.[392]

Some of the popular customs observed in this region were more specifically redolent of a Catholic past, such as those brought to light in an enquiry of between 1575 and 1590 including 'wearing [Rosary] beads' and 'fasting at St Anthonie's fast' - the vigil of the feast-day, on 17 January, of St Antony of Egypt or of Anthony of Padua on 13 June - and there was a report of a woman who believed it was unlucky to start any new work on a Friday, a legacy of popular superstition, albeit loosely linked to the Catholic festal cycle, that would no doubt have been out of kilter with the sober Tridentine Catholicism of the likes of John Vaux.[393] Clearly, these inherited practices, like the Sunday sports detailed by Robinson, continued to prevail in the Lakes region, with the kind of persistence over time that often characterises vernacular and local cultures, even when they become vestigial and their original meaning is over-laid. Personal names honouring saints and left over from a Catholic past include 2.3% of baptisms in Cumbria in 1642 by the name of Anthony, and there were 52 occurrences of Mungo, the 'pet form' of the name of the popular regional saint Kentigern, a figure excised from Vaux's saintly gallery. In this this hand-me-down nomenclature provided no incontrovertible evidence of an explicit commitment to Catholic faith, but rather that 'Godparent-naming or family lineage had probably replaced any direct link with the patron saint as a means of transmission by the sixteenth century'.[394]

Thus for officialdom to detect evidence of Catholic commitment in the survival of folk habits that had been passed down the generations was to see a Roman Catholic presence where there was none, and the innocuous, inherited words and customs would probably have been best left alone by the authorities, until they faded away over time.

For the campaigns against Sunday recreations, against passed-down customs and demotic entertainments, games and sports gave religious reform a divisive effect, muting its more widespread appeal, making it socially, culturally and educationally selective. Kendal, in the jurisdiction of the diocese of Chester, was Cumbria's most notable instance of the success of reform - and of its relative failure, in the sense of its inability to create a homogeneous Protestant urban society. The threatened survival of Kendal's originally medieval annual Corpus Christi play, organised every June by the town's trade guilds, focused a fission in the town that was moral, cultural, and class-based. In 1586, when, amidst a 'general cry for the reinstitution of the Corpus Christy play', the question was raised of a licence to permit the performance and other 'delights and fantasyes', it was clear that the defence of this memorial of 'former tyme' was in the hands of the 'common inhabitants' who 'do covytt and earnestly crye for the having the Corpus Xtii yearlye': the suggestion is of 'a strongly puritan corporation restraining the excesses of the godless masses'. Official suspicion, in the context of the controversy over the survival of the play, of 'shooting in long bows' suggests that the same kind of imperative that guided the criminalisation of games also motivated the campaign against the Corpus Christi enactment as a long-standing feature of the 'ritual year'. In 1605 the play was suspended, redolent of 'popery' in the year of the Gunpowder Plot, only to survive for another 20 years until its eventual suppression, apparently in 1625.[395]

The fact that it may have taken 40 years to end this piece of ancestral street theatre suggests that there existed a powerful resistance to imposed cultural innovation in late Elizabethan and early Stuart Kendal, a movement of socio-cultural defence spearheaded by the town's lower classes. What emerged was a division in the town between one community, that of the 'godly', and another, that of those 'reputed particularly godless'.[396]

Opposition from the town's lower classes to social, cultural and religious innovation and reform in Elizabethan and Stuart Kendal may also have been a reflection of the social stratification of the townscape. The district around the parish church, Kirkland, which was officially outside the town limits, may have been a lower-class outlier, with 'lots of yards filled with cottages'. An object of puritan loathing, the phallic symbol of the maypole, was lodged there, the subject of a 'city father's complaint in 1589 ... removed by the [puritan] commonwealth', and the 'godly' vicar Ralph Tyrer found the whole district to be 'near the church, far away from God.'[397]

In Kendal Ralph Tyrer, vicar from 1592 to 1627, was the model of the kind of preaching minister on whose sermons depended the success or otherwise of the Anglican Reformation on the local, and especially on the urban, level. Tyrer represented the fulfilment of the kind of aspiration for Kendal that had been expressed in the records of an episcopal visitation in 1578 that the congregation might 'have everie sondaie in the yeare a sermon to their great cofort and ediyfieinge'.[398]

A preacher with a national reputation, Tyrer had his 'five godly and learned sermons preached at Kendal' published in London in 1602, and the local author Richard Brathwaite celebrated the Kendalians' good fortune:

.By th' grave and reuerend Pastor which they haue; Whose life and doctrine are so ioint together, (As both sincere, there's no defect in either.) [399]

With his education in puritan Cambridge - 'Cambridge sped [favoured] me', reads the brass memorial plaque inserted into the floor of the parish church - Tyrer was an ideal answer to the call made by Kendal in 1578 for the town to have the service of 'a learned preacher'.[400]

Yet Tyrer's ministry in Kendal was at best only a partial and a contentious success and his disappointment at the limits of his achievement is evident in remarks on his memorial plaque. Kendal only 'caught' this unhappy, homesick Londoner, leading him into a life of 'labour', 'sickness' and 'death'. And it may have been a kind of vindictiveness that induced him to endow scholarships to his church's patron, Trinity College, Cambridge, not for local youths, but for boys out of London's top schools, Westminster and St Paul's. There was bitterness, too, in Tyrer's taunt that the mere 'country village' of Kendal had been undeservedly raised (in 1576) to the status of a corporate borough:

> Tyrer's disparaging outsider attitude to Kendal people - his basic mistrust for folk who always preferred to hear the flute and the pipe in the alehouse over any sermon in the church - was, apparently, fully repaid by locals, who seem to have been the main source of the 'tedious discontentments' from which his ministry suffered. The bickering and quarrelling can have done nothing to advance the ongoing cause of Reformation in Kendal.[401]

Thus the success of the mission of the Church of England, especially during Tyrer's lengthy ministry, was restricted by the involvement of the Church in largely unpopular campaigns against recreation and popular sociability, a contest over values and lifestyle in which the question of the Corpus Christi play was a rallying point for rival forces.

Finally, a key factor in the inability of the late Tudor and early Stuart Church in Kendal to maintain a socially inclusive presence in the town was to be found in the nature of the worship that was decided upon in the parish church: the resolutions of 1578 calling for the appointment of 'a learned preacher' also specified the removal and sale of the organ, the proceeds to be devoted to building repairs. Further:

> That all such stipende and portyons of money as were wont to be given to the organ plaier and other unnecessary clerks [clerics] be wholie employed to the stipend of that preacher and the rest to be supplyed by the contribucion of the well disposed pichioners of the said parishe.[402]

The story of the vicissitudes of church organs of 16th-and 17th-century England is a vital chapter in the religious contestation of that age. Survivors from the pre-Reformation Catholic middle ages, they were condemned by Grindal. In 1562 a motion in the Church's Convocation to remove them from all churches was defeated by only a single vote and a puritan-inspired proposal to do away with them in cathedrals was rejected in c. 1586; in c. 1570 'organs were newly all removed or terminally neglected' and most remaining parish organs were destroyed in 1644 under puritan legislation.[403] Kendal Holy Trinity's elimination of its organ was a local initiative that got rid of this instrument.

It was also a one-sided change, inasmuch as it envisaged only one form - a sermon-based one - of parish worship, to which the income transferred from the silencing of the organ was to be dedicated. While no mention was made in the reforms of 1578 for the administration of communion or for any music, stress on preaching was insistent: members of the corporation were to have a chapel to themselves 'to heare dyvyne service and sermons'; a new loft would allow 'the Justices of peace and gentlemen with wives and childers [to] sitt to heare sermons and Dyvyne Service if they will duringe the sermon and service tyme ... the aldermen and his brethren to sitt ... to heare sermons'.[404]

While the meticulously detailed seating arrangements - 'the

Justices of peace and gentlemen with wives and childers' - inevitably reflected a hierarchical society, the virtual identification of parish worship with (lengthy) sermonising created a cultural and educational cleavage in which a largely non-literate plebeian population was excluded from any full involvement in an order of service that was conducted by the 'learned' preacher and aimed at an educated elite 'of the well disposed pichioners' who were attuned to a taxingly cerebral puritan variant of Christianity: 'a 'bible-based religion which appealed to the thinking literate, protestantism was adopted enthusiastically among the middling sort, rather than the under class'.[405] The threat to the success of the Elizabethan and early Stuart Church of England in winning over the urban community as a whole arose, then, from the Church's own combination of intrusive moral policing with a social-class-based pressure to convert a parish congregation into a conventicle or a seminar.

The progress of Protestant reform in early Stuart Cumbria was impeded by the brevity of a succession of episcopates at Carlisle: Robert Snoden, or Snowden, was appointed in 1616 and died in 1621; Richard Milbourne, appointed in 1621, died in 1624; Richard Senhouse was installed in 1624 and died as a result of a fall from his horse two years later; the Dean of Carlisle from 1622 to 1626, Francis White (1564?-1638), became Bishop in 1626 and was transferred to Norwich in 1629. The longest tenure between the death of Bishop Robinson in 1616 and the outbreak of the civil wars in 1642 was that of Barnabas Potter, from 1629 to 1642.[406]

Brief though his occupancy of the see was, Francis White's episcopate represented the arrival in the diocese of an unfolding form of non-Calvinist Anglican churchmanship. This modification of the Church of England's Protestant identity can be traced back to the writings of the theologian Bishop Richard

Hooker (c. 1554-1600), the author of the six-volume *Treatise on the Laws of Ecclesiastical Polity* (published in instalments from 1594). Hooker, who saw the Church of England as a middle way between the contrary extremes of papal Rome and those of Calvinist Geneva and as existing in essential, albeit reformed, continuity with the *Ecclesia Anglicana* of the middle ages, 'alloted a relatively minor role to preaching in the scheme of salvation ... [and] stressed the prime importance of the Eucharist in worship'. Meanwhile, critiques of Calvin's doctrine of predestination were under way at Cambridge in the 1590s.[407]

A further development in the Stuart Church of England's counter-Calvinist revisionism was the rise of the party, of which Francis White was a leading adherent, known as Arminian, named after a reaction, which gathered momentum in the Protestant Netherlands, against strict Calvinism: this movement is termed Laudian in England, from its leadership by William Laud (1573-1645), Bishop of St David's from 1621 to 1626, of Bath and Wells from 1626 to 1628, of London between 1628 and 1633 and Archbishop of Canterbury from 1633 to 1645. Laudianism recovered its leading role in the worship of the Church of England following the restoration of the Stuart monarchy in 1660.

A 'High Church' ideology, Arminianism disputed the Calvinist doctrine of predestination, according to which some were elected to eternal salvation and others to everlasting damnation. Grounded in doctrinal foundations in Hooker, the Laudians saw the Church as an avenue, through its sacraments, and above all through the eucharist, to divine grace, and holy communion, which was given 'a special value as the highest form of prayer', was at least as important as preaching in the Church's mission.[408]

Reverence for the eucharist was given recognition in

churches when, under Laud's Archiepiscopal Visitation regulations of 1634, the communion tables were removed from the body of the church to an 'altar-wise' position in the east end of the building and railed, requiring communicants to receive the sacrament kneeling at the rail, not standing or sitting. The Laudians also accorded a special status to the clergy and to episcopacy 'by divine right', bishops being 'endowed by God with special authority as guardians of the Christian tradition'.[409]

The Laudian party also upheld an authoritarian royalism and opposed puritan strictures over Sunday: the Declaration of Sports was reissued, by the movement's strong supporter Charles I, in the year when Laud became archbishop. The Laudians were not Roman Catholics but were the spiritual ancestors of what would later be known as the 'Anglo-Catholic' grouping in the Church of England. They insisted on the wearing of the surplice, upheld sacred music and the use of the organ and took issue with puritan iconoclasm, demanding close attention to the good condition and repair of church and cathedral buildings, as well as respect for their historic 'monuments or ornaments'. Their liturgical programme involved:

> .The consecration of the [eucharistic] elements, the sign of the cross at baptism, the consecration of church structures and objects, the blessing after the marriage and at the end of the service, the confirmation of the young, churching after childbirth, and hearing confessions, and of course the ordination of priests and deacons.

All these features appeared to the Laudians' many foes to be a frontal neo-Catholic attack - illicit 'innovations' - on the established doctrines and practices of the English Protestant Reformation, the revisions being represented as 'a plain device to usher in the Mass'.[410]

Even so, the impact of the Laudian reforms could be expected to be felt in Carlisle during Francis White's tenure. His own associations indicate his prominent position within the Laudian fraternity. In 1622 he led conferences opposing Catholic disputants, management of the third of which 'was entrusted to William Laud', to whom White's *Treatise of the Sabbath-Day* of 1635, commending a balanced approach to the conduct of Sunday, was dedicated. In December 1626, White was consecrated Bishop of Carlisle by prelates including the Bishop of Durham, Laud's patron Richard Neile (1562-1640). The sermon at the consecration was preached by John Cosin (1594-1672), who was to emerge after his appointment as Bishop of Durham in 1660 as the most important Laudian influence in the far north. In 1626 White and Cosin were both involved in a debate against two Calvinist theologians.[411]

Bishop White was, then, a deeply committed Laudian whose 78 *Articles to be enquired of in the Diocese of Carlisle in the Visitation of the Reverend Father in God, Frances [sic], Bishop of Carlisle* of February 1628 announced the arrival in the diocese of Carlisle of the High Church ecclesiastical restoration, signalled by the content and language of the instructions on holy communion. Whereas Bishop Robinson's Visitation Article made no mention of the frequency of the distribution of the eucharist, White was adamant that what he termed 'the blessed sacrament of the Lord's Supper' be 'duely and reuerently administered every moneth, 'or thrice euery yeere at least', and demanded to know if it was:

> deliuered unto or receiued by any of the communicants within your parish that unruerently sit or stand, or doe not deuoutly and humbly kneele upon their knees.[412]

As with Laud, reverence for the communion inspired

White's regulations:

> whether [the table] is so used out of time of diuine service or sermon as is not agreeable to the holy use of it as by sitting on it, or by throwing hats on it, or writing on it, or is it abused to other prophaner uses.[413]

As for the minister's vestments, whereas Robinson was content to enquire 'whether dooth yor minister usually weare the surplesse whyle he ys saying the publicke prayers & ministering the Sacraments', White insisted on 'a comely large and fine surplice' - as standard liturgical dress: did the parson 'wear the surplice and dothe he never omit wearing such'? The era of image-breaking was also to come to an end, with the Article 'Whether hath any in your parish defaced, or caused to be defaced, any monuments or ornaments in your church?' Then, on other aspects of the puritan agenda, where the 1603 Millenary Petition had requested individual let-outs over such usages as the wearing of the surplice, the Sign of the Cross, the use of the ring in marriage and bowing at the recitation of the name of Jesus, White demanded uniform enforcement: did the minister always use the Sign of the Cross in baptism? Did he always use the ring in marriage? Did congregations show 'all duly and lowly reuerence when the blessed name of the Lord Jesus is mentioned?'- the inherited Catholic practice of bowing at the name of Jesus.[414]

Thus on one point after another, Bishop White's regulations put forward a ritualised form of Anglicanism and opposed puritanism over the appearance of the church, the dress of its ministry and the behaviour of congregations: they were to kneel and stand at the Creed and key prayers, bow at the 'holy name', remain hatless and stay for the whole service, not just the sermon. There was a provision for 'auricular', that is individual, confession of sins to the minister (which the Book of Common Prayer 'continued to allow').[415]

The extent to which these Laudian reforms were implemented in parish churches in Cumbria is not known, though the region might have fallen into the category where 'in some rural areas ... shortage of funds probably hindered the introduction of new rituals and fittings'.[416] Yet where the changes were effected, and where congregants were required to behave in reverential ways during worship, even the least liturgically literate of parishioners would be able to see that sweeping ecclesiastical alterations were under way, that order and ceremony were in vogue and that the Sacraments and the elaborate mode of their celebration were restored.

The next occupant of the see, the Kendal-born Barnabas, or Barnabie, Potter (1577-1642), is difficult to classify in terms of the polarisations in the Stuart Church of England. On the one hand, the historian Thomas Fuller (1608-61) recalled that 'he was commonly called the puritannical Bishop; and they would say of him in the times of King James "that organs would blow him out of the church"'. He was, however, appointed chaplain-in-ordinary to the then Prince Charles and served as a court preacher for ten years, being made chief almoner in 1628 to the king, who 'held him in high esteem'; he 'was liked by Charles I in spite of his Puritan leanings' and was appointed 'promptly' by the king to Carlisle in 1629.[417]

The difficulty over Potter's ecclesiastical alignment is the unlikelihood of a 'puritannical' cleric's holding high court offices and of being appointed to a bishopric by a king who preferred individuals who assented to his own views, including his High Church ecclesiastical position.The mystery is deepened by the statement that 'so strongly did he attack the corruptions which had sprung into the Church that he was censured as popish', an

Bishop Barnabas Potter

allegation that 'he took so much to heart that he fell sick and died'.[418]

There was, however, nothing 'popish' or Laudian in Potter's 55 Visitation Articles of 1629. Instead of White's insistence on the invariable wearing of the surplice by the parson, there was only the question of whether or not he 'usually' put it on. As with Robinson's Articles, holy communion is not mentioned, nor is auricular confession. Robinson's ordinance on Sunday amusements is carried over from the latter's Articles, along with his condemnation of 'superstitious' practices and processions at funerals.[419]

The extent to which Potter broke with White's Laudian policies was most evident in the condition of Carlisle Cathedral during his episcopate. Elizabeth I had loved sacred music and retained it in the Chapel Royal, while under her influence the cathedrals were 'emboldened to follow suit.' During the Laudian ascendancy, the English and Welsh cathedrals became foci of High Church practice.[420]

Carlisle Cathedral was, however, emphatically not in that group. In 1634, mid-way through Potter's tenure, three army officers from Norwich, visiting Cumberland, found no evidence of a Laudian transformation in the Cathedral - far from it. The trio observed the poor quality of music, which fell far below

Laudian standards, the visitors commenting that the singing resembled that of the unaccompanied Psalms that were in use in pubic worship in Calvinist Scotland: 'The organ and the voices did well agree, the one being like a shrill bag pipe; the other the Scottish tone'. There was also flagrant departure from Laudian norms in the dispensing of holy communion, 'administered and receiv'd in a wild and unreverent manner'.[421]

The state of the Cathedral building, neglected over the course of a century since the dissolution of the Priory, was also deplorable from a High Church viewpoint, 'like a great wild country church, as it appeared outwardly, so it was inwardly neither beautify'd nor adorn'd one whit'. This state of affairs prompted the king himself to write in September 1639 to the Dean, Thomas Comber (1575-1654), alluding to his special concern for the Cathedral as a royal property, from its foundation by Henry I:

> Our Cathedral Church of Carlisle is fallen exceedingly into decay and indeed so far that if there be not present care taken for the repair thereof, it cannot be long upheld.[422]

A stern kingly rebuke informed Comber that:

> your long continued together with some negligence of your predecessors, have hastened this fabric, which should have been upheld both by your charge and care, towards the ruin in which it is now likely to fall without speedy supply.[423]

Energised, no doubt, by this royal intervention, Potter discussed the matter with Comber and in December wrote to the Secretary of State to give:

> .an account of my care to see His Majesty's royal and religious commands performed for the repairing of the Cathedral Church of Carlisle.

Potter mentioned a possible request for the necessary funding from the Dean and Chapter but Comber's 'response was anything but enthusiastic'. In 1639, however, there may have been a tidying-up operation in the form of demolition of some old Priory buildings.[424]

By 1640, after decades of neglect, the state of Carlisle Cathedral had deteriorated so much that only some selective demolition could save the structure as a whole. During the first civil war between Charles I and parliament, between 1642 and 1646, from October 1644 to June 1645, Parliament's Scottish allies laid siege to Carlisle, and, upon its surrender, gave an undertaking that no damage would be done to the city's churches: the Scottish occupation lasted until December 1646, during which period the Cathedral was safe.[425]

At the end of 1646 Parliament assumed control of the city, which was captured by royalists in a second civil war in 1648, but then, following the defeat of the royalist offensive, was captured by Oliver Cromwell (1599-1658) on behalf of Parliament in October 1648. Following the assumption of Parliamentarian control, partial demolition took place in about 1649, with the removal of five bays of the nave, in effect St Mary's church, the 'greater part of the Norman nave ... the church's lowest point ... [leaving] not much more than half a cathedral'.[426]

There has been a tradition in the historical literature of viewing the taking down of the five bays as an act of vandalism, motivated by Calvinist bigotry. Thus the royalist Anglican clergyman Hugh Todd (c. 1658-1728) claimed that this partial reduction of the fabric was only the prelude to a plan 'to pull down the whole Cathedrall', a design that was thwarted only by the restoration of Anglican monarchy in England in 1660, which 'put an end to these and such like sacriligious intencons'.[427]

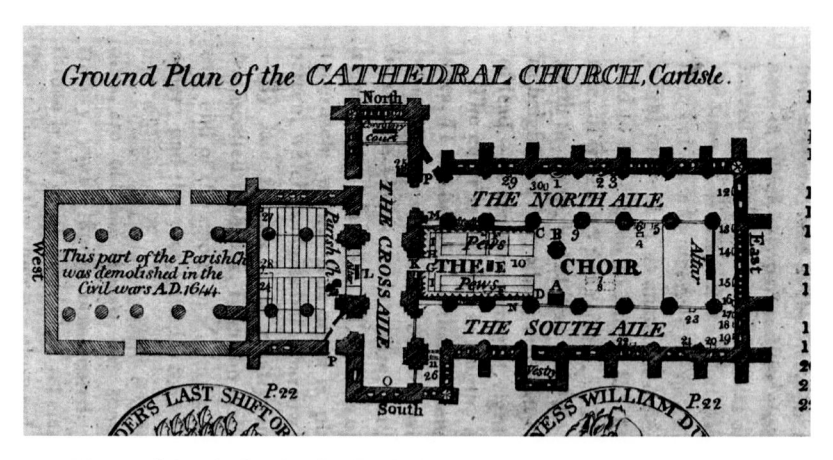

Plan of Carlisle Cathedral showing the demolished bays. Jollie, 1811

Omitting any mention of the parlous condition of the Cathedral building as Charles I had found it to be in, Nicolson and Burn recalled that:

.The body of St Mary's church, which is the cathedral, was before the civil wars in [1642] a spacious building, comprehending all the western part of the church from the great tower, and extending in length 135 feet. But this being deemed superfluous by the fanatical reformers, was in great measure demolished ... and the materials applied to build a guard house at every gate.[428]

A descriptive history of the British cathedrals published in 1816 contains a particularly colourful version of the story of the alterations as the outcome of the passions of 'vandal bands', making it one of the 'infernal acts of delirious despotism committed by those infuriate fanatics'.[429]

An account of the removal of the bays as motivated by misplaced puritan zeal is, however, the reverse of the truth of the matter, for England's puritan and Parliamentarian authorities were deeply concerned that the population should have ready access to safe parish churches, and 'the destruction of the nave was a considered act based on its derelict condition and the proximity of St Cuthbert's Church' (bearing in mind that, with Parliament's abolition of episcopacy in England and Wales in 1643, there was no function of cathedrals as seats of Bishop and cathedral clergy). In 1649 parliament's detailed attention to the state of the building was signalled in the attention paid to 'the viewes of judicious workmen' on site and the recognition that alterations 'will cost fyve hundred pounds att the least, which seems to us very necessary there being but one other church (likewise very ruinous) in all that citty' - only two run-down place of worship hardly being adequate for a population of perhaps about 2,000.[430]

Parliament's practical concern for St Mary's was further advanced in 1652 by a payment of £340 to two of the city's leading puritan figures, the former Cromwellian captain Thomas Craister, mayor in 1649-51, and Cuthbert Studholme, mayor in 1652, 'for repairs to the Great Church of Carlisle', leading to the construction of a new west end and roof repairs.[431]

Contrary to some features in the historiographical tradition, Carlisle Cathedral thus received more care from the puritan regimes of the 1640s and 1650s than from any other civil or ecclesiastical establishment in England since the Reformation. Likewise, in 1658 the Council of State in Whitehall made a grant of £25 to repair the 'decayed' parsonage in Penrith, with an allowance of £30 for Greystoke.[432]

Towards the end of the English Republic in the late 1650s, further work was carried out at Carlisle Cathedral in the shape of new bells:

.Towards the end of Elizabeth I's reign ... the English ... invented a game with their church bells not found anywhere else in Europe.They called it change-ringing and developed a huge enthusiasm for it .... . Change-ringing became part of the fun of being an English Protestant.[433]

It is not always generally recognised that the puritan movement was all about the fun of being an English Protestant, but in 1658 three new bells were hung in the Cathedral tower, one of them inscribed:

This ring was made six tunable bells at the charge of the Lord Howard and the gentry of the county and city, and officers of the garrison by the advice of Mayor Jeremiah Tolhurst, Governor of the garrison.[434]

The 'tunable' - melodious - objects, which were made for the pleasure given by the change-ringing of a peal of bells, were installed courtesy of two of the most important individuals in the puritan system in mid-17th-century Carlisle and Cumberland: Charles Howard (1628-85), Cromwell's Major- General - military governor - of Cumberland, Westmorland and Northumberland and a member of one of the puritan 'gathered' churches, and Jeremiah Tolhurst (1615-71), an officer in the Parliamentarian New Model Army and Howard's deputy governor of Carlisle from 1655 to 1660. Their initiative - what David Weston calls 'the strangest piece of work at this time' - was 'hardly the action of those who have only destruction in mind'.[435]

The revolutionary decades of the 1640s and 50s witnessed the overturning of the episcopal system that had been assembled in the Elizabethan settlement of religion of 1559. Following the outbreak, in August 1642, of civil war between a High Church-oriented king and the puritan-dominated Long Parliament that

Charles been compelled to summon in 1640, the prospects arose of a Calvinistic puritan ecclesiastical establishment in the far north-west. A petition to Parliament of that August from the Kendal area - the 'Barony' in Westmorland - focused heavily on religion as the *casus belli* between the contesting forces, taking aim at the liturgical revisions brought in by the Laudians and praising Parliament's

> endeavours to preserve the true reformed Protestant Religion without mixture or composition, against those subtle [sly] Innovators that have long laboured to hinder and calumniate the power and practise thereof ... by Innovations in Religion.

In November the Long Parliament showed the same concern with the religious issue in the northern counties, alleging that the crown's ranks were filled with Catholics and urging the creation of a military alliance 'to suppress and subdue the Popish and malignant [royalist] party in the said several counties ... the Papists and other malignant and ill-affected persons'.[436]

By 1643 Parliament's lack of military success against the crown's forces necessitated an alliance with the Scots, who had gone to war against the king, alienated by his attempted imposition of Anglican forms of worship on their Reformed Church. The price of this alliance was Parliament's acceptance of Scotland's Calvinist Solemn League and Covenant and, in 1645, in place of abandoned episcopacy, the adoption of the Presbyterian form of church government, which involved the equality of status of ministers, the involvement of lay elders in ecclesiastical concerns and a pyramidal territorial organisation, with the unit known as the classis at its base. Could a Presbyterian Church truly replace its Anglican predecessor as a comprehensive and inclusive national establishment of religion? Would Cumbrian clergy in post accept the new ecclesiastical order that was trialled in the Solemn League and Covenant in sufficient numbers to allow it to function?

The answer is that attempts to enforce acceptance of the Covenant in Cumbria revealed resistance to it by a strong Anglican opposition. In the Westmorland division known as the Barony, Richard Archer, the incumbent at Windermere, was 'a non-covenanter and disaffected': illustrating the difficulty of replacing anti-Presbyterians with supporters of the system, Archer remained in place until his death in 1653. Henry Wilson, the minister at Grasmere, was 'a notorious malignant and articled [wrote] against the Parliament'. A Mr Johnson, the parson at Burton, was an unconvincing convert, 'one who hath formerlie complied with the [Anglican royalist] enimie, but hath since taken the Covenant'. In Westmorland's sub-division called the Bottom, the ministers of Brough-under-Stainmore, Musgrave, Long Marton and Cliburn all fell into the category of 'a non-covenanter and disaffected'. Again revealing the difficulty of removing opponents of the new Presbyterian establishment, William Richardson of Brough retained his position until the restoration of the Anglican monarchy in 1660. Robert Simpson at Ormside, and Bongate in Appleby, was 'a non-covenanter and a pluralist' - a holder of more than one benefice. The minister at Kirkby Thore was 'a malignant and pluralist lately come from the King's quarters' at York. The parsons of Appleby and Newbiggin refused the Covenant, while the incumbents at Clifton, Morland and Askham were, like their colleague at Burton-in-Kendal, converts the depth of whose sincerity could not be ascertained - 'formerly complied with the enemy, but [had] since taken the Covenant'. In Westmorland, a majority of 12 'known opponents of Presbyterianism or very doubtful supporters of that system' confronted 11 who were 'presumably Presbyterian'. Making up for the recalcitrance of the clergy,

Kendal parish had 12 Presbyterian lay elders, recruited from the local elite. However, as far as the clergy were concerned, the prospects for setting up a thorough-going Presbyterian system in Cumbria depended on the complete elimination of clerics who were of a basically Anglican-royalist cast.[437]

Expulsions of outright opponents of that system were quite numerous in Cumbria - 21 in the territory of the diocese and ten in the Chester deaneries of Coupland and Kendal, while George Buchanan, vicar of Kirkby Lonsdale, 'a deep sufferer ' for 'his Constancy to the Church in the worst of times' was imprisoned for three years. Yet the necessary 'process of ejection and substitution seems hardly to have touched Westmorland, at all events, in the early years of the [puritan] Commonwealth ... [and] though the Presbyterian system was the law of the land from 1645 to 1660, it was put completely into practice in very few counties, and Westmorland was not one of these counties'. There is 'no evidence that a Classis ever existed in Westmorland ... [and] here, as almost everywhere in the country, Presbyterianism was not the form of church government favoured by a majority of the people ... the type of religion favoured by the Parliament was not very acceptable'.[438]

Yet if the above comments suggest that Cumbrians resentfully and passively put up with political and ecclesiastical innovations imposed on them from above, a riot in the Barony in August 1647, which was directed against the local branch of a Parliamentarian body, the Committee for the Sequestration of Delinquents' [royalists'] Estates, set up in 1643, directed active violence against the Long Parliament's measures. The members of the Committee reported how on Tuesday 9 August nine men led:

many others to the number of four hundred or thereabouts, all

Inhabitants within the Barony of Kendal aforesaid, [who] did in a rebellious and riotous manner, assemble themselves together within the said Barony, armed with Muskets, Swords, Pikes, Handguns, and other Instruments of War, to the great terror and affrightment of all peaceable and well-affected persons thereabouts.[439]

On Wednesday 10 August the rioters marched on Kendal, to a house in the town where the Committee was 'consulting how to discharge the Trust reposed in them by ... Parliament', and:

the aforesaid Persons, with a great Number more, all armed, and many of them with their swords drawn, Matches lighted, and other Instruments of War in their hands, did violently enter the Chamber where the said Committee were so sitting and discharging their duties.[440]

Kendal's municipal corporation was committed to the Presbyterian way and had set up a local classis. Revealing the discord between the pro-Presbyterian governing body and opposition to the system in the area, the rioters 'apprehended' the mayor of Kendal, Allan Gilpin, along with the rest of the Committee and took them to the house of a Kendal 'Malignant', where they:

set guards upon them, till Thursday afternoon the next following; during which Time and after (they continuing in Arms until the Sunday Morning next following) they uttered many Menaces and Threats against the said Committee, declaring themselves both by their Words and Actions to be opposite to any Parliamentary power ... [they] stood for God and the King ... And, to testify their further malignity, they seized upon the Magazine and Arms provided for the Parliament's Service and Defence of the said Barony.[441]

The rioters also 'apprehended and imprisoned Mr. Henry

Massey, Minister of the said Town, a Man ever well-affected to the Parliament'. An associate of the Westmorland puritan leader Philip Lord Wharton (1613-96), Henry Masy (or Massey) was appointed minister of Kendal in November 1646. As a 'rigid Presbyterian', a 'rigidly Presbyterian divine', a 'strictly Presbyterian' cleric whose 'constant regret was that the full Presbyterian system was not in operation', Masy was an obvious target for the hatred of the Kendal rioters. Their animosity would have made it ever clearer to him 'that Presbyterianism never had the shadow of a chance either in Westmorland or Cumberland', and that Westmorland was 'rotten' because the 'honest party' had little support in it.[442]

Even so, efforts continued to establish the Presbyterian structures. Lancashire was one of the few English counties where the system took root and, following the 1647 riot, six Lancashire Presbyterian gentry were brought in to firm up the Westmorland Committee for Sequestrations. In March 1650 the Long Parliament passed an Act For the Better Propagating and Preaching of the Gospel of Jesus Christ in the Four Northern Counties - Cumberland, Westmorland, Northumberland and Durham.[443]

The Act was a special measure introduced in Westminster to take account of the fact that Parliament's approved system had little indigenous support in the far north, and in particular 'that there was no Classis in any of the four counties, for otherwise there would have been no need for many of [the Act's] provisions'. It is true that in Penrith, for example, a Presbyterian presence emerged, under the leadership, from 1649, of the Lancastrian Roger Baldwin (1624-95), a graduate of the Calvinist Universities of Glasgow and Edinburgh and a cleric who was accorded the customary plaudits of the Presbyterian ministry - a 'godlie and Orthodox [strict Calvinist] devine … a good

Scriptural Preacher. A Judicious Divine'. [444]

Baldwin's congregation would have worshipped according to the Directory for the Public Worship of God, which was formulated by the Presbyterian-led Westminster Assembly of Divines (initiated in 1643) and authorised by Parliament in 1645, in place of the officially suppressed Book of Common Prayer. Baldwin and his congregants had the use of St Andrew's parish church - but the link between the church and the wider urban community was reduced as a result of parliamentary legislation of 1654 in favour of non-religious civil marriages, and between that date and 1660 no weddings were recorded in the parish register.[445]

The Presbyterian church order continued to enjoy state support, allowing its officials to exercise coercive powers over the clergy. In 1649, a leading Cumberland Presbyterian lay member, the Penrith merchant Thomas Langhorne, was appointed as a commissioner 'to receive all Articles or Charge against any scandalous Ecclesiasticall person, having any place in the said counties'. Langhorne was also a close associate of the puritan magnates who were responsible for executing the government's religious measures in the north - Philip Lord Wharton, Charles Howard and Sir Arthur Hesilrige (or Haselrig, d. 1661).[446]

However, from the time of its inception onwards a would-be Presbyterian system in Cumbria faced too much rivalry from other religious groupings, from the Catholics, the Anglicans and the new, more radical, elements, for it to prevail as a single established church, even with state support. A vital Presbyterian aspiration in the direction of an exclusive ecclesiastical monopoly was set out in the text of the 1643 Solemn League and Covenant in which the subscribers (in theory, in England all adult males) would bring about the elimination of 'popery, episcopacy, heresy, and schism', so 'that the Lord may be one and his name one in the three kingdoms' of England, Ireland and Scotland.[447]

Yet apart from the fact that 'the English people would never let themselves be forced into an ecclesiastical strait-jacket in which only a few of them felt comfortable', the basic problem in imposing an authoritarian Presbyterian uniformity was the absence of the machinery of enforcing conformity: the regulatory Court of High Commission, which had been set up to maintain uniformity in the Church of England, was suppressed by the Long Parliament in July 1641; before its abolition, a division of the court for the ecclesiastical province of York had 'taken a leading part in the repression of recusancy'.[448]

Yet an effective repression of 'popery' as presaged in the Covenant did not come about in Stuart Cumbria. Nationwide, persecution of the recusants was partly alleviated under James I, and the English Catholic 'mission' was reorganised in 1623: in the latter year a leading member of the Benedictine Order, Augustine Smith, was present in Cumberland. In 1632 four 'secular' priests (i.e. not members of religious orders) were working in Cumberland and Westmorland, plus a Benedictine and a Jesuit - admittedly not many in comparison with the 16 priests active in County Durham - but Cumbria had its own problems of 'remoteness and inaccessibility',while the presence of the lone Jesuit in 1632 heralded an extension of the missionary range of the Society of Jesus from the north-east to Westmorland in 1638-9, amid profile-raising claims to perform exorcisms.[449]

As for the Catholic laity, there is the frequently cited quotation from the most authoritative historian of post-Reformation English Catholicism:

By the Civil War, except for one or two isolated households of the Howards and a couple of more firmly seated gentry families like the Curwens of Workington and the Stricklands of Sizergh [Cumbrian society] had lost all connection with Catholicism.[450]

J. A. Hilton adds, of Cumbrian Catholics, that:

the organisation of the [Catholic] mission had nourished Lancashire and the North-east at the expense of Cumbria. ... The Cumbrian mountains had not defended but defeated Catholicism. [451]

To set those generalisations in context, however, in 1617 Carlisle's Bishop Snowden recorded 80 recusants in his diocese and, although only 132 Cumbrian Catholics refused to accept Parliament's 1641 Protestation in defence of 'the true reformed protestant religion', there were Catholic clusters in Wetheral, Castle Carrock and Hesket; Bolton (Cumberland) housed 14 individuals, Cockermouth 13, St Bees 11, Brampton ten, and Brough-under-Stainmore 19. The recorded numbers of Catholic families among the landed gentry rose from 18 out of 141 in 1600 (13%) to 35 out of 180 (19% in 1642). If, overall, the demography of the Catholic laity was in low figures (compared, for example, with some parts of Lancashire), compensation was forthcoming in the form of the wealth and status of some of the recusant elite. The convert Lord William Howard, with his library and Benedictine chaplain, maintained a Catholic establishment at Naworth in Gilsland. Sir Francis Salkeld (d. 1702) of Whitehall, with estates in Cumberland, Westmorland, Lancashire and Yorkshire, had an income of rents of £110 pa; the properties of the Curwen family of Workington had a value of £679 in 1660 and those of the Ducketts of Grayrigg a valuation of £260 in 1642.[452]

Grayrigg itself, among the six northern constablewicks of the Barony of Kendal, returned 25 recusants in 1641, compared with 30 in Skelsmergh and Patton and 22 in Whinfell. The totals for the nothern constableswicks increased from 61 in 1626 to 105 in 1641. In the southern constablewicks, Beetham had 28 in 1641, up from ten in 1626, but Kendal reached only 11 in 1641, although increasing from three in 1626. The combined total for the two constablewicks rose from 85 in 1626 to 157 in 1641 and in the whole Barony, consisting of 48 constablewicks, recusant numbers nearly doubled from 105 to 195 over the same years. On the basis of such data, charting a tangible revival in recusant fortunes over the course of the decades, Lance Thwaytes observed that:

> The suggestion that by the Civil War Cumbrian society in Westmorland had lost all connection with Catholicism, except for the Stricklands of Sizergh, is not accurate and the solutions suggested for the alleged mystery of the vanishing Cumbrian Catholics are not really necessary.[453]

In Furness, the fortunes of the Catholic presence largely depended on the families of the Kirkbys, Bardseys, Knipes, Rawlinsons and Prestons, the last-named being 'the prime standard-bearers of Furness gentry recusancy'. Between the late 1580s and 1678 the Prestons maintained a chaplaincy at their property known as the Manor, with a priest or priests on hand.[454]

Sir John Preston of the Manor was a leading figure in the re-assertion of Cumbrian Catholicism through the enlistment of the community's gentry on the royalist side during the civil wars including, in Furness, the Knipes of Rampside and the Catholic members of the family of the Rawlinsons of Cark Hall. In 1644 Sir John Preston, who had been made a baronet for his earlier military service on the king's side, took part in a skirmish near the Manor and later died from the head injuries he received in the engagement.[455]

Sir John's death in battle typified the royalist activism of some of the English and Welsh Catholic landed class in the civil wars. They had the Stuart crown to thank for the Compositions, a fiscal deal compounding for recusancy fines which 'provided English Catholics with a framework for survival in the years leading up to the civil war': under Charles I 'many agreed that Catholics had not fared so well since the reign of Mary Tudor'; [456] and the recusants, as the Solemn League and Covenant warned them, had, it would appear, nothing to hope, and everything to fear, from a Parliamentarian and Presbyterian civil war victory.

It was to be expected, then, that in Cumbria, as elsewhere, Catholics would rally to the king's cause, and it suited Parliamentarian propaganda, which dwelt constantly on an alleged line-up between royalism and 'popery', to report that this was the case, that in Cumberland and Westmorland, where 'not ten of the Gentry ... may I dare say not so many, have proved Cordiall to the state', 'the whole gentry are Malignants, Delinquents [cavaliers in arms in the first civil war], Papists, Popish or base Temporisers'.[457]

Yet despite Parliamentarian propaganda and the undeniable royalist heroism of such a one as Sir John Preston, the royalist military commitment of Cumbrian Catholics, at least *en masse*, should not be over-stated, since stereotypical allegations of a large scale Catholic-royalist wartime alliance in the Lake Counties may be undermined by citing numerical evidence. This indicates that 'Whatever the Parliamentarians thought, Cumberland and Westmorland were not strongholds of papist superstition which filled the ranks of Royalist officers': in 1642, 19% - 35 - of gentry families had a Catholic presence and in 28 families the head was a Catholic - 15 of whom were neutral in the first civil war. Research on the religious affiliations of the Cumbrian officer corps would seem to confirm a low correspondence between Catholic profession and royalist military commitment: Cumbria had no Catholic lieutenant-colonels, compared with seven in Yorkshire and nine in Lancashire, and no Catholic majors, as against ten in Yorkshire.[458]

That said, Catholic gentry enlistment in the king's forces at commissioned officer level was likely to be higher in counties with relatively high recusant populations such as Northumberland, where 39.5% of the 43 royalist commanders were Catholic, and Lancashire, where 59.7 % of the total were recusants. These, however, were 'unrepresentative shires with relatively strong Catholic populations and traditions of recusant militancy' [459] - a group to which Cumberland and Westmorland did not belong.

Even so, the Catholic element in the Cumbrian officer corps was by no means negligible, for the Catholic colonels were of the highest echelon of the Cumberland gentry - Sir Francis Howard (1588-1660) and Thomas Howard, both of Corby. There may be some doubt over 'the religious persuasion' of Sir William Hudleston (1603-1669) of Millom, the 'noted Royalist, who raised a regiment for the King', but, given the imperative in that period to conceal an illicit faith, it is as likely as not that Hudleston, like Sir Robert Strickland, who was 'never convicted of recusancy', was at least a covert Romanist, while his relative Andrew Hudleston (1603-72) of Hutton John 'served in the Royalist army and was fined as a papist and delinquent'.[460]

Thus, to turn the number count on its head, it might be said not that as *few* as 46% of gentry recusants, made up of 18 individuals, 'actively supported the Royalist cause in the first [civil] war but that as *many* as that percentage and number - nearly half the total - did so. Thus in so far as the Covenant placed at the head of its list of priorities the destruction of 'popery', it was failing, as far as Cumbria was concerned, for a regional Catholic surge came about as a factor in the civil war alliance between the recusant population, at least on the higher social levels, and the royalist cause. A further alleviation came about in 1650 when Parliament, despite the Covenant's threat to destroy 'popery', repealed the recusancy laws which prescribed heavy fines for absence from parish worship.[461]

Further, as Lord Protector between 1653 and 1658, Cromwell, not a Presbyterian, 'lifted almost all the penalties on Catholics introduced by the governments of Elizabeth I and James I. Under Cromwell there were no penalties for failure to attend Protestant services, and very little prosecution for attending Mass': 'what is reputed to be England's oldest Catholic register dates from Cromwell's regime, in 1657'. Even though Catholic landowners who had fought for the king had their estates confiscated, Cumbrian Catholics, like their co-religionists elsewhere in the country, would have benefitted from Cromwell's *de facto* religious toleration.[462]

In second place after the elimination of 'popery' in the list of aspirations of the subscribers to the Solemn League and Covenant came that of episcopacy, or 'prelacy'. As a formal structure of ecclesiastical governance, the national hierarchy of bishops and their subordinates was abolished by the Long Parliament in 1643. If, however, 'prelacy' was given a more generic meaning of the Anglicanism of the Book of Common Prayer, it did not disappear from Cumbria during the Presbyterian regime. The character of episcopalian Anglicanism as the correlate of loyalty to the king, and vice-versa, was to the fore in John Chambers, the parson of Allhallows, 'tenderer of the [royalist] oath for Lord Newcastle, a preacher for the [royalist] enemy, a common-prayer-book man'.[463] (William Cavendish [1592-1676], 9th baron and 1st earl of Ogle, 1st duke of Newcastle, was the leading royalist commander in the north.)

The most influential Cumbrian representative of the

Lady Anne Clifford in the Great Picture from Appleby Castle

Anglican way, which was centred on the outlawed Book of Common Prayer, was Lady Anne Clifford (1590-1676) at Appleby. It is true that Lady Anne's brand of Anglicanism harked back to the strongly Protestant Elizabethan style of her puritan-inclined mother, Margaret Russell (d. 1616), countess of Cumberland. The Laudian revival passed Anne by and she retained the 'Elizabethan Protestant passion for sermons and for scripture'. It was even the case that, always a pragmatic realist and survivor, her 'traditionalist "low church" brand of Protestantism could accommodate the Calvinistic and Presbyterian regime that was introduced into the parish churches of Appleby in the 1640s and 50s'. This 'devout and studious' lady was also a moral puritan who 'derived her ideas as to right and wrong from the Old Testament' and who, after the restoration of the monarchy in 1660, kept away from debauched court of Charles II (r. 1649-85). [464]

Lady Anne was, however, a consistent adherent of the

Church of England, a person whose 'firme hope and resolution', set out in her will of 1674, was 'by God's grace, to dye a true childe of the Church of England and a professor of the true orthodox faith and religion and mainetained in that church in which myselfe was borne, bred and educated by my blessed mother'. Richard Spence writes that 'two of the constants which infused Anne's outlook were her Anglican faith and noble beneficence'.[465]

The countess was probably too cautious, in a dangerous time, to make a parade of her Anglicanism in her letters or diaries and, in an altercation in Appleby in 1651 with the 'terribly phanatical' radical puritan army commander Thomas Harrison (1606-60), the dispute concerned her royalist politics rather than her Church of England faith. She was, however, at odds with a salient feature of the puritan cultural campaign of the period, the abrogation of Christmas. This festival was observed in the Church of England as 'The Nativity of Our Lord, or the Birthday of Christ Commonly Called Christmas Day', but was attacked in a 1643 parliamentary Ordinance for 'giving liberty to carnal and sensual delights', was suppressed, along with Easter and Whitsun, in another Ordinance, of 1644, and was condemned in the 1645 Directory for the Public Worship of God. Nevertheless, in 1651 Lady Anne recorded 'And that Christmas I kept here at Aplebie Castle (as I had done the Christmas before at Skipton)'.[466]

At the heart of the Anglican survival during the years of the Church's official suppression was the maintenance and observance of the Book of Common Prayer. Lady Anne's secretary, George Sedgwick, suggested that she maintained Common Prayer worship - but kept out of trouble for it by having contacts in high places:

.in the worst of times ... duly in her own private chapel where she never failed to be present at it, though she was threatened with sequestration [confiscation of property]. Yet by means of her honourable friends and relations in both houses of parliament she always escaped it.[467] Canon Bouch added that Lady Anne Clifford 'was a devoted adherent of the Church and much attached to its liturgy. It is typical of her that even during the [puritan] Commonwealth years she refused to communicate, except according to the Prayer Book, and kept ... the rules and forms of sound words prescribed by the Rubrics [liturgical directions in the Book of Common Prayer].'[468]

In this way, Lady Anne Clifford typified a Cumbrian Anglican retention of the use of the Book of Common Prayer as the touchstone of the continuing existence of the Church of England, a situation which was also reflected in the recollections of life in the parish of Sebergham by the Carlisle Recorder Thomas Denton (d. 1698) to the effect that 'the Common Prayer was read in the church ... in all the late time of trouble, and we never had a phanatick [puritan] in the parish, neither then nor since'.[469]

Nor was Prayer Book Anglicanism in Cumbria necessarily a hole-in-the-corner subterfuge. Having come into his estate in 1653, throughout the remainder of the decade the Westmorland squire Daniel Fleming (1633-1701) 'surreptitiously worshipped according to the rites of the banned Book of Common Prayer'. He was, however, married in 1655 not 'surreptitiously' but overtly, and indeed defiantly, 'before a great many Persons of Quallity ... according to the Forme of Solemnization of Matrimonie in the Book of Common-Prayer'. The service was conducted by Thomas Smith (1614-1702), who was to be Bishop of Carlisle from 1684.[470]

This Anglican survivalism in Cumbria in the 1640s and 1650s provides proof of the 'failure of State Presbytery' [471] to impose an exclusive religious monopoly. In a third area of the Covenant's programme, that of the eradication of 'heresy and schism', there arose further serious inability to enforce uniformity.

For Presbyterians their form of church order, grounded in the model of the Apostolic Church, as restored in Geneva by John Calvin, represented 'the *jus divinum* [divine right] of presbyterianism'. However, the Presbyterian-dominated Westminster Assembly of Divines contained a minority of five ministers, who, while sharing the theological orthodoxy, including acceptance of absolute predestination, that was derived from Calvin, were committed to a more decentralised ecclesiology known as Independency. Those arrangements were based on the autonomy of the individual church, each one of which was ideally to be composed of 'visible saints', an ecclesiology that was partly derived from the practice of puritan New England. Strongly supported by Cromwell and by many soldiers in Parliament's New Model Army, Independency (or 'Congregrationalism') made powerful strides in England and Wales in the 1640s and 1650s. Even so, the Independents' belief that their ecclesiastical model 'was primitive in that it represented the earliest form of church order', collided with the Presbyterians' claim that their structure was validated in the New Testament. Thus Independency could thereby be seen as tantamount to the heresy and schism that were condemned in the Solemn League and Covenant, a literary offensive delivered by the Presbyterian zealot Thomas Edwards (1599-1647) in his *Antapologia* of 1644.[472] The division over church order between the two main arms of English Calvinism exposed the fallacy of the Covenant's vision of uniformity and nullified any effective mechanism for enforcing a Presbyterian ecclesiastical monopoly.

Under the influence of the town's patron Algernon Percy (1602-68), 10th earl of Northumberland, and of the neighbouring Lawsons of Isel, Cockermouth, a chapelry within the parish of Brigham, became linked with Wigton as 'the other Roundhead town' in Cumberland, 'a stronghold of the Puritan party', a 'den of Puritanism'. However, the church that was formed in the town in October 1651, to come under the inspiration of an outstanding puritan minister of northern England, George Larkham (c. 1639-1700), was 'an Independent church acknowledging no outside human authority, having the character of a 'gathered' community of 'saints', as well as having pastoral responsibilities towards the wider local community.[473]

Attempts to mend the rifts between the Presbyterian and Independent wings of English Calvinism included the joint Independent-Presbyterian Cumberland and Westmorland Association of July 1653. This fusion, promoted by the Greystoke Presbyterian pastor Richard Gilpin (d. 1700), was a defensive alliance to protect the Calvinistic heritage in Cumbria from new and more radical doctrinal insights.[474]

Yet this would-be defensive Calvinistic rapprochement came on the scene too late, because a new form of Christianity had already emerged in Cumberland and Westmorland, making the Lake Counties the birthplace of Quakerism, the faith of the 'Friends'. This new arrival on the denominational scene - in the 'most remarkable episode in the religious history of Westmorland', which 'became a stronghold of the new sect' - offered a response to 'a widespread quest in mid-17th-century England for a form of Christianity that was less dogmatically precise and less preoccupied with human guilt, reprobation and predestination than was the prevailing orthodox Calvinism of the period', for the leading Quaker founder George Fox (1624-91) affirmed 'the potential for goodness in all men and women' and taught that 'every [person] had received from the Lord a measure of light which, if followed, would lead him to the Light of Life'... that 'every [person] was enlightened by the divine light of Christ'. This was an interior form of faith that dispensed with the external sacraments of baptism and communion, which had no prescribed liturgy or clerical ministry and which proclaimed peace, simplicity of life and the equality of men and women.[475]

The particular regional factors that predisposed the Lake Counties to the new faith included the long-standing deficiencies of the 'Established Church in a [region] split between a small isolated diocese of Carlisle and the huge unwieldy diocese of Chester and its 3 deaneries of Kendal, Coupland and Furness (under the Archdeaconry of Richmond) ... Quakers were most numerous where parishes were largest, clergy neglectful and landowners relatively impotent.'[476]

Fox made his first evangelising appearance in the north with his preaching, in June 1652, at Firbank Fell, near Sedbergh, addressing a large audience of the pursuants of an experiential faith who were known as Seekers. These women and men accepted the ministry of the preachers John Audland and Francis Howgill (1618-69) and were centred on the Preston Patrick district of Westmorland, which was the matrix of the expansion of the infant Quaker movement into the south of England.[477] Although in his *Journal* (published posthumously, in 1694) the Leicestershire man George Fox put himself in control of the narrative of early Friends' history, emphasising his own leadership, the character of Quakerism as a Cumbrian phenomenon is underscored by the number of its evangelists belonging to the region: they included the author and preacher Francis Howgill, a leader at Firbank chapel; the controversialist and itinerant minister Edward Burrough (1634-63), from the

Barony of Kendal; the Kendal-born Firbank chapel preacher John Audland; the author John Camm (1604?-56) of Camsgill; and the itinerant preacher, author and controversialist George Whitehead (1636?-1723) of Orton in Westmorland - 'names written large in the history of the Quakers movement' to whose 'labours in various parts of the country the movement owes much of the success that attended it during the 17th Century'.[478]

While Independents supported a degree of religious toleration, the acceptance by the Friends of a human capacity for good, plus their denial of predestination and acceptance of free will, both of which seemed to align them with Catholicism, endangered the pillars of the Reformed Calvinist doctrine that was held in common by Independents and Presbyterians alike, the Quakers putting forward alternative beliefs, such as acceptance of the value of good works, that became attractive to many in the ranks of the Independents. This radical new gospel brought about widespread departures from Independency in favour of what the Cockermouth Independent minister George Larkham, who was confronted by Fox at Embleton near Cockermouth in 1653, called 'that sweeping errour of Quakerisme, which shook the church in respect to many members'.[479]

Even harsher terms than those were used of the Friends by the Kirkby Stephen minister, Philip Lord Wharton's appointee Francis Higginson, who in 1653 traced the origins of the Quaker incursion to the events at Firbank Fell in 1652, when 'there came or rather crept unawares into the County of Westmorland, George Fox, James Nailer ... Satan's seedsmen'. Higginson was acclaimed by the leading New England Independent minister Cotton Mather (1663-1728) as the opponent of 'the prodigious and Comprehensive Heresy Quakerism', which had its 'first outbreaking in that very place [Westmorland]; and a multitude of People being bewitched therein it was a great affliction to this worthy man'. (Fox's fellow 'seedsman' in the Cumbrian Quaker pentecost of 1652 was James Nayler (1617-60), who was imprisoned in Appleby in 1653 for claiming that 'Christ was in him' and who was to be savagely punished in 1653 for an allegedly blasphemous parody of Jesus's Palm Sunday entry into Jerusalem.)[480]

Following the gathering on Firbank Fell and preaching in the chapel at Preston Patrick, Fox became the direct founder of what was to become one of England's major Quaker urban centres, when he:

> went to Kendal, where a meeting was appointed in the town-hall; in which I declared the word of life to the people, shewing them 'how they might come to the saving knowledge of Christ, and have a right understanding of the Holy Scriptures, opening to them what it was that would lead them into the way of reconciliation with God, and what would be their condemnation'.[481]

Although George Fox shared the leadership of early Quakerism with other figures, from the far north, his charisma, certainty, self-promotion, physical toughness, courage and longevity made him stand out as the early movement's *primus inter pares* and most effective itinerant missionary. From Kendal Fox proceeded to Underbarrow, where he preached in the chapel, when 'many of Crook and Underbarrow were convinced [converted] that day', and crossed over from Westmorland to Newton, in Cartmel, and on to Lindale.[482]

In 1652 Fox acquired a northern base and refuge, as he proceeded from Lindale 'to Ulverstone and so to Swarthmore to Judge Fell's - the home of the Vice-Chancellor of the Duchy of Lancaster and judge of assize for the Chester and North Wales

Swarthmoor Hall in 1860

Circuit, Thomas Fell (1598-1658). Fell 'tolerated and protected' Fox and, without being converted to Quakerism, allowed the use of Swarthmoor Hall for Friends' religious meetings, 'a shelter and a family-hearth for Quakerism'. At Swarthmoor, Fox first met Judge Fell's 'fervent' wife Margaret, whom he was to marry in 1669, after Fell's death, and who was to be a leading Quaker figure in her own right. Fox preached in the Furness villages and paid a return visit to Westmorland.[483]

The following year saw George Fox extending his mission into Cumberland from his base at Swarthmoor, preaching in the church in Bootle and in Millom and moving north along the coast. Reports of 'great threatenings' that 'if ever I came there they would take away my life' only made him feel 'drawn to go' on into Cumberland. Near Cockermouth, Fox encountered 'twelve soldiers and their wives from Carlisle; and the county people came in, like as it had been to a fair', and at Brigham he debated with John Wilkinson, the 'preacher in great repute, who had three parishes under him' and whom Fox was to win over to his faith in 1654: Wilkinson went on to be 'one of George Fox's ablest lieutenants'.[484]

The Cumberland mission was now at a crescendo of revivalist zeal and:

> Many hundreds were convinced that day, who received the Lord Jesus Christ and his free teaching with gladness .... The soldiers also were convinced and their wives, and continued with me till first day [Sunday].[485]

Passing by Caldbeck, and perhaps visiting Wigton, Fox was now approaching Carlisle, there to encounter the most tumultuous episode in his initial missionary career in Cumberland, opening up the sharp discords in the city's religious life, and delivering a deeply challenging message: he used the dismissive terms 'steeple-house' for a parish church and 'priest' for an established minister:

> I went into the steeple-house; and after the priest had done, I preached the truth to the People ... the priest got away and the magistrates desired me to go out of the steeple-house. But I still declared the way of the Lord unto them ... so that the people trembled and shook; some of them feared it would have fallen down on their heads. The magistrates wives were in a rage and strove mightily to have been at me; but the soldiers and friendly people stood thick about me. At length the rude people in the city rose and came with staves and stones into the steeple-house, crying 'Down with these round-headed rogues'. Whereupon the governor [Charles Howard] sent a file or two of musqueters into the steeple-house, to appease the tumult and commanded all the other soldiers out. So those

soldiers took me by the hand in a friendly manner and said they would have me along with them. When we came into the street the city was in an uproar; the governor came down and some of the soldiers were put into prison.[486]

These turbulent scenes in Carlisle need to be put into the national context of the year 1653, the *annus mirabilis* of the English puritan revolution, when Cromwell's convening of the Nominated Assembly ('Barebones Parliament'), based on the 'gathered' churches, promised to usher in a millenarian Zion in England, with Christ's second coming in prospect. Fox's visionary preaching was a local manifestation of the high excitement of that year. He was, and set out to be, a polarising figure, and his intentionally disturbing sermon, presumably in St Mary's, exposed and intensified the divisions in the city. On the one hand, opposed to Fox were the corporation, typified by Presbyterian magistrates such as Cuthbert Studholme (d. 1668), mayor in 1652,[487] and the magistrates' wives. Sharing the appetite of those women for using force against Fox, the 'rude' - rough, lower class - populace probably perceived in Fox's message a variant of the 'roundhead' puritan assaults on popular culture and amusements. On Fox's side, on the other hand, were some 'friendly people' and soldiers of the garrison, forming a protective cordon around him.

It has already been seen that at Cockermouth Fox was attended by a dozen troopers from Carlisle and their wives and that the 'soldiers also were convinced and their wives'. Many troops of Cromwell's army were attracted to the radical religious stance of the Baptists, whose acceptance of voluntary church membership by virtue of adult baptism seemed to conservative observers to open the door to social and religious anarchy. It was 'the Baptist congregation in Carlisle [that] went over *en bloc* to the Friends, including the "Pasteur"'.[488]

Whether or not the soldiers who supported Fox were of the Baptist persuasion, they in effect mutinied in his defence, and were consequently imprisoned: members of an armed force that was supposed, under Governor Howard's orders, to 'appease the tumult' that had been provoked by Fox refused to do so. The machinery of coercion to impose uniformity had simply broken down.

The sequel proves the impotence of enforcement of the period's religious laws. Fox's sense of himself as Christlike - that he was God's son and had seen His face - was among those that Parliament's Blasphemy Act of August 1650 defined as intolerable and criminal, punishable by banishment, and if that was refused, hanging, and yet soldiers of the garrison upheld his right to state that conviction. Fox's detention was brief and 'after I came out of Carlisle prison aforesaid I went into the Abbey chamber'.[489]

Further evidence of the non-enforcement of religious repression in Carlisle, in the very same year that Fox faced, and evaded, a potential grave sentence for blasphemy, comes from the speed with which a Quaker meeting and its premises were established in the city, 'amongst the earliest in the country to possess a meeting house':

> though few in number, they were concerned for some provision to be made towards a meeting to be held some times in Carlisle; and one Thomas Bewly of Haltcliffe Hall [with whom Fox had stayed near Caldbeck en route to Carlisle], bought a house in the Abbey [Close] for a meeting house for the furtherance of the work of Truth.

These were the 'Abbey chambers', former Priory premises, to which Fox repaired after his release from Carlisle prison; there the Friends continued to meet, untroubled by the authorities, for the rest of the 1650s and 'many comfortable meetings Friends had in it'.[490]

It was not as if the mainstream Calvinist clergy of the region did not seek the suppression of the intruder, and a new attempt at forging a Cumberland and Westmorland Presbyterian-Independent Association was made in 1656 in the context of fear that:

> Satan is enraged ... and ... desgorgeth from his hateful stomack a swarm of Quakers; these... came upon us like a furious Torrent; all is on fire on the sudden, many are unsettled; the foundations shaken, and some *apostazise*; here we are beaten off and are forced to lay other things aside, that we might more fully binde ourselves to quench these flames.[491]

Yet the effectiveness of efforts to quench the Quaker flames was low, certainly as far as concerned Fox's itinerant mission, which was carefully chronicled in his *Journal*. Two points arise from Fox's narrative, both of them illustrating the failure of religious repression in Cumberland and Westmorland in the 1650s. The first of these is Fox's extraordinary freedom of movement, taking in, at various dates, Gilsland, Langlands, Holm Cultram, Keswick, Kendal, Strickland Head, Pardsey Crag and Wigton. He aimed his message at all sorts and conditions of men and women, and in 1657 at Strickland Head:

> where most of the gentry of that country being gathered to an horse race, not far off from the [Quaker] meeting, I was moved to go and declare the truth unto them. [492]

The second point concerning the weakness of the machinery to enforce intolerance in Cromwellian Cumbria is the freedom and extent of Quaker assembly and unimpeded conversions when, for example, 'a large meeting there is gathered in the Lord' and at Langlands, near Uldale, there was a 'very large' assembly, for 'most of the people had so forsaken the priests that the steeple-houses in some places stood empty'.[493]

Thus, if in the 1650s Westmorland and Cumberland were the birthplace of Quakerism, these counties also gave rise to a religiously pluralist society, as the enforcement of uniformity failed. The Calvinistic Presbyterian and Independent churches themselves acquired a recognised status that was to be transformed after 1662 into Protestant Nonconformity. As elsewhere in the country, Anglicans continued to worship covertly according to the Book of Common Prayer. Catholic gentry asserted their presence, enlisting as royalists in arms, and the new wave of Quakerism found a lasting place in a novel multi-denominational regional society. As will be seen, after the restoration of Anglican monarchy in 1660, and until the passage of the Toleration Act in 1689, efforts were made over three decades, under the aegis of parliament, the state, the landed ruling class and the Church of England, to reassert credal uniformity through persecution of dissidents. These endeavours failed, as in the 1689 Toleration Act England and Wales discovered a formula for (Protestant) religious pluralism and inter-denominational practical tolerance that had been first introduced in Interregnum Cumbria.

Cromwell's death in September 1658 set in motion the chain of events leading to the restoration of monarchy in the person of Charles II in the spring of 1660, accompanied by the reintroduction of the crown's ecclesiastical ally, the Church of England.

The restored Church had an episcopalian structure from which any attempts to inject Presbyterian modifications were repulsed following the restoration. Preceded by legislation of 1660 which permitted the return of dispossessed Anglican priests to their cures, the Act of Uniformity of 1662 required, as a condition of a cleric's retaining a benefice, complete compliance with the entirety of the Book of Common Prayer (itself revised in a neo-Laudian direction) and the Thirty-Nine Articles, abjuration of the Solemn League and Covenant and of resistance to the crown, as well as episcopal ordination.[494]

As a direct result of the Act, nationwide over 936 clergy were expelled from the Church of England before the end of 1662, contributing substantially to the total of 1,760 ejected between 1660 and 1663 and providing the newly emergent Nonconformist (or Dissenting) congregations with their clerical leadership.[495]

The low numbers of the ejected in Westmorland confirms the paucity of the puritan clerical presence in the county in the two decades before 1660: the Nonconformist historian of the ejections nationwide, Edmund Calamy (1671-1732), in *The Nonconformist's Memorial: being an Account of the Ministers who were Ejected or Silenced after the Restoration particularly by the Act of Uniformity* (published in 1702), listed six removals in Westmorland - those of the ministers of Askham, Barton, Crossby-on-the Hill, Halton Chapel, Kendal and Staveley. For Cumberland Calamy counted 23 parochial evictions, 'chiefly by the Act of Uniformity', from Addingham, Bowness, Brampton, Bridekirk, Carlisle, Cockermouth, Croglin, Crosby, Crosthwaite, Edenhall, Egremont, Greystoke, Hutton-in-the Forest, St John's Chapel, Kirkandrews ... Lazonby, Melmerby, Penrith, Plumbland, Sowerby, Thursby, Torpenhow and Wetheral, plus three others 'preaching at various places in the county contrary to the Uniformity Act'. Nathaniel Burnand was expelled from Brampton, 'an area of strong non-conformity [where] the inconvenience of a Parish church 1½ miles from the town became an important consideration' in the vitality of Dissent and he 'remained about the neighbourhood and Alston Moor for, at least, ten years, preaching as he had opportunity'.[496]

In the 1650s, the Independent minister of Cockermouth, George Larkham, had achieved prominence in the puritan movement nationally, acting as a delegate at the Independents' national assembly at the Savoy in London in 1658. At the restoration, he was sure to be a target for the county's newly assertive royalist elite, led by Sir George Fletcher (c. 1663-1700) of Cockermouth and Hutton-in-the-Forest. Fletcher formed an alliance with the Anglican parson Robert Rickerby who had been dispossessed in 1650 of his living of Cockermouth and was now, successfully at it turned out, seeking reinstitution. Despite a petition to Fletcher from 'the inhabitants of the town of Cockermouth' to be allowed to retain Larkham - confirming the town's image as a puritan place - in November 1660, along with the Bridekirk minister George Benson, Larkham was 'put forth' from his post, becoming a fugitive, with a warrant directed against him in July 1663.[497]

At Carlisle, Timothy Tullie had appeared to conform to the puritan system and was appointed to St Mary's in 1656. However, he remained an Anglican at heart and refused the Solemn League and Covenant in 1646. At the restoration, Tullie was reconciled to the Church of England and became a Canon of York Minster, leaving Carlisle to escape the local stigma of his ostensible puritan period. His fellow at St Cuthbert's, Comfort Starr (1624-1711) was ejected soon after the restoration and in advance of the Act of Uniformity.[498]

The return of the Church of England found the diocese of Carlisle to be in a 'pitiable condition'. Some of the parochial livings were vacant, and the dire state of the diocese was encapsulated in the condition of the Cathedral, where the west end was ruinous and the Dean's and Prebends' premises could not be lived in. Rose Castle had suffered considerable damage.

The new Bishop, Richard Sterne (1596-1683, Bishop 1660-4), had to address these problems, including structural repairs: the rebuilding of the Deanery and the prebendal houses was undertaken and the chapel at Rose Castle made good. Sterne was also a leading figure on the Laudian wing of the Church of England and his episcopate saw the return of ritual to the worship of Carlisle Cathedral, with fine choral music performed at holy communion.[499]

In his bid to regain his throne, and in order to broaden the base of his support, in April 1660 Charles II had issued his Declaration of Breda, a manifesto for his recall to his kingdom, promising religious toleration. Subsequently, however, the general election of 1661 saw the return to parliament of a majority made up of 'cavaliers', hardline Church of England royalists who were determined to hound the Nonconformists and impose an exclusively monarchist and Anglican settlement on the country.

Typical of the new legislation that followed, forming the repressive 'Clarendon Code' of 1661-70, was the 'Quaker Act' of 1661, which made illegal the Friends' conscientious scruples against swearing oaths. The Corporations Act of 1661 aimed to eliminate the Nonconformists from the municipal governing bodies by making urban local government an Anglican monopoly: under its provisions five members were put out of the Kendal corporation, plus three pre-1660 corporation officials, two of whom were later presented for Nonconformity. The main agent for this drive in Cumberland and Westmorland was the royalist civil war veteran Sir Philip Musgrave (1607-78) of Eden Hall, a member of the parliamentary committee that drafted the Corporations Act and who described himself as 'a state physician and courses about to Kendal, Appleby and Carlisle to purge the corporations'. A devout Anglican, as MP for Westmorland from

1661 to 1678 Musgrave was proud of being 'esteemed to be an instrument in the House of Commons in crossing the desires of those who did desire the procuring a toleration of different opinions in matters of religion'.[500]

The repressive policies of the 1660s, contravening the Breda Declaration - 'an enormous decline of official toleration from the Breda high point to the Clarendon Code low' - provoked a violent reaction among some Dissenters, a movement of protest that was focussed on the far north. As Musgrave told the deputy lieutenants of the Westmorland militia in 1663, the state's surveillance had unearthed a radical conspiracy and 'the King has knowledge of a fanatical [Nonconformist] design at hand, of which the scene will first appear in the northern parts'. The scene of armed resistance in Westmorland in October 1663 was at Kaber Rigg, near Kirkby Stephen, an uprising led by Cromwell's governor of Appleby Castle, Captain Robert Atkinson, and aiming to capture Appleby and Carlisle Castles.[501]

On the night of 12 October Atkinson and about 20 associates, expecting reinforcements from Kendal, assembled at Kaber Rigg, planning to take Appleby Castle and seize both Musgrave and the government tax receipts stored in the castle. When the Kendal contingent failed to put in an appearance, Atkinson dismissed his troops and the Kaber Rigg enterprise collapsed, Atkinson being hanged, on Musgrave's initiative, in September 1664.[502]

It would be easy to discount this rising, along with others at around the same time in County Durham and in the North and West Ridings, as harmless fiascos, unlikely to upset a secure restoration settlement. Royalist contemporaries, however, emphasised the threats to security posed by the sects and in Cumbria pointed to a perceived link between sedition and the Friends, who were represented as social radicals and anarchists, refusing to pay tithes or swear oaths, practising egalitarian speech and body language and holding extreme religious views: Musgrave reported that 'Those in authority can hardly bear the insolence of the Quakers, who meet 200 or more every week ... stricter courses should be taken with them, and a few horse [cavalry] kept in constant pay in Carlisle'. They were, he alleged, 'a dangerous people' who 'had a deep hand' in radical militancy in the area in 1663.[503]

The area's Quakers, however, were not prepared to accept repression lying down: in 1675, Sir Christopher Philipson (1646-1709), a deputy lieutenant under Daniel Fleming's command, wrote to the latter to inform him that:

> .the Quakers of Windermere ... are grown very preremptory, and presumptuously meet in great assemblies in opposition to the parson, before the Church, and intend *nolens volens* [like it or not] to have another meeting on Sunday three weeks.

That meeting was held, Philipson taking part in efforts to suppress it, and he and Fleming convicted eight preachers and over 50 other Friends.[504]

Fear of the connection between religious dissidence and political subversion and of the 'growing and dangerous practices of seditious sectaries' inspired parliament's Conventicle Act of 1664 (renewed, with modifications, in 1670) which set fines on individuals of up to £5 for each first offence of attendance at a meeting for religious worship made up of more than five people and not in accordance with the liturgy of the Church of England; for a second offence the penalty was six months imprisonment and for a third transportation to the colonies for seven years.[505]

The impact of the Act on local Dissenting congregations varied according to the zeal of local magistrates and Anglican clergy, the Cockermouth church being the victim of a 'reign of terror', carefully recorded by Larkham in his church book, validating the congregation's claim to be at one with the oppressed Christian community of the New Testament: the year of the passage of the Uniformity Act was 'one of the yeares of the captivity of the Churches, and of the passion and the interest of Christ'. One evasive tactic on their part was to divide the congregation up into smaller 'parcells' so as to get round the figure specified in the Conventicle Act: on one occasion, 'the church brake up their publike manner of meeting together in regard of an evill Act of Parliament passed against meeting above five in a company'. The Cockermouth Independents also made life difficult for the authorities by playing a cat-and-mouse game, keeping on the move, assembling 'sometimes at one place and sometimes at another', 'forced to get into holes in this day'. The members also devised ingenious strategies of concealment, secrecy and counter-surveillance which are familiar from the long history of proscribed dissident groups, appointing agents 'to give notice where the meetings would be [only] the day before the meetings'.[506]

Among the members of his own congregation Larkham was the principal victim of persecution, being imprisoned for three years in York Castle. However, all the members of his church encountered in various degrees the traumas of religious repression - everything from excommunication, social marginalisation and criminalisation of individuals to the threat of sky-high fines and mounting legal penalties: the vicar Rickerby even refused burials in the churchyard to Nonconformists. Inevitably in these circumstances, there were cases of 'sad Apostacy & backsliding of some of the members', though probably leaving behind a core of deeply committed adherents.[507]

The Presbyterian congregation in Penrith did not undergo the same degree of harassment as did the Independents of

Cockermouth and survived the departure of the minister Roger Baldwin, to rise in numbers from 41 to 46 by 1676, liable for prosecution and excommunication for absence from parish worship but shepherded by the merchant Thomas Langhorne. With its tightly concentrated townscape, Penrith could be closely watched by the authorities so that at uncertain times the congregation spread out to the nearby village of Penruddock, to worship, under the ministry of Anthony Sleigh, at the home of John Noble (d. 1708).[508]

In the longer run, ambivalence and a moderate official regime seem to have governed the lives of Penrith's Presbyterians: a Presbyterian brazier, the Wordsworths' maternal ancestor William Cookson, was denounced as a Nonconformist in 1669, excommunicated in 1682 and absolved in the following year, but also supplied St Andrew's church with iron and lead building materials and served as a churchwarden at St Andrew's in 1673 and 1684.[509]

Following the departures of Comfort Starr, Carlisle's Presbyterian Nonconformist congregation was weaker numerically and socially than Penrith's and was under the direct oversight of the 'strong and aggressive Churchman' Bishop Sterne. Fourteen men and women were presented in c. 1666 for not attending parish worship at St Cuthbert's but in 1669 only four or five Nonconformists were recorded at meetings in the whole of the Carlisle Deanery, though a survey of 1676 gave 22 Protestant Nonconformists (and two Catholics) in the two Carlisle parishes, compared with 46 in Penrith. Thereafter, the city's Presbyterians were reported to be 'a poor inconsiderable people to carry on the work of the Gospell' and needing outside funding to continue in existence. Sample numbers of Nonconformists elsewhere in Cumbria ranged from 63 in Cockermouth to 88 in Kirkoswald, an important Dissenting location.[510]

Cessation of persecution was offered to the nation's non-Anglican religious communities in Charles II's Declaration of Indulgence of March 1672. In this, the king, attempting to create national unity in a war against the Dutch Republic and adhering to the tolerationist policies that he had set out in the Declaration of Breda, announced that 'the Execution of all ... Penal Laws in Matters Ecclesiastical against whatsoever Sort of Nonconformists or Recusants be immediately suspended', subject to a form of licensing.[511]

The regional take-up rate of applications to license meetings was low - 15 in Cumberland, (out of 1,610 nationwide), compared with 108 in Devon, 103 in London and 52 in Lancashire, reflecting the small numbers of Dissenters in the Lake Counties and the lack of the kind of large urban centres to which the English Nonconformists were increasingly gravitating. Two licences were taken out for Carlisle, in the house of Barbara Studholme, the widow of a Cromwellian mayor, and now registered as Independent. A licence was obtained for worship in the Penrith home of Thomas Langhorne. In Cockermouth Larkham responded to the Declaration with the height of enthusiasm and his 'church had an open meeting ... (liberty being granted the week before by King & councell unexpectedly'), holding worship before a licence was received, though that was subsequently put right. Few Quakers applied for licences.[512]

Some - Larkham was, clearly, not one of them - took objection to the Declaration on the constitutionalist grounds that it was a unilateral royal action, annulling parliamentary legislation. Alongside that was another perceived threat, apparent in the Declaration's extension of its benevolence to 'nonconformists or recusants' - the latter word usually being paired with 'popish' - and its granting a share in liberation to 'recusants of the Roman Catholic religion ... to whom we ... indulge them their share in the common exemption from the executing the penal laws and the exercise of their worship in their private houses only'.[513]

The response to this modest alleviation, permitting the Catholic nobility and gentry to do what they were accustomed to do anyway, and have Mass said in their country houses, was explosive, in the context of a national paranoia over 'popery', its alleged idolatry, superstition, brutality and historic cruelty and its hostility to England's interest, in alliance with Catholic and absolutist France. Putting the king under heavy financial pressure, parliament enforced the withdrawal of the Declaration and in 1673 passed the first Test Act - 'an Act for preventing danger which may happen from Popish recusants' - debarring Catholics from posts in the civil or military services. The resignation of the king's brother and heir presumptive, James (1633-1701), duke of York, from the office of Lord High Admiral on the grounds of his Catholic faith gave rise to a suspicion of a royal court riddled with 'popery': 'Fear of popery, of France and of arbitrary government started to replace fear of Dissent', and in 1674 and 1675 the king ordered the enforcement of the anti-Catholic penal laws.[514]

In Cumbria Catholic houses were now searched, though the Catholic and patriotic Sir Thomas Strickland (1621-94) of Sizergh in Westmorland, MP for the county from 1661, swore that he would defend the king against the pope. Those proceeded against included Francis Howard (1635-1702) of Corby and his wife Anne, Sir Francis Salkeld of Whitehall, Henry Curwen (1661-1725) and five other Curwens of Camerton, Katherine Curwen of Workington Hall, the Skeltons of Branthwaite and the Porters of Colton: this enforcement of the penal laws showed up the continuing presence of the Catholic religion among the county's landed families.[515]

Among county families, the religious position of the Curwens of Workington may be a matter of speculation, the historian of the family stating that, about the religion of the family to the 1660s 'I know little'. That said, few could have made a more eloquent statement of his Church of England loyalty than Sir Patricius Curwen (1601-64), perhaps clearing up any ambiguity over his family's religious alignment:

> utterly abhor and renounce all Idolatry and Superstition [Catholicism] all Heresy and Schism [Nonconformity] and whatsoever is contrary to sound religion and the word of God Professing myself with my whole Heart to believe all the Articles of the Christian Faith and the whole Doctrine of the Protestant Religion taught and maintained in the Church of England.[516]

Curwen would have been prudent to profess his Protestantism, because the issue of Catholicism was increasingly coming to dominate English politics, despite its adherents' numbers as only 2% of the country's population (only 0.5% - 111 adults - in the diocese of Carlisle in 1676). But it was fear and paranoia rather than statistical analysis that fed anti-popery, and from August 1678 both factors were aroused by allegations coming from Titus Oates (1649-1705) and Israel Tonge (1621-80) of a Catholic plot to assassinate Charles II and set fire to London. The parliament elected in 1661 was dissolved, and between 1679 and 1681 a series of parliaments, controlled by the newly formed Whig party, which was masterminded by Anthony Ashley Cooper (1621-83), 1st earl of Shaftesbury, demanded Exclusion Acts to prevent the succession to the throne of the duke of York, on the grounds that his status as heir encouraged Catholic conspiracy: the agitation was sustained by a massive pamphlet campaign, by vitriolic sermons and by skilfully orchestrated street demonstrations in the capital.[517]

By 1681 basic flaws in the policy of 'Exclusion', plus some acts of Whig extremism, created a reaction in favour of the Whigs' rivals, the royalist and Anglican Tories, supporters of York's legitimate hereditary succession. During the Exclusion crisis, the Nonconformists, whose religious views predisposed them to anti-Catholicism, had given their electoral support to Whig parliamentary candidates. In the nationwide 'Tory reaction' that followed 1681, persecution was renewed against the Dissenters, a process that was especially well documented in the case of Cockermouth, where in 1683-4:

> The day is black & gloomy. We are straitned as to former Liberty [during the Whig ascendancy of 1679-81] ... to seek the lord till these evil days passe away. ... meetings now are very difficult to be kept up. The Lord open againe the doore of Liberty. O guide & protect thy pore people, O gracious Lord.

In August 1684 'A very sad providence then falling in, shut up the churches door' and in January 1685 'Severall of the church were indited for a riot upon the account of meeting contrary to an act against conventicles'.[518]

No-one was to know what royal religious policies were to be forthcoming following the peaceful accession of the duke of York as James II upon Charles II's death in February 1685. By April 1687, however, the king's aims had solidified sufficiently to produce a new royal Declaration of Indulgence, followed by a second a year later.

A remarkably advanced, enlightened and progressive text and a milestone in the history of religious toleration in Europe and America, the Declaration took its stand on 'Liberty of Conscience ... on just and equal Foundation' on 'the free

241

Exercise of ... Religion' and insistence that 'Conscience ought not to be constrained' nor 'People forced in matters of meer Religion [their religion only]'. The Declaration announced that:

> the Execution of all ... Penal Laws in Matters Ecclesiastical, for not comeing to Church, or not Receiving the Sacrament, or for any other Nonconformity to the Religion Established in any manner whatsoever be immediately suspended.

All subjects were given 'Leave to Meet and Serve God after their own way and Manner'.[519] The Declaration, though aborted by the forces of intolerance, presaged a situation in which the modern state, keeping the peace between rival religions, observing variants of *laïcité*, becomes religiously neutral and free of the shackles of maintaining any established church and from the pressure to repress dissent away from any majority denomination.

There were varying responses to the Declaration from the Dissenting churches, since some of their members feared an irreparable breach with the Church of England if they welcomed it or were alarmed at the allegedly unconstitutional cancellation of Acts of Parliament by the monarch acting alone, or were offended by the enfranchisement of Catholic worship that was guaranteed by the sweeping liberalisations contained in the Declaration. Large numbers of Dissenters, however, welcomed the promise of toleration after decades of spasmodic repression, none more so than those of Cockermouth, where in May 1687 George Larkham's 'church kept a solemne day of thanksgiving upon the account of the Kings declaration of liberty' and the Friends opened a meeting house in the following year, as they did at Colthouse, near Hawkshead, and in Kendal. A highly favourable reception of the Declaration came from an address sent by a Friend, James Park, to the Quakers of the northern counties:

> And, dear Friends, sensibly prize this great mercy and kindness, from God, that the King out of his favour hath extended liberty for us, to meet together, to serve and worship God, and for such an openness as there by now appears in most places in the nation for people to hear God's privy Truth declared, whereby the Truth of God may spread and come to be known in the earth. [520]

Needless to say, Catholics were included in this liberalisation of religious dissidence: in July 1687 the Westmorland-born Vicar Apostolic (Bishop with direct authorisation from Rome) Bishop John Leyburne, 1620-1702) began a national tour to dispense the Sacrament of Confirmation to the Catholic laity, involving, in Cumberland, 126 Confirmations at Corby and 22 at Greystoke and in Westmorland a total of 224 (or 226) at Sizergh, at Dodding Green near Kendal (the largest proportion, reflecting the distribution of Catholics within the Barony), and at Witherslack.[521]

In 1687-8 James II extended his offensive against the penal laws by campaigning for the repeal of the first Test Act of 1673, which refused entry by Catholics into military and civil employment under the crown, and for the abrogation of its sequel, the 1678 second Test Act, which excluded them from both Houses of Parliament. In order to achieve repeal, the king winnowed out from the county commisions of the peace and the municipal corporations opponents of repeal and authorised questions to be directed to the political elites of the regions on their willingness to stand for a new parliament on a repeal ticket, on their preparedness to vote for candidates so pledged and on their general attitudes to religious toleration and harmony.

In order to elicit the responses from Cumberland and

Westmorland, the Lord Lieutenant of the two counties, Sir Richard Graham (1648-95), 1st Viscount Preston, convened a meeting of the gentry at the George Inn in Penrith in January 1688. There the deferentially expressed, but unmistakably negative, responses of the majority of the Cumbrian gentry to the two substantive questions gave notice of the resistance of the Anglican ruling class to any changes in legislation that would make inroads on the privileged position of the Church of England in the nation's life.[522]

Alongside his canvassing of the upper classes to concur with his policies, the king addressed himself to the electorate in the towns and cities, which returned the great majority of MPs to the House of Commons, aiming to influence elections by altering the religious make-up of the municipal corporations, where an Anglican monopoly of membership had been guaranteed by the Corporations Act of 1661. In various parliamentary boroughs, the king was able to install into civic governing bodies members of his coalition - compliant Anglicans and believers in 'non-resistance' and monarchical absolutism by divine right, various Dissenters, and Catholics - but in the pivotal parliamentary constituency of Carlisle, the Nonconformist element was numerically and socially too weak to build a political presence on, so that in the case of the county town James drafted on to the corporation 'a solid cohort of openly Catholic gentry, now being given the chance of fulfilling the ambition of playing a role in the governance of their communities', a 'Catholic ascendancy' that reached its zenith in late Stuart Carlisle.[523]

By the end of 1688 James II had lost too much support from the ruling class and the Anglican majority of the population to be able to resist an invasion by the Dutch Protestant leader William of Orange (1650-1702): James left the country in December and William and his wife, James II's elder daughter

Mary (1666-94), became joint sovereigns, with parliamentary assent, in February 1689.

King James, nevertheless, had put the question of religious toleration at the head of the political agenda and that issue needed to be faced as the new reign began. As answers to the king's third question, on tolerance, showed, general attitudes to religious diversity were improving and it would have been unthinkable to revert to the harsh anti-Nonconformist policies of the Tory Reaction. Thus the Toleration Act of 1689 provided freedom of worship to Protestant Nonconformists who accepted the doctrine of the Trinity, abandoning the Conventicle Act, though leaving the Dissenters as second-class subjects in such area as admission to the universities and local government. The Catholics, by the same token, were third-class people, their religious worship proscribed for virtually the whole of the 18th century as England (Great Britain from the 1707 Act of Union with Scotland onwards) remained a confessional state until the 19th century, and the emancipatory vision proclaimed in the Declaration of Indulgence was deferred.

Below these level of high politics, Stuart Cumbrians were affected by the 'witch craze' that swept over Europe and the American colonies in the 17th century, a mass response to war, climate crisis, and a general overdose of religious passion and confrontation. In 1650 Carlisle corporation made a payment 'for the witchfynder' but in August 1684 William Nicolson recorded an acquital in a prosecution: 'witch of Ainstable clear'd'. If this verdict presaged a dawning scepticism over the colletive witchcraft hysteria, even at the end of the century, in 1699 a Greystoke parishioner was presented at court 'for going to witches and wizards, as is reported by common fame and his own relacon [confession]'. [524]

Endnotes

1 David Miles, *The Tribes of Britain* (London: Phoenix p'back, 2006), p. 73; Tom Clare and David M. Wilkinson, 'Moor Divock revisited: some new sites, survey and interpretations', *Transactions of the Cumberland and Westmorland Antiquarian and Archaeological Society*, Third Series (hereafter *CW3*), Volume VI (2006), p. 9; Percival Turnbull and Deborah Walsh, 'A Prehistoric ritual sequence at Oddendal, near Shap', *Transactions of the Cumberland and Westmorland Antiquarian and Archaeological Society,* New Series (hereafter *CW2*), Volume XCVII (1997), p.11.

2 T. Clare, 'Some Cumbrian stone circles in perspective', *CW2*, Volume LXXV (1975), pp. 13-14.

3 V. E. Turner, 'Shapbeck Stone Circle', *CW2*, Volume LXXXVI (1986), pp. 248-50; Robert Gambles, *Man in Lakeland* (foreword by William Rollinson, Clapham, North Yorks.: Dalesman Books p'back, 1975), pp. 66-7; Chris Barringer, *The Lake District* (National Trust Histories, Series Editor Richard Muir, London: Willow Books Collins in association with the National Trust, 1984), pp. 25-6; Ernest H. Rudkin, *Some Reflections based upon Lakeland and the Pennines* (foreword by W. F. Bussel, Driffield, Glos.: Horsley & Dawson, nd.), p. 29.

4 William Hutchinson, *The History of the County of Cumberland* (2 vols., Carlisle: F. Jollie, 1794-1797, Republished, with a new introduction by C. Roy Hudleston, Wakefield: EP Publishing in collaboration with Cumberland County Library, 1974), Volume I, pp. 250-1. See also Stephen Hood, 'Cumbrian stone circles, the calendar and the issue of the Druids', *CW3*, Volume IV (2004), pp. 1-25. Although the megaliths were not artefacts of the later, Iron Age, Druidic cult, subsequent generations might have adapted the already ancient phenomena, looking 'back on the memorials of their ancestors and [incorporating] these older monuments into their own living societies': A. W. Hoaen & H. L. Loney, 'Bronze and Iron Age connections: memory and persistence in Matterdale, Cumbria', *CW3*, Volume IV (2004), p. 51. However, if there was a Druidic religious system in the Lakes region, it remains elusive, since, apparently, the Druids distrusted the written word, committing 'vast quantities of poetry' to memory: F. J. Carruthers, *People called Cumbri* (London: Robert Hale, 1979), p. 64.

5 Paul N. K. Frodsham, 'Two Newly Discovered Cup and Ring Marked Stones from Penrith and Hallbankgate, with a Gazetteer of all known Megalithic Carvings from Cumbria', *CW2*, Volume LXXXIX (1989), p. 17; Steven Hood and Douglas Wilson, 'Further Investigations into the astronomical alignments at Cumbrian prehistoric sites', *CW3*, Volume III

(2003), p. 203; Steven Hood, 'The Great Cumbrian Stone Circles, their Environs and the Moon', *CW3*, Volume XII (2012), p. 5; Tom Clare, 'A Magical Thing: The Layout of the Long Meg Enclosures', *CW3*, Volume IX (2009), p. 27.

6 H. A.W. Bure, 'The stone circle of Long Meg and Her Daughters, Little Salkeld', *CW2*, Volume XCIV (1994), pp. 1,9,10.

7 Barry M. Marsden, *Discovering Regional Archaeology North West England* ... (Series editor: James Dryer,Tring, Herts.: Shire Publications, p'back, nd.), p. 9; J. A. Dixon and Clare Fell, 'Some Bronze Age burial circles at Lacra, near Kirksanton', *CW2*, Volume XLVIII (1949), p. 19; C. Roy Hudleston, 'Askew of Standing Stones', *CW2*, Volume LXXIX (1979), p. 57; T. G. E. Powell, 'The tumulus at Skelmore Heads near Ulverston', *CW2*, Volume LXXII (1972), pp. 54, 55.

8 Tom Clare, 'The magic of stone axe production', *CW3*, Volume IV (2004), p. 248; Joseph Nicolson and Richard Burn, *The History and Antiquities of the Counties of Westmorland and Cumberland* (2 vols., London: W. Strachan and T. Cadell, 1777, Republished with Introduction by B. C. Jones, Wakefield, West Yorkshire: EP. Publishing in collaboration with Cumbria County Library, 1976), Volume I, p.529; Percival Turnbull, 'A Lost Bronze Bucket from Westmorland', *CW2*, Volume XCV (1995), pp. 55, 58.

9 Steven Hood, 'New evidence for Prehistoric activity in and around Dean Parish', CW3, Volume V (2005), p. 5..

10 John Zant, 'The Roman Army in Carlisle', in Mark Brennand and Keith J. Stringer, eds., *The Making of Carlisle from Romans to Railways* (Kendal: Cumberland and Westmorland Antiquarian and Archaeological Society, General Editor Jean Turnbull, Extra Series NO. XXXV, 2011), Ch. 3, pp. 33-52.

11 For Roman religion in the Lakes region: David Shotter, *Romans and Britons in North-West England* (Revised edn., Lancaster: Centre for North-West Regional Studies, Series Editor Jean Turnbull, 2004), pp. 123-132; L. Allason-Jones, 'An Eagle Mount from Carlisle', *CW2*, Volume LXXXV (1985), pp. 262-6. A similar petition is found on another eagle mount: P.M. Cracknell, 'Part of an Eagle Mount from Beckfoot', *CW3*, Volume XI (2011), pp. 227-9.

12 G. R. Stephens and M.G. Jarrett, 'Two Altars of cohors IV Gallorum from Castlesteads', *CW2*, Volume LXXXV (1985), pp. 77-80: these may be 3rd century.

13 Martin Henig and Martin Millett, 'An intaglio from Carlisle', *CW2*, Volume LXXXVI (1986), pp. 258-9.

14 R.W. Davies, 'Cohors I Hispanorum and the Garrison of Maryport', *CW2*, Volume LXXVII (1977), pp. 7-8. Under the Emperor Gaius Julius Caesar Octavianus (Augustus, r. 31 BC-AD 14) Jupiter Augustus was designated as the protective deity of the reigning head of the state.

15 Michael A. Mullett, *A New History of Penrith Book I From Pre-History to the Close of the Middle Ages* (Carlisle: Bookcase, 2017), pp. 9-10.

16 Colin Richardson, 'A catalogue of recent acquisitions to Tullie House Museum and reported finds from the Cumbrian area 1990-1966. Part II: Reported finds', *CW2*, Volume XCIX (1999), pp. 21-2; Hadrian's Wall Trust, *Hadrian's Wall Country Romans in Cumbria Hadrian's Wall and the Coastal Defences* (np., 2013), p. 11.

17 Nicholas Higham and Barri Jones, *The Carvetii* (Peoples of Roman Britain General Editor Keith Branigan, Gloucester: Alan Sutton, 1985); Catherine Ross, 'The Carvetii - a Pro-Roman Community', *CW3*, Volume XII (2012), pp. 55-68; B. J. N. Edwards & D.C. A. Shotter, 'Two Roman Milestones from the Penrith area', *CW3*, Volume V (2005), p. 68; David Shotter, 'Roman Carlisle Its People and Their Lives', in Brennand and Stringer, eds., *The Making of Carlisle*, ch. 4, p. 62; David J. Breeze, 'Civil Government in the North: the Carvetii, Brigantes and Rome', *CW3*, Volume VIII (2008), pp. 63-72.

18 Stuart Noon and David Shotter, 'Two Roman epigraphic fragments from Old Carlisle', *CW3*, Volume XIV (2014), p. 283. 'Old Carlisle' is the name given to the fort and civilian settlement ten miles south-west of Carlisle.

19 R. S. O. Tomlin and R. G. Annis, 'A Roman Altar from Carlisle Castle', *CW2*, Volume LXXXIX (1989), p. 81. 'Queen Juno', wife of Jupiter, was the Roman state's most important goddess. Minerva was the female patron of arts and crafts; 'Father Mars' was concerned with war, hunting and farming. From the reign of Augustus onwards, sessions of the Roman Senate were opened with sacrifices to the deity Victory: Tim Cornell and John Matthews, *Atlas of the Roman World* (Amsterdam: Time-Life Books, 1995), p.193.

20 Ian Caruana, 'An Altar to Victory from the Birdoswald sector of Hadrian's Wall', *CW2*, Volume LXXXVI (1986), p. 263; R. W. Davies, 'A note on some Roman soldiers in quarries', *CW2*, Volume LXVIII (1968), p. 25.

21 Richardson, 'Catalogue of recent acquisitions' (*CW2*, 1999), p. 20; Colin Richardson, 'A collection of Roman and later finds from Kirkby Thore, 1985-1988', *CW2*, Volume XCVII (1997), pp. 63-4.

22 Colin Richardson, 'A Catalogue of Recent Acquisitions to Carlisle Museum and Reported Finds from the Cumbrian Area', *CW2*, Volume XC

(1990), pp. 29-31; R. P. Wright, 'The discovery of Roman altars at Busbridge Hale, near Godalming, Surrey', *CW2*, Volume LXXV (1975), pp. 93-4.

23 J. Alan Biggins and David J. A. Taylor, 'The Roman Fort at Castlesteads, Cumbria: a Geophysical Survey of the Vicus', *CW3*, Volume VII (2007), p. 17; Eric Birley, 'Some Roman military inscriptions', *CW2*, Volume LI (1952), pp. 69-70; Matthew Symonds, 'Terminating milecastle 50: ritual activity in the Hadrian's Wall milecastles', *CW3*, Volume 18 (2018), p. 79; Janet Webster, 'A bronze incense container in the form of Bacchus from Carlisle', *CW2*, Volume LXXIII (1973), pp. 90-3.

24 R. S. O. Tomlin, 'A Roman tombstone from Brougham Castle (BROCAVM) near Penrith', *CW2*, Volume LXXVI (1976), p. 3; Breeze, 'Civil Government and the North', p. 67; Shotter, 'Roman Carlisle', p. 66; John Thorley, 'The Ambleside Roman Gravestone', *CW3*, Volume II (2002), pp. 51-2; D.C.A. Shotter, 'The murder of Flavius Romanus at Ambleside: a possible context', *CW3*, Volume III (2003), pp. 228-31; Manuel Fernández Götz and John Reid, 'Ambleside Roman fort under attack: New research on a forgotten battle in the Lake District', *Cumberland and Westmorland Antiquarian and Archaeological Society News*, Autumn 2022, No. 10, p. 9; T. Patten, 'The Roman Cemetery on London Road, Carlisle', *CW2*, Volume LXXIV (1974), p. 10.

25 D. P. Dymond, review of M. J. T. Lewis, *Temples in Roman Britain* (1966), *Northern History* (hereafter *NH*), Volume II, 1967), pp. 165-6; Birley, 'Some Roman military inscriptions', pp. 67-8; Wright, 'The discovery of Roman altars', pp. 92-3.

26 Miranda J. Green, 'A Celtic God from Netherby, Cumbria', *CW2*, Volume LXXXIII (1983), pp. 42-3.

27 Daniel W. Elsworth, 'Carved stone heads from the Furness and Cartmel Peninsulas', *CW3*, Volume VI (2006), p. 240; C. Richardson, 'Stone Head from Millom', *CW2*, Volume LXXVIII (1978), pp. 211-12; W. Fletcher, 'Cairns at Mecklen Park, Santon Bridge', *CW2*, Volume LXXXV (1985), pp. 15-16; R.C. Turner, 'Another Cumbrian Bog Body, found in Seascale Moss in 1834', *CW2*, Volume LXXXIX (1989), pp. 21-23; Ian Caruana and J. C. Coulston, 'A Roman Bridge Stone from the River Eden, Carlisle', *CW2*, Volume LXXXVII (1987), pp. 44-5.

28 G. R. Stephens, 'An Altar to Vulcan from Maryport', *CW2*, Volume LXXXVIII (1988), pp. 29-31.

29 Symonds, 'Terminating Milecastle 50', p. 70.

30 Tom Garlick, *Romans in the Lake District* (Foreword by Eric Birley,

Clapham, Yorks: Dalesman Publishing p'back, 2nd edn., 1972), p. 29. The 'Horned God of the Brigantes' may in fact have been the horned god of the Carvetii, whose name may mean 'stag people': A. R. Birley,' The Frontier People of Roman Britain' (review article), *NH*, Volume II (1967), p. 149; B. J. N. Edwards, 'The "caput Carvetiorum" and the putative god of the tribe', *CW3*, Volume VI (2006), p. 225; W. Douglas Simpson, 'Brocavum, Ninekirks and Brougham: a study in continuity', *CW2*, Volume LVIII (1959), p. 70; Wright, 'The discovery of Roman altars', p. 91; J. Hughes, 'Roman altar from Old Carlisle', *CW2*, Volume LXXII (1972), p. 334.

31 Symonds, 'Terminating Milecastle 50', p. 70.

32 Martin Henig, 'Intaglios from Castleheads and the Roman fort at Kirkbride', *CW2*, Volume LXXII (1972), p. 59.

33 Stephen Johnson, *Later Roman Britain* (London and Henley: Routledge and Kegan Paul, 1980), p. 33; Shotter, *Romans and Britons*, pp. 128-9.

34 Charles Phythian-Adams, *Land of the Cumbrians A study in British provincial origins A.D. 400-1120* (Maps by Kenneth Smith, Aldershot, Hants: Scholar Press; Brookfield, VT: Ashgate Publishing, 1996), p. 48.

35 Michael Walsh, ed., *Dictionary of Christian Biography* (London and New York: Continuum p'back, 2001), pp. 842-3, 920.

36 Richard P. McBrien, General Editor, *The HarperCollins Encyclopedia of Catholicism* (New York: HarperCollins, 1995) p. 829; John Robinson, 'Notes on Brampton Old Church', *CW2*, Volume LXXXII (1982), p. 73; Robert Gambles, *The Story of the Lakeland Dales* (Chichester, West Sussex: Phillimore, 1997) pp. 138-9.

37 Douglas Simpson, 'Brocavum, Ninekirks and Brougham', pp. 73-5 38 Rex Gardner, 'Kentigern, Columba, and Oswald': The Ripon Connection', *NH*, Volume XXXV (1999), p. 15, n. 62.

39 Gardner, 'Kentigern, Columba, and Oswald', pp 14-16; Diana Whaley, *A Dictionary of Lake District Place-Names* (Nottingham: English Place-Names Society Regional Series, General Editor Richard Coats, Volume 1, 2006) pp. 245, 88. A further example of a 'well indicating that St Kentigern preached and baptised' at the site comes from Castle Sowerby, whose medieval church was dedicated to him: Sheila Ricketts, *Lakeland Country Churches A Visitor's Guide* (Illustrations by Edmund Blood, Maryport: Ellenbank Press, 1994), pp. 103-4.

An early well, dedicated to St Gregory (r. 590-694), the bishop of Rome who, in 596, sent the monk Augustine (d. 604) to convert the English, may be dated to a point in time before the Norman Conquest: Peter Lucas, 'A South Westmorland Medieval Holy Well?' The Case of St. Gregory's Well, Preston

Patrick', *CW3*, Volume XIV (2014), p. 133.

40 https://en.wikipedia.org/wiki/Cuthbert, 2/11; John Satchell, 'A History of Meathop Woods', *CW2*, Volume LXXXIII (1983), p. 31; E. J. Crowe, 'The Earliest Christian Community', *CW2*, Volume LXXXIV (1984), pp. 63-4; Phythian-Adams, *Land of the Cumbrians*, p. 91. The probable derivation of nearby Cark from the Cymric *carreg* (Whaley, *Dictionary of Lake District Place-Names*, p. 66) would confirm the Celtic identity of the area; Crowe, 'Earliest Christian Community', p. 65.

41 V. Tudor, 'St Cuthbert and Cumbria', *CW2*, Volume LXXXIV (1984), pp. 67, 68, 73.

42 Barringer, *The Lake District*, pp. 33-4; George Thomson, 'The Dalston discoid marker', *CW3*, Volume IX (2009), p. 54.

43 Mary C. Fair, 'The West Cumberland group of pre-Norman crosses', *CW2*, Volume L (1951), pp. 91-4.

44 William Rollinson, *A History of Cumberland and Westmorland* (Drawings by David Kirk, Cartography by Alan Hodgkiss and Joan Treasure, The Darwen County History Series, Chichester, Sussex: Phillimore, 1978), p. 30; Pevsner, in John Parker, *Cumbria A Guide to the Lake District and its County* (Edinburgh and London: John Bartholomew, 1977), p.60.

45 Lord Harlech, *Illustrated Regional Guides to Ancient Monuments ... Volume I Northern England* (London: HMSO, 1951), p. 24; P. A. Wilson, 'Eaglesfield: the place, the name, the burials', *CW2*, Volume LXXVIII (1978), p. 48.

46 Parker, *Cumbria*, p. 60

47 Richard N. Bailey, 'The meaning of the Viking-age shaft at Dacre', *CW2*, Volume LXXVII (1977), pp. 61-70.

48 Gambles, *The Story of the Lakeland Dales*, p. 130.

49 Fair, 'The West Cumberland group', pp. 93-4; Matthew Hyde and Nikolaus Pevsner, *Cumbria Cumberland, Westmorland and Furness* (The Buildings of England Founding Editor: Nikolaus Pevsner, New Haven, CT, and London: Yale University Press, 2010), p. 369; Revised Adrian Room, *Brewer's Dictionary of Phrase and Fable* (Millennium edn., London: Cassell, 2001), pp. 841, 773, 1291, 711, 560.

50 James Wilson, ed., *The Victoria History of the Counties of England A History of Cumberland, Volume I*, (Westminster: Archibald Constable, 1901), p. 267; Hyde and Pevsner, *Cumbria*, p. 367. The triquetra is an ornament consisting of three interlaced arcs, familiar in early northern European religious art.

51 Wilson, ed., *Victoria History of Cumberland*, I, p. 267; W.G. Collingwood, *The Lake Counties* (ed. and revised William Rollinson, London: J. M. Dent, 1988), p. 65.

52 Hyde and Pevsner, *Cumbria*, p. 20.

53 Mullett, *Penrith I*, pp. 27-8; Daniel W. Elsworth, 'Knockross, Bowness-on-Solway: Rediscovered but Still Lost', *CW3*, Volume 16 (2016), p. 249; Mullett, *Penrith* I, p. 31; Amy R. Miller, 'A Second "Saint's Tomb" at Gosforth, Cumbria', *CW3*, Volume XII (2012), p. 93.

54 R. D. Ellwood, 'A Cross from Nether Denton Church', *CW2*, Volume XLII (1942), pp. 149-150; Hyde and Pevsner, *Cumbria*, p. 333.

55 Ellwood, 'A Cross from Nether Denton', p. 151; Corinne Jouanno, 'Romanesque Art', in André Vauchez, with Barrie Dobson and Michael Lapige, eds., *Encylopedia of the Middle Ages* (2 vols., trans. Adrian Waldord, Paris: Éditions du Cerf; Cambridge: James Cape; Rome: Città Nuova, 2000) II, p. 1254; McBrien, ed., *Encyclopedia of Catholicism*, p. 383.

56 R. M. Newman, N. J. Hair, C. L. E. Howard Davies, C. Brooks and A.White, 'Excavations at Penrith Market, 1990', *CW2*, Volume C (2000), p. 107; Mullett, *Penrith I*, p. 33.

57 J.C. Dickinson, 'Proceedings', summer 1961, *CW2*, Volume LXII (1962), pp. 331-2.

58 Phythian-Adams, *Land of the Cumbrians*, p. 95; Barringer,*The Lake District*, p. 43; Hyde and Pevsner, *Cumbria*, pp. 367, 647, 458, 469, 307, 308, 104, 473, 522, 320, 144, 333, 474.

58 G. W. S Barrow, 'Northern English Society in the Twelfth and Thirteenth Centuries', *NH*, Volume IV (1969), p. 8.

60 Hyde and Pevsner, *Cumbria*, pp. 20, 458; George Washington, 'The Border Heritage, 1066-1292', *CW2*, Volume LXII (1962), pp. 106-7; O.R. Bagot, 'Proceedings', *CW2*, Volume LXV (1965), p. 436: the dates are 1090-1097 for Heversham.

61 W. H. Chippindall, 'Kirkby Lonsdale Church. A Suggestion', *CW2*, Volume XXXVII (1937), pp. 40-1.

62 C. Roy Hudleston and R. S. Boumphrey, *Cumberland Families and Heraldry* ... (Illustrated by J. Hughes *et al.*, Kendal: Cumberland and Westmorland Antiquarian and Archaeological Society, Extra Series Vol. XXIII, 1978), p. 225; Washington,'The Border Heritage', pp. 106-7.

63 George Washington, 'The Parentage of William de Lancaster, lord of Kendal', *CW2*, Volume LXII (1962), pp. 97-9.

64 F. B. Swift and C. G. Bulman, 'Ireby Church', *CW2*, Volume LXV (1965), pp. 224-5; Hyde and Pevsner, *Cumbria*, p. 421.

65 Ian Caruana, 'Excavations on the Medieval Church of St Thomas, Farlam', *CW2*, Volume XCII (1992), p. 123; C. Richardson, 'Note on a Grave-Slab in a Distington garden', *CW2*, Volume LXXVIII (1978), pp. 212-14. Barringer,*The Lake District*, p. 43; Hyde and Pevsner, *Cumbria*, pp. 367, 647, 458, 469, 307, 308, 104, 473, 522, 320, 144, 333, 474.

66 F H. Marshall, 'Proceedings', *CW2*, Volume LXII (1962), pp. 333-5.

67 C. M. L. Bouch, *Prelates and People of the Lake Counties A History of the Diocese of Carlisle 1113-1933* (Kendal: Titus Wilson, 1948), pp. 157, 174, 160; Janet Martin, 'The Building and Endowment of Finsthwaite Church and School, 1723-4', *CW2*, Volume LXXXIV (1984), p. 125.

68 Bouch, *Prelates and People*, pp. 157, 174, 160; Martin, 'The Building and Endowment', p. 125

69 R.B. Dobson, 'Cathedral Chapters and Cathedral Cities: York, Durham and Carlisle in the Fifteenth Century', *NH*, Volume XIX (1983), p. 19; Bouch, *Prelates and People*, p. 3; John K. Walton, 'Cumbrian Identities: Some Historical Contexts', *CW3*, Volume X (2010), p. 19.

70 David Weston, 'The Medieval Church in Carlisle', in Brennand and Stringer, eds., *The Making of Carlisle*, pp. 104-106; C. G. Bulman, 'The Norman Priory Church at Carlisle', *CW2*, Volume XLII (1942), p. 66.

71 Bulman, 'The Norman Priory Church', p. 66; Weston, 'The Medieval Church', pp. 120, 139; *St Cuthbert's Church and The Tithe Barn* (Pamphlet: St Cuthberts Church/ Blackfriars Street, Carlisle).

72 J. L. Hobbs, 'Conishead Priory', *CW2*, Volume LXII (1962), p. 337; Bouch, *Prelates and People*, pp. 6, 8; Hudleston and Boumphrey, *Cumberland Families and Heraldry*, p. 258.

73 John Todd, 'The boundary of the lands of Lanercost Priory at Hare Hill', *CW3*, Volume VI (2006), p. 58; J. C. Dickinson,'A Note on the Foundation of Lanercost Priory', *CW2*, Volume XLII (1942), P. 183; Hudleston and Boumphrey, *Cumberland Families and Heraldry*, p. 351; Hyde and Pevsner, *Cumbria*, p 479; *The Lake District and Lancashire* (London: The Reader's Digest Association for the Automobile Association,1988), p. 89.

74 J. R. H. Moorman, 'The estates of the Lanercost Canons, with some notes on the history of the Priory', *CW2*, Volume XLVIII (1949), pp. 83, 85, 91-2; Lorna M. Mullett, 'A case study of Lanercost, Priory', Unpublished Research Paper, 2021, citing Henry Summerson and Stuart Harrison, *Lanercost Priory, Cumbria* (Kendal: Cumberland and Westmorland Antiquarian and Archaeological Society Research Series, No. 10, 2000), p. 16.

75 Hyde and Pevsner, *Cumbria*, p. 267; Chris Wild & Christine Howard Davis, 'Excavations at Priory Gardens, Cartmel', *CW2*, Volume C (2000), pp 161-2; Parker, *Cumbria*, p. 79; Thomas West, *The Antiquities of Furness; Or, An Account of the Royal Abbey of St. Mary* ... (London: J. Johnson *et al.*, 1774, Republished Beckermet, Cumbria: Michael Moon, 1977), p. 185.

76 Harry Hawkins and John Thorley,'The Premonstratensian House of Canons at Preston Patrick, *CW3*, Volume XII (2012), pp. 107, 109, 110; Carl Richardson, *Cumbrian Abbeys A review of mediaeval abbeys and priories in Cumbria* ... (Carlisle: North Cumbria Imprint, 1991), p.25; Hudleston and Boumphrey, *Cumberland Families and Heraldry*, p.79.

77 Rita Wood, 'The Two Tympana at Long Marton Church', *CW3*, Volume 18 (2018), pp. 123-40; Hyde and Pevsner, *Cumbria*, p. 499.

78 Percival Turnbull and Deborah Walsh, 'Monastic Remains at Ravenstonedale', *CW2*, Volume XCII (1992), p. 67; Hyde and Pevsner, *Cumbria*, p. 586; Angus J. L. Winchester, ed., *Cumbria: An Historical Gazetteer* (Lancaster: Lancaster University Regional History Centre in Association with the Cumbria History Trust, 2016), p. 250.

79 Wilson, 'Ecclesiastical History: Religious Houses', in Wilson ed., *Victoria History of Cumberland Volume II* (Haymarket: James Street, 1905), p. 184, 185; Matthew Railton *et al.*, 'Cumwhinton: Archaeological investigation of a medieval rural site', *CW3*, Volume XIII (2013), p. 66.

80 Hyde and Pevsner, *Cumbria*, p. 353.

81 G. W. S Barrow, 'King David I, Earl Henry and Cumbria', *CW2*, Volume XCIX (1999), pp. 123-4; Winchester,ed., *Cumbria: An Historical Gazetteer*, p. 164; Bouch, *Prelates and People*, p. 6; Wilson, 'Ecclesiastical History: Religious Houses', p. 162; Hyde and Pevsner, *Cumbria*, p. 87; Paul Gibbons *et.al.*, 'Excavations and Observations at Kirkby Thore', *CW2*, Volume LXXXIX (1989), p. 113; B. C. Jones, 'Historical development of Annetwell Street, Carlisle', *CW2*, Volume XCIX (1999), p. 129.

82 Wilson, 'Ecclesiastical History: Religious Houses', pp. 174-5; Hyde and Pevsner, *Cumbria*, 213-15; John Thorley,'The Estates of Calder Abbey', *CW3*, Volume IV (2004), pp. 133-4; John Thorley, 'The Hesleyside charters, the Salkelds of Whitehall, and the Carltons of Hesleyside', *CW3*, Volume VII (2007), pp. 73-4.

83 John M. Todd, 'St Bega: Cult, Fact or Legend?', *CW2*, Volume LXXX (1980), p. 23; Todd, 'The pre-Conquest Church of St Bees, Cumbria: a possible minster', *CW3*, Volume III (2003), pp. 97, 105; Gambles, *The Story of the Lakeland Dales*, p. 67.

84 John M. Todd, 'St Bega: Cult, Fact or Legend?', *CW2*, Volume LXXX

(1980), p. 23; John M. Todd, 'The pre-Conquest Church of St Bees, Cumbria: a possible minster', *CW3*, Volume III (2003), pp. 97, 105; Gambles, *The Story of the Lakeland Dales*, p. 67.

85 Hyde and Pevsner, *Cumbria*, pp. 115; Wilson, 'Ecclesiastical History: Religious Houses', p. 189.

86 C. G. Bulman, 'Carlisle Cathedral and its development in the thirteenth and fourteenth centuries', *CW2*, Volume XLIX (1950), pp. 88-9, 96-7; David W.V. Weston, *Carlisle Cathedral History* (Carlisle: Bookcase, 2000), p. 12; Hyde and Pevsner, *Cumbria*, p. 224.

87 H. Summerson, 'The King's *Clericulus*: The Life and Career of Silvester de Everdon, Bishop of Carlisle, 1247-1254', *NH*, Volume XXVIII (1992), p. 71; Bouch, *Prelates and People*, pp. 13-14.

88 Summerson, 'The King's *Clericulus*', pp. 71-6.

89 Summerson, 'The King's *Clericulus*', pp. 79-88.

90 Summerson, 'The King's *Clericulus*', pp. 89, 91. Crown control over this royal diocese was made further apparent in 1279, when the canons were heavily fined for electing a bishop without the king's licence: Summerson, 'The King's *Clericulus*', p. 91.

91 Henry Summerson, *Medieval Carlisle The City and the Borders from the Late Eleventh to the Mid-Sixteenth Century* (2 vols., Kendal: The Cumberland and Westmorland Antiquarian and Archaeological Society Extra Series XXV, 1993) I, pp. 116, 160, II, p. 435; Weston, 'The Medieval Church', p. 113; D.R. Perriam 'An Unrecorded Carlisle church: the church of the Holy Trinity, Caldewgate', *CW2*, Volume LXXIX (1979), p. 54-5. The chapel's dedication to the Holy Trinity probably dates it to the period after 1162, when the martyr Thomas Becket (c. 1118-70) chose to be consecrated archbishop on that feastday: B. C. Jones, 'Notes on Caldewgate', *ibid.*, pp. 53-4, 55; F. L. Cross, ed., *The Oxford Dictionary of the Christian Church* (London: Oxford University Press, 1961), p. 1377.

92 Weston, 'The Medieval Church', p. 111-122; B.C. Jones, 'The Topography of Medieval Carlisle', *CW2*, Volume LXXVI (1976), p. 95; Summerson, *Medieval Carlisle*, I, p. 11, 64, 160; B.C. Jones, 'St Alban's church and graveyard, Carlisle', *CW2*, Volume XC (1990), p. 167.

93 W. G. Wiseman, 'The Medieval Hospitals of Cumbria', *CW2*, Volume LXXXVII (1987), p. 83; Daniel Le Blévek, 'Hospital, Hospice', in Vauchez *et al.*, eds., *Encyclopedia of the Middle Ages*, pp. 691-2.

94 Weston, 'The Medieval Church', pp. 117- 18; W. G. Wiseman, 'The hospital of St. Nicholas, Carlisle, and its masters; Part 1 - the period up to 1333', CW2, Volume XCV (1995), pp. 93-4, 97-8; Bouch, *Prelates and*

People, p.79; Summerson, *Medieval Carlisle*, I p. 206; Christine Howard-Davis and Mark Leah, 'Excavations at St Nicholas Yard, Carlisle, 1996-7', *CW2*, Volume XCIX (1999), pp. 89, 112-13.

95 W. G. Wisemam, 'The hospital of St Nicholas, Carlisle, and its masters. Part 2 - the period from 1333', *CW2*, Volume XCVI (1996), p. 61.

96 Henry Summerson, *Medieval Carlisle The City and the Borders from the Late Eleventh to the Mid-Sixteenth Century* 2 Vols, Kendal: Cumberland and Westmorland Antiquarian and Archaeological Society Extra Series, 1993, I, p, 155-6

97 Mike Salter, *The Old Parish Churches of Cumbria* (Malvern, Worcs.: Folly Publications, 1998), p. 34; F. B. Swift, 'Proceedings', *CW2*, Volume LXV (1965), p. 429; Hyde and Pevsner, *Cumbria*, p. 210; Mary C. Fair, 'The Church of the Holy Trinity, Millom', *CW2*, Volume XXXVII (1937), pp.89, 94; Hudleston and Boumphrey, *Cumberland Families and Heraldry*, p. 25; Winchester, ed., *Cumbria: An Historical Gazetteer*, p. 21.

98 F. B Swift, 'The parish and church of Castle Sowerby' and J. Hughes, 'An architectural description of the church', *CW2*, Volume LXXIII (1973), pp. 170-2.

99 Wilson, 'Ecclesiastical History: Religious Houses', p. 181; John M. Todd, 'Civil Engineering, c. 1250: the St Bees Mill Leat', *CW2*, Volume LXXXV (1985), pp. 124, 127; J. and P. J. Cherry, 'Recording of a monastic grange at Orton', *CW3*, Volume IV (2004), p. 266; Thorley, 'The Hesleyside charters', p. 74; J. C. Dickinson, 'Three pre-Reformation documents concerning South Cumbria', *CW2*, Volume LXXXVI (1986), pp. 130-1. A unit of account, the mark was worth 2/3 of a pound - 13s 4d.

100 Thorley, 'The Hesleyside charters', pp. 82, 74..

101 Hudleston and Boumphrey, *Cumberland Families and Heraldry*, p. 115; John Thorley, 'The Hesleyside charters', *CW3*, Volume VII (2007), pp. 76-8; Wilson, 'Ecclesiastical History: Religious Houses', pp. 176, 177.

102 Roy Millward and Adrian Robinson, *The Lake District* (London: Eyre & Spottiswoode, 1970), pp. 157-8.

103 Gambles, *The Story of the Lakeland Dales*, p. 67; Jamie Lund, 'A history of Wray Castle Estate, Claife', *CW3*, Volume II (2002), p. 231.

104 Hyde and Pevsner, *Cumbria*, pp. 352, 399; J. A. Tuck, 'War and Society in the Medieval North', *NH*, Volume XXI (1985), p. 36; Henry L. Widdup, *The Story of Christianity in Cumbria a geographical appraisal* (Kendal: Titus Wilson, 1981), p. 43.

105 Millward and Robinson, *The Lake District*, pp. 160-1.

106 Gambles, *The Story of the Lakeland Dales*, p. 67, Millward and Robinson, *The Lake District,* pp. 159-60. However, the idea that sheep were the mainstay of Cumbrian medieval farming has been challenged. In 1297 Furness had 482 oxen, 186 cows and 5000 sheep over four estates but most of the sheep were on the Yorkshire estate. The north in the 13th century was essentially cattle country: *Cumbria Local History Federation*, Bulletin 90, 2022, p. 5.

107 Barringer, *The Lake District*, pp. 40-1; John Satchell, 'A History of Meathop Woods. Part I -Prehistory', *CW2*, Volume LXXXIII (1983), p. 25; Tuck, 'War and Society', p. 36.

108 Widdup, *Christianity in Cumbria*, pp. 42-3.

109 West, *Antiquities of Furness*, p.73; Widdup, *Christianity in Cumbria*, p. 43; Bouch, *Prelates and People*, pp. 473-4; Gambles, *The Story of the Lakeland Dales*, p. 69.

110 Millward and Robinson, *The Lake District*, p. 157; Solemnes.com/sites/default/files/upload/pdf/rule_of_St_Benedict.pdf.

111 F. L. Cross, *The Oxford Dictionary of the Christian Church* (London: Oxford University Press, 1961), pp. 97-8

112 Widdup, *Christianity in Cumbria*, pp. 42-33.

113 West, *Antiquities of Furness*, pp. 21, 34-5.

114 West, *Antiquities of Furness*, p. 61.

115 Bouch, *Prelates and People*, p. 174.

116 Hyde and Pevsner, *Cumbria*, pp. 252, 353, 356; West, *Antiquities of Furness*, pp.94-5.

117 West, *Antiquities of Furness*, 94; Hyde and Pevsner, *Cumbria*, p. 357.

118 Michael Carter, 'An unexplored 14th-century source for the history of Furness Abbey', *CW3*, Volume 22 (2022), p. 96.

119 Jean-François Genest, 'Clairvaux', Pierre Bonnerue, 'Lectio Divina', in Vauchez *et al.*, eds., *Enyclopedia of the Middle Age*, I, pp. 313, II, 835-6.

120 Michael Mullett, 'The Reformation in the parish of Whalley', in Robert Poole, ed., *The Lancashire Witches Histories and Stories* (Manchester and New York: Manchester University Press, 2002), p. 93.

121 https://en.wikipedia.org/wiki/Jocelyn _ of_Furness.

122 Michael Walsh, ed., *Dictionary of Christian Biography* (London and New York: Continuum p'back, 2001), p. 998; Carter, 'An Unexplored Source', p. 96.

123 Marshall, 'Proceedings', *CW2*, Volume LXII, 1962), p. 333; Carter, 'An

unexplored source', p. 96.

124 htpps://en.wikipedia.org.wiki/Ranulf_Higden.

125 Carter, 'An unexplored source', p. 101, n. 3; François Suard, 'Geoffrey of Monmouth (c. 1110-1155)', in Vauchez, et al., eds., Encyclopedia of the Middle Ages, I, p. 594..

126 Suard, 'Geoffrey of Monmouth', p. 594; David Williamson, *Brewer's British Royalty A Phrase and Fable Dictionary* (London: Cassell, 1966), p. 113.

127 François Suard, 'Arthur', in Vauchez *et al.*, eds., *Encyclopedia of the Middle Ages*, I, pp. 115-16.

128 Wilson, 'Ecclesiastical History: Religious Houses', p. 154; https://atticbooks.ca/products/106992.

129 Jones, 'Historical development of Annetwell Street', *CW2*, Volume XCIX (1999), p. 119.

130 Moorman, 'The estates of the Lanercost Canons', pp. 100-101; Hyde and Pevsner, *Cumbria*, p. 479.

131 Wilson, 'Ecclesiastical History: Religious Houses', p. 157.

132 Moorman, 'The estates of the Lanercost Canons', p. 103.

133 Hyde and Pevsner, *Cumbria*, p. 633; John Zant, 'Archaeological Investigations on the A66 at Temple Sowerby 2006-2007', *CW3*, Volume IX (2009), p. 29; G. Jones, 'Some sources of Loans and Credit in Cumbria before the rise of the banks', *CW2*, Volume LXXV (1975), p. 276.

134 Summerson, *Medieval Carlisle*, I, p. 161; Bouch, *Prelates and People*, p. 49.

135 Weston, 'The Medieval Church', p.113; Summerson, *Medieval Carlisle*, I, p, 161; Philip Cracknell, 'Four pieces of sculpture from Devonshire Street, Carlisle', *CW2*, Volume XCVIII (1998), p. 309; R. H. Moorman, 'Some Franciscans of Carlisle', *CW2*, Volume XLIX (1950), p. 74.

136 Moorman, 'Some Franciscans of Carlisle', pp. 81-3.

137 Jones, 'The Topography of Medieval Carlisle', *CW2*, Volume LXXVI (1976), p. 87; Weston, 'The Medieval Church', pp. 115-16; Summerson, *Medieval Carlisle*, I, p. 161.

138 Summerson, *Medieval Carlisle*, I, p. 204; Henry Summerson, *Edward I at Carlisle: King and Parliament in 1307* (Kendal: Cumberland and Westmorland Antiquarian and Archaeological Society, General Editor Jean Turnbull, Tract Series XXIII, 2011), p. 30.

139 Martin Railton, 'Appleby Archaeology Group reveal the site of

Appleby's medieval friary', *Cumberland and Westmorland Antiquarian and Archaeologic Society News*, Autumn 2022, No. 10, p.8; awhistory.co.uk/files/module_document_pdfs/Appleby_in_Westmorland_fact_sheet.pdf; https://www.heritagegateway.org.uk.

140 Mullett, *Penrith I*, pp. 64-6.

141 Bouch, *Prelates and People*, pp. 64-5.

142 Bouch, *Prelates and People*, pp. 64-5; Hyde and Pevsner, *Cumbria*, pp. 554-5, 383.

143 Summerson, *Medieval Carlisle*, I, p. 226; John Robinson, 'Notes on Brampton Old Church' *CW2*, Volume LXXXII (1982), p. 75

144 C.M L. Bouch, 'Rose Castle', *CW2*, Volume LVI (1957), pp. 132-4.

145 C. J. McNamee, 'William Wallace's Invasion of Northern England in 1297', *NH*, Volume 26 (1990), p. 48

146 M. J. Kennedy, 'John Halton, Bishop of Carlisle, 1292-1324', *CW2*, Volume LXXIII (1973), p. 94.

147 Kennedy, 'John Halton', p. 101, 110; *The Softback Preview The Concise Dictionary of National Biography* ... (3 vols., London: Oxford University Press 1992), II, 199; Bouch, *Prelates and People*, p. 89.

148 Mullett, *Penrith I*, pp. 93-5.

149 Mullett, *Penrith I*, p. 95; Hugh Owen, *The Lowther Family Eight Hundred Years of 'A Family of Ancient Gentry and Worship'* ... (Chichester: Phillimore, 1990), pp. 35-6.

150 Bouch, *Prelates and People*, pp.110-12; Tuck, 'War and Society', p. 50.

151 Bulman, 'Carlisle Cathedral and its development', p. 104; Weston, *Carlisle Cathedral History*, p 14. Decorated is the term used in architectural history for the fashion that was dominant in England between c. 1290 and c. 1350, taking its name from the elaborate window tracery of the period: Hyde and Pevsner, *Cumbria*, p.718 .

152 Bulman, 'Carlisle Cathedral and its development', pp. 106, 109; Weston, *Carlisle Cathedral History*, p. 14.

153 Bouch, *Prelates and People*, p. 72; Hyde and Pevsner, *Cumbria*, pp. 226, 231.

154 Ricketts, *Lakeland Country Churches*, pp. 16-17; Hyde and Pevsner, *Cumbria*, p. 188; W. Douglas Simpson, 'Brough-under-Stainmore: The Castle and the Church', *CW2*, Volume XLVI (1947), pp. 282-3.

155 Hyde and Pevsner, *Cumbria*, p. 645; F. B. Swift, 'Part I Uldale church: history and changes', *CW2*, Volume LIX (1960), pp 51-2; *idem*, 'St Mary's

Chapel, Uldale', *CW2*, Volume LXXVII (1977), p. 181.

156 Chippindall [?], 'Kirkby Lonsdale Church', p. 42; Hyde and Pevsner, *Cumbria*, p. 458; Robinson, 'Notes on Brampton Old Church', pp. 74-5; Hyde and Pevsner, *Cumbria*, p. 279.

157 Hyde and Pevsner, *Cumbria*, p. 385; Bouch, *Prelates and People*, pp. 96-7.

158 Hyde and Pevsner, *Cumbria*, p. 385; N.Hudleston, 'Proceedings', *CW2*, Volume LXV (1965), p. 431; Salter, *Old Parish Churches of Cumbria*, p. 54.

159 Swift and Hughes, 'The parish and church of Castle Sowerby', p 176.

160 J. Hughes, 'Recent discoveries at St Oswalds' Church, Dean', *CW2*, Volume LXVIII (1968), p. 35; F. B. Marshall, 'Proceedings, summer 1961', *CW2*,Volume LXII (1962) , p. 334; B. J. N. Edwards, 'The damaged carvings on the font, St Kentigern's Church, Gt Crosthwaite', *CW3*, Volume IV (2004), pp. 257-63; Hyde and Pevsner, *Cumbria*, p. 315; C. M. L. Bouch and G. P. Jones, with R. W. Brunskill, *A Short Economic and Social History of the Lake Counties 1500-1830* (Manchester: Manchester University Press, 1961), p. 60.

161 Colin Richardson, 'A Catalogue of recent acquisitions to Tullie House Museum and reported finds from the Cumbrian area, 1990-1996. Part I: Tullie House accessions', *CW2*, Volume XCVIII (1998), pp. 40-2; Hyde and Pevsner, *Cumbria*, p. 539.

162 B. L. Thompson, 'Westmorland church bells', *CW2*, Volume LXX (1970), pp. 52-3; Hyde and Pevsner, *Cumbria*, 507.

163 Thompson, 'Westmorland church bells', pp. 52-4; Mary C. Fair, 'Three West Cumberland Notes', *CW2*, LI (1952), pp. 93-4; Mary C. Fair, 'The pre-reformation church bells of West Cumberland', *CW2*, Volume XLVIII (1949), pp. 110-13.

164 Richardson, 'A Catalogue of Recent Acquisitions', *CW2*, Volume XC (1990), p. 46.

165 Richardson, 'A Catalogue of Recent Acquisitions', *CW*, Volume XCIX (1999), pp. 32-3.

166 John Marsh, 'List of objects found by metal detectorists in the Kendal area in recent years', *CW2*, Volume XCVI (1996), pp. 238-40; Ian Caruana, 'A Possible Medieval Votive Coin from Cumbria', *CW2*, Volume XCI (1991), p. 293.

167 Iris Origo, *The World of San Bernardino* (London: The Reprint Society, 1964), p. 118; Richard Asquith, 'Serving the Needs of a Lakeland Parish:

Kendal in the Late Middle Ages', *CW3*, Volume 17 (2017), p. 93; Richardson, 'A catalogue of recent acquisitions', *CW2*, Volume XCIX (1999), pp. 26-7; Pers. Comm. Jane Platt.

168 Caruana, 'A Medieval Votive Coin', pp. 292-4.

169 Weston, *Carlisle Cathedral History*, p. 17; Hyde and Pevsner, *Cumbria*, p. 232. The wyvern was a monster resembling a dragon, and the griffin was a beast with the body and legs of a lion, the beak and wings of an eagle.

170 Thirlie Grundy, 'The Misericords of Carlisle Cathedral: their carver and his pysche', *CW2*, Volume XCIV (1994), p. 91.

171 Hyde and Pevsner, *Cumbria*, p. 232.

172 Mullett, *Penrith* I, pp. 108-9.

173 Summerson, *Medieval Carlisle*, I, pp. 325, 350, II, p. 591; https://en.wikisource.org/wiki/Dictionary_-of-National-Biography,-1885-1900/Merke,_-Thomas, 1./4

174 Bouch, *Prelates and People*, p. 101; https://en.wikisource.org/wiki/Dictionary_of_National_Biography,_1885-190/Merke,_Thomas, pp.1/4.

175 Bouch, *Prelates and People*, p. 102.

176 Bouch, *Prelates and People*, p. 102.

177 Bouch, *Prelates and People*, p. 102; https://en.wikisource.org/wiki/Dictionary_of_National_Biography,_1885-1900/Merke,Thomas, 2/4; May McKisack, *The Fourteenth Century 1307-1399* (The Oxford History of England, ed. Sir George Clark, Oxford: Clarendon, 1971), p. 494.

178 https://en.wikisource.org/wiki/Dictionary_of_National_Biography,_1885-1900/Merke,Thomas,3/4;Wilson, 'Ecclesiastical History', p. 43.

179 Bouch, *Prelates and People*, p. 103; https://en.wikisource.org/wiki/Dictionary_of_National_Biography,_1885-1900/Merke, Thomas, 3/4.

180 https://en.wikisource.org.wiki/Dictionary_of_National_Biography,_1885-1900/Merke,Thomas, 3/4-4/4; Bouch, *Prelates and People*, pp. 103-5.

181 Room, Rev., *Brewers' Dictionary of Phrase and Fable*, p. 302.

182 Nicolson and Burn, *The History and Antiquities*, II, p. 271.

183 June C. F. Barnes, 'The Coronation of the Virgin or the Apotheosis of King Richard the Second? Considering a boss on the pulpitium screen in Carlisle Cathedral', *CW3*, Volume 18 (2018), pp. 141-5.

184 Pete and Linda Murray, *The Oxford Companion to Christian Art and Architecture* (Oxford and New York: Oxford University Press, 1996), p. 335.

185   https://en.wikipedia.org/wiki/Labours_of_the_Months#:~:text, 1/4-2/4.
186   Weston, *Carlisle Cathedral History*, pp. 14-15, 64.
187   Hyde and Pevsner, *Cumbria*, p. 229; Weston, *Carlisle Cathedral History*, pp. 64-5; Perrin Mane, 'Labours of the Months', in Vauchez *et al.*, eds., *Encyclopedia of the Middle Ages*, II, p. 812.
188   Mane, 'Labours of the Months', p. 812; McBrien, ed., *Encyclopedia of Catholicism*, p. 225.
189   André Vauchez, 'Benedict of Nursia, Benedictine Rule', in Vauchez, *et al.*, eds., *Encyclopedia of the Middle Ages*, I, p. 167; Bernard Chevalier, 'Labour' in *ibid.*, II, pp. 811-12.
190   Weston, *Carlisle Cathedral History*, p. 65.
191   Margaret Briggs, 'The carvings of Labours of the Months in Carlisle Cathedral', *CW3*, Volume V (2005), p. 133.
192   Hyde and Pevsner, *Cumbria*, p. 232.
193   McBrien, ed., *Encylopedia of Catholicism*, pp. 113-18; Cross, ed., *Dictionary of the Christian Church*, p. 569.
194   McBrien, ed., *Encyclopedia of Catholicism*, p. 114.
195   *Chambers's Encyclopædia New Edition*, Volume X (London: George Newnes, 1961), p. 493.
196   Weston, *Carlisle Cathedral History*, p. 68. The word 'yam' is still Cumberland dialect for 'home'.
197   McBrien, ed., *Encyclopedia of Catholicism*, p. 63; Walsh, ed., *Dictionary of Christian Biography*, p. 80.
198   Weston, *Carlisle Cathedral History*, p. 70.
200   Cross, ed., *Dictionary of the Christian Church*, p. 148. 'Laiking' is still Cumberland dialect for playing.
201   Weston, *Carlisle Cathedral History*, p. 69.
202   Weston, *Carlisle Cathedral History*, p. 69.
203   V. Tudor, 'St Cuthbert and Cumbria', *CW2*, Volume LXXXIV (1984), p. 68.
204   Today the parish church of Distington, near the coast, south of Workington, is dedicated to the Holy Spirit but in 1653 it was 'The Church of St Cuthbert' and possessed a medieval treble bell inscribed '*Sancte Cuthberte Ora Pro Nobis* - St Cuthbert, Pray for us'. It has been suggested, therefore, 'that Distington was the last halting place for the monks conveying the saint's body, before they embarked on the crossing to Whithorn': Mary C. Fair, 'The Lost Dedication of Distington Church', *CW2*,

Volume LI (1952), pp. 92-3; D. P. Kirkby, 'Strathclyde and Cumbria: a survey of historical development to 1092', *CW2*, Volume LXII (1962), p. 82; Daniel W. Elsworth, 'Low Tide and a Red Horse: St Cuthbert's Relics and Morecambe Bay', *CW3*, Volume XIII (2013), pp. 67-72.

205 https://en.wikipedia.org/wiki/Cuthbert, 4/11; Cross, ed., *Dictionary of the Christian Church*, p. 997.

206 https://en.wikipedia.org/wiki/Cuthbert, 4/11.

207 McBrien, ed., *Encyclopedia of Catholicism*, p. 1096.

208 Patrick J. Geary, 'Relics', in Vauchez *et al.*, eds., *Encyclopedia of the Middle Ages*, II, 1222.

209 Weston, *Carlisle Cathedral History*, p. 69.

210 Weston, *Carlisle Cathedral History*, p. 67.

211 Cross, ed., *Dictionary of the Christian Church*, p. 354, 72-3; McBrien, ed., *Encyclopedia of Catholicism*, pp. 74-6.

212 McBrien, ed., *Encylopedia of Catholicism*, p. 74.

213 Weston, *Carlisle Cathedral History*, p. 71.

214 Weston, *Carlisle Cathedral History*, p. 71.

215 Weston, *Carlisle Cathedral History*, p. 71; p 71; McBrien, ed., *Encyclopedia of Catholicism*, p. 45.

216 Weston, *Carlisle Cathedral History*, p. 71.

217 Weston, *Carlisle Cathedral History*, p. 71.

218 Cross, ed., *Dictionary of the Christian Church*, p. 711; Room, Rev., *Brewer's Dictionary of Phrase and Fable*, p. 629.

219 Weston, *Carlisle Cathedral History*, p. 71; Clemens Jöckle, *Encyclopedia of Saints* (trans. German Translation Centre, London: Parkgate Books, 1997), p. 327.

220 Weston, *Carlisle Cathedral History*, p. 71.

221 Weston, *Carlisle Cathedral History*, p. 71; Jöckle, *Encyclopedia of Saints*, p. 240.

222 Weston, *Carlisle Cathedral History*, p. 71.

223 Peter Stanford, Foreword by Karen Armstrong, *A Life of Christ* (np.: Quercus, 2009, pp. 154-5; Eamon Duffy, *The Stripping of the Altars Tradtional Religion in England c.1400-c. 1580* (New Haven, CT, and London: Yale University Press p'back, 1992), p. 239.

224 Cross, ed., *Dictionary of the Christian Church*, pp. 391, 610; Michael A. Mullett, *John Calvin* (Routledge Historical Biographies Series Editor:

Robert Pearce, London and New York: Routledge, 2006), p. 219; Bernard M. G. Reardon, *Religious Thought in the Reformation* (London and New York: Longman p'back, 1981), p. 195.

225 Weston, *Carlisle Cathedral History*, p. 71; McBrien, ed., *Encyclopedia of Catholicism*, p. 1253; Jöckle, *Encyclopedia of Saints*, p. 434.

226 Weston, *Carlisle Cathedral History*, p. 71; Jöckle, *Encyclopedia of Saints*, p. 228.

227 Weston, *Carlisle Cathedral History*, p. 71; Jöckle, *Encyclopedia of Saints*, p. 369.

228 Weston, *Carlisle Cathedral History*, p. 71; Jöckle, *Encyclopedia of Saints*, p. 54.

229 McBrien, ed., *Encyclopedia of Catholicism*, p. 142.

230 Weston, *Carlisle Cathedral History*, p. 71; Room, Rev., *Brewer's Dictionary of Phrase and Fable*, p. 1634; Jöckle, *Encyclopedia of Saints*, p. 316.

231 Weston, *Carlisle Cathedral History*, p. 71; Room, Rev., *Brewer's Dictionary of Phrase and Fable*, p. 1634; Jöckle, *Encylopedia of Saints*, p. 316.

232 Weston, *Carlisle Cathedral History*, p. 71; Cross, ed., *Dictionary of the Christian Church*, p. 1337

233 Dominique Rigaux, 'Judas', in Vauchez, *et al.*, eds., *Encylopedia of the Middle Ages*, I, p. 789.

234 Jöckle, *Encylopedia of Saints*, p. 52.

235 Jöckle, *Encyclopedia of Saints*, p. 316; Cross, ed., *Dictionary of the Christian Church*, p. 144.

236 Dobson, 'Cathedral Chapters and Cathedral Cities', pp. 2-3.

237 Dobson, 'Cathedral Chapters and Cathedral Cities', pp. 24, 26, 37; Summerson, *Medieval Carlisle*, II, p. 618; C.R. Davey, 'The Carlisle Tithe Barn', *CW2*, Volume LXXII (1972), pp. 74-5.

238 Cross, ed., *Dictionary of the Christian Church*, p. 262.

239 Wilson, 'Religious Houses', p. 139; Dobson, 'Cathedral Chapters and Cathedral Cities', p. 42.

240 Dobson, 'Cathedral Chapters and Cathedral Cities', pp. 42-3; Wilson, 'Ecclesiastical History', pp. 44-5.

241 Hyde and Pevsner, *Cumbria*, pp. 232-3; C. G. Bulman, 'The Gondibour and Salkeld Screens in Carlisle Cathedral', *CW2*, Volume LVI (1957), pp. 112-12; Weston, *Carlisle Cathedral History*, p. 51.

242 Weston, *Carlisle Cathedral History*, p. 32; Hugh Vaux, 'Two Cumbrian Chantries, Hutton-in-the-Forest (Bramwra) and Edenhall: a response to plague and economic change', *CW3*, Volume 21 (2021), p. 106.

243 Cross, ed., *Dictionary of the Christian Church*, p. 262.

244 Cross, ed., *Dictionary of the Christian Church*, p. 263.

245 R. L. Storey, 'The Chantries of Cumberland and Westmorland. Part II', *CW2*, Volume LXII (1962), p. 152.

246 M.A. Clark, 'Richard Robinson, clerk, chantry priest of Brigham', *CW2*, Volume LXXXVIII (1988), pp. 98-9.

247 Susan E. James, 'Parr Memorials in Kendal Parish Church', *CW2*, Volume XCII (1992), pp. 99-103.

248 Nicolson and Burn, *The History and Antiquities*, II, p. 411; Bouch, *Prelates and People*, p. 190; Storey, 'Chantries of Cumberland and Westmorland', pp 152-3, 166, 169-70.

249 Helen M Jewell, '"The Bringing Up of Children in Good Learning and Manners": a survey of Secular Educational Provision in the North of Engand, c.1350-1550', *NH*, Volume XVIII (1982), p. 6.

250 Storey, 'Chantries of Cumberland and Westmorland', pp. 169-70.

251 In *The Stripping of the Altars*, p. 3, Eamon Duffy uses the term 'traditional religion' as a phrase that does 'justice to the shared and inherited character of the religious beliefs and practices of the people' and also 'to indicate the general character of a religious culture which was rooted in a repertoire of inherited beliefs and symbols while remaining capable of enormous flexibility and variety'.

252 M. A. Clark, 'Reformation in the Far North: Cumbria and the Church, 1500-1571', *NH*, Volume XXXII (1996), p.88

253 Summerson, *Medieval Carlisle*, II, p. 618.

254 David Williamson ed., *Brewer's British Royalty A Phrase and Fable Dictionary* (London: Cassell, 1996), p. 293.

255 Peter Biller, 'Lollards', in Vauchez *et al.* eds., *Encyclopedia of the Middle Ages*, II, pp. 861-2; S. H. Steinberg and I. H. Evans, eds., *Steinberg's Dictionary of British History* (2nd edn., London: Book Club Associates, 1974), p. 212; Bouch, *Prelates and People*, p.134.

256 Bouch, *Prelates and People*, p. 134.

257 McBrien, ed., *Encyclopedia of Catholicism*, p. 239; Duffy, *Stripping of the Altars*, p. 54.

258 Summerson, *Medieval Carlisle*, II, p. 618.

259 Summerson, *Medieval Carlisle*, II, p. 613.

260 Summerson, *Medieval Carlisle*, II, p. 618; W. Douglas Simpson, 'Brough-under-Stainmore: The Castle and the Church', *CW2*, Volume XLVI (1947), p. 282.

261 F. J. Field, 'The Carvings in the Entrance to Major MacIvor's Cell, Carlisle Castle', *CW2*, Volume XXXVII (1937), pp. 13-23.

262 G. A. Behrens, 'Conservation Work on the Cartmel Fell Figure of Christ', *CW2*, Volume LXXXII (1982), p. 124; Gambles, *The Story of the Lakeland Dales*, p. 88; Hyde and Pevsner, *Cumbria*, p. 273, attribute the foundation to Antony Knipe (d. 1500): in 1561 Antony Knipe testified that in 1506 his father William and others had been responsible for the erection of the chapel: Sam Taylor, *Cartmel People and Priory* (Photographs by Hilary Forrest, Kendal: Titus Wilson 1955), p. 141.

263 Hyde and Pevsner, *Cumbria*, p. 274; Thomas Davidson and J. Liddell Geddie, eds., *Chambers's Twentieth Century Dictionary of the English Language* ... (London and Edinburgh: W & R. Chambers, 1921), p. 993.

264 Jöckle, *Encyclopedia of Saints*, p. 29.

265 Hyde and Pevsner, *Cumbria*, p. 274.

266 J. C. Dickinson, *The Land of Cartmel A History* (Kendal: Titus Wilson, 1980), p. 86; Taylor, *Cartmel People and Priory*, p. 139.

267 Duffy, *Stripping of the Altars*, pp. 245, 243-48.

268 Duffy, *Stripping of the Altars*, pp. 355-7; C. Roy Hudleston, 'A Kendal will of 1522', *CW2*, Volume LVIII (1959), pp. 183-4.

269 Hudleston, 'A Kendal will', pp. 183-4.

270 M. A. Clark, 'Kendal: the Protestant exception', *CW2*, Volume XCV (1995), p. 138; Duffy, *Stripping of the Altars*, p. 369.

271 Hyde and Pevsner, *Cumbria*, p. 430; Michael Mullett, 'The Urban Reformation in North-West England', *North West Catholic History*, Volume XXXI (2004), p. 8.

272 Hyde and Pevsner, *Cumbria*, p. 232; Bulman, 'Gondibour and Salkeld screens', p. 120.

273 Hyde and Pevsner, *Cumbria*, p. 232; Salkeld, 'Lancelot Salkeld', p. 149.

274 Hyde and Pevsner, *Cumbria*, p. 232.

275 Bulman, 'Gondibour and Salkeld screens', p. 120; Duffy, *Stripping of the Altars*, p. 248.

276 Bulman, 'Gondibour and Salkeld screens', p. 117.

277 Duffy, *Stripping of the Altars*, ch. 11; Diarmaid MacCulloch, *Thomas*

Cromwell A Life (London: Allen Lane, 2018), pp. 414-15, 453, 460.

278 Michael A. Mullett, '"for the helthe of my Soul": the will of John Hoton of Penrith', *CW3*, Volume 19 (2019), p. 276.

279 Michael Mullett, *Historical Dictionary of the Reformation and Counter-Reformation* (Historical Dictionaries of Religions, Philosophies, and Movements Jon Woronoff, Series Editor, No 100., Lanham, MD, Toronto and Plymouth, 2010), p. 206.

280 Clark, 'Reformation in the Far North', p. 87; Bouch, *Prelates and People*, p. 183.

281 West, *Antiquities of Furness*, Appendix, No. X (4). Salley's comments contained a double affront on the king, not only on his headship of the Church but on his status as a 'secular knave' - a common layman.

282 Bouch, *Prelates and People*, p. 183.

283 Bouch, *Prelates and People*, p. 178.

284 Bouch, *Prelates and People*, p. 182.

285 Clark, 'Reformation in the Far North', p. 81; Bouch, *Prelates and People*, p. 182.

286 Wilson, 'Religious Houses', pp. 170, 160.

287 Anne C. Parkinson, *A History of Catholicism in the Furness Peninsula, 1127-1997* (Lancaster: University of Lancaster Centre for North-West Regional Studies, 1998), p. 13.

288 Michael A. Mullett, *A New History of Penrith Book II: Penrith under the Tudors* (Carlisle: Bookcase, 2017), pp. 27-8, 34; Susan M. Keeling, 'The Reformation in the Anglo-Scottish Border Counties', *NH*, Volume XV (1979), p.33 .

289 Mullett, *Penrith II*, pp. 28-9.

290 Mullett, *Historical Dictionary of the Reformation*, pp. 374-5; Mullett, *Penrith II*, p.33.

291 Clark, 'Reformation in the Far North', p. 82.

292 Wilson, 'Ecclesiastical History', p. 54.

293 Bouch, Jones and Brunskill, *Economic and Social History*, p. 58.

294 Wilson, 'Ecclesiastical History', p. 55.

295 Duffy, *Stripping of the Altars*, chs. 11, 12.

296 Mullett, *Historical Dictionary of the Reformation*, p. 174.

297 Mullett, *Historical Dictionary of the Reformation*, p. 33; W. R. Cooper, ed., *The New Testament Translated by William Tyndale* ... (Preface by David

Daniell, London: The British Library, 2000), p.v.

298 *Concise Dictionary of National Biography*, II, p. 32; Wilson, 'Ecclesiastical History', p. 58, n. 4; Williamson, *Brewer's Dictionary of British Royalty*, p. 69.

299 Susan James, 'The Devotional Writings of Queen Catherine Parr', *CW2*, Volume LXXXII (1982), p.136; Susan E. James, 'Queen Kateryn Parr', *CW2*, Volume LXXXVIII (1988), p. 113; Don Matzat, *Katherine Parr Opportunist, Queen, Reformer A Theological Perspective* (Stroud, Glos.: Amberley Publishing 2020, p. 14; Roger Bingham, *Kendal A Social History* (Milnthorpe, Cumbria: Cicerone Press, 1992), p. 392.

300 James, 'The Devotional Writings', p. 136; James, 'Queen Kateryn Parr', p. 113; Bouch, 'Churchwardens' Accounts of Great Salkeld', p. 134.

301 Parkinson, *Catholicism in the Furness Peninsula*, p. 19; Bouch, 'Churchwardens' Accounts of Great Salkeld', p. 134.

302 *The First and Second Prayer Books of King Edward the Sixth* (Everyman's Library NO 448, London and Toronto: J. M. Dent; New York: E. P. Dutton, 1927), pp. 4-5.

303 Matzat, *Katherine Parr*, p.16; M. A. Clark, 'Richard Robinson, chantry priest of Brigham', *CW2*, Volume LXXXVIII (1988), p 104.

304 Parkinson, *Catholicism in the Furness Peninsula*, p. 19; Bouch, 'Churchwardens' Accounts of Great Salkeld', p. 134.

305 Clark, 'Reformation in the Far North', p. 84; Kenneth Hylson-Smith, *The Churches in England from Elizabeth I to Elizabeth II Volume I: 1558-1688* (London: SCM Press, 1996), p. 33.

306 Bouch, *Prelates and People*, p. 194; Mullett, *Penrith II*, p. 38.

307 *Concise Dictionary of National Biography*, III, pp. 2231-2; Summerson, *Medieval Carlisle*, II, p. 635; Margaret Clark, 'Contrary Clerics: two Tudor bishops of Carlisle', *CW3*, Volume I, 2001), p. 69; Clark,'Reformation in the Far North', p. 85; Summerson, *Medieval Carlisle*, II, p. 639; Wilson, 'Ecclesiastical History', p. 59; Bouch, *Prelates and People*, p. 194. Because of Protestant acceptance of clerical marriage, married clergy were likely to have adopted Protestant faith, so that the 93 ejections of clerics in Essex (Bouch, *Prelates and People*, p. 194, n.), mostly for having married, is evidence for the strength of the Protestant religion in the south-eastern county, just as the low rate of dismissals on grounds of marriage offers proof of minimal clerical Protestantisation in the diocese of Carlisle.

308 Bouch, *Prelates and People*, p. 194. In the *Actes and Monuments of the Church* ('Foxe's Book of Martyrs', 1563) the Protestant martyrologist John Foxe (1516-87) recorded a Marian victim of Cumberland origins, Isabel,

the wife of John Foster of Fleet Street, London: she 'was born in Greystock, in the diocese of Carlisle' and was burned to death for heresy in 1556 (Bouch, *Prelates and People*, p. 194, n.).

309 Summerson, *Medieval Carlisle*, II, p. 635; Bouch, *Prelates and People*, p. 197.

310 Clark, 'Contrary Clerics', p. 76.

311 Bouch, *Prelates and People*, p. 200; Widdup, *Christianity in Cumbria*, p. 70; J. A. Hilton, 'The Cumbrian Catholics', *NH*, Volume XVI (1980), pp. 35, 43. Ellerton was subjected only to 'gentlemanly talks' in York and faced no further disciplinary action: Mullett, *Penrith II*, p. 43.

312 S. M. Keeling, 'The Reformation in the Anglo-Scottish Border Country', *NH*, Volume XV (1979), pp. 35-6

313 Keeling, 'Reformation in the Border Counties', p. 25; Mullett, *Dictionary of the Reformation*, p. 221; Bouch, *Prelates and People*, p. 201; John Todd and Mary Todd, 'Archbishop Grindal's birthplace: Cross Hill, St Bees, Cumbria', *CW2*, Volume XCIX (1999), p. 186.

314 Todd and Todd, 'Grindal's birthplace', p. 186; Keeling, 'Reformation in the Border Counties', p. 39. Best believed that JPs who were unfavourable to religious reform were efficient at their work as magistrates and should be continued in office: Clark, 'Reformation in the Far North', p. 86.

315 Mullett, *Penrith II*, pp. 22-3; Bouch, *Prelates and People*, p. 207, n.; Summerson, *Medieval Carlisle*, II, p. 645.

316 Henry Summerson, *'An Ancient Squires Family': The history of the Aglionbys c. 1130-2002* (Carlisle: Bookcase, 2007), p. 47: in 1571, however, the bishop awarded Aglionby a 21-year lease on a mill': Bouch, *Prelates and People*, p. 200; Keeling, 'Reformation in the Border Counties', p. 39.

317 Bouch, *Prelates and People*, p. 201.

318 Keeling, 'Reformation in the Border Counties', p. 39.

319 Bouch, *Prelates and People*, p. 201.

320 Bouch, *Prelates and People*, pp. 202, 200-1; Bouch, Jones and Brunskill, *Economic and Social History*, p. 23; Summerson, *Medieval Carlisle*, p. 645.

321 Hilton, 'The Cumbrian Catholics', pp. 43-4.

322 Bouch, *Prelates and People*, p. 205.

323 Mullett, *Penrith II*, pp. 78-89.

324 Dick White, '"Sizergh to be burnt within two days"', Sizergh Castle and the Gordon Riots', *CW3*, Volume VI, (2006), p. 103; Nicolson and Burn, *The History and Antiquities*, I, p. 100.

325 Mullett, *Penrith II*, p. 43-4, 66, 61, 62, 44. 45; Wilson, 'Ecclesiastical History', p. 82, n. 2;

326 Summerson, *Medieval Carlisle*, II, p. 645; Keeling, 'Reformation in the Border Counties', p. 36; Bouch, *Prelates and People*, p. 206.

327 Clark, 'Reformation in the Far North', p. 78; Mullett, 'Urban Reformation', p. 11.

328 Bouch, *Prelates and People*, p. 206.

329 Hilton, 'The Cumbrian Catholics', p. 44; Bouch, 'Churchwardens' Accounts of Great Salkeld', p. 138.

330 Michael A. Mullett, *Catholics in Britain and Ireland, 1558-1829* (Social History in Perspective General Editor: Jeremy Black, Basingstoke, Hants.: Macmillan Press, New York: St Martin's Press, 1998), pp. 1, 14, 15; Steinberg and Evans, eds., *Steinberg's Dictionary of British History*, p. 314; Wilson, 'Ecclesiastical History', p. 82.

331 Mullett, *Dictionary of the Reformation*, p. 221-2, 170; Patrick McGrath, *Papists and Puritans under Elizabeth I* (Blandford History Series, General Editor R. W. Harris, London: Blandford Press, 1967), pp. 149-53; Mullett, *Catholics in Britain and Ireland*, p. 15; Bouch, *Prelates and People*, p. 208.

332 Bouch, *Prelates and People*, p. 208; Wilson, 'Ecclesiastical History', p. 82.

333 Bouch, *Prelates and People*, p. 209.

334 Michael Mullett, *The Counter-Reformation and the Catholic Reformation in Early Modern Europe* (Lancaster Pamphlets General Editors Eric J. Evans and P. D. King, London and New York: Routledge 1995), *passim; idem*, *The Catholic Reformation* (London and New York: Routledge, 1999), *passim*; Widdup, *Christianity in Cumbria*, p.71; Bouch, Jones and Brunskill, *Economic and Social History*, p. 82.

335 Hilton, 'The Cumbrian Catholics', pp. 45, 47; Hudleston and Boumphrey, *Cumberland Families and Heraldry*, p. 271.

336 Hilton, 'The Cumbrian Catholics', p. 46.

337 Mullett, *Penrith II*, pp. 48-9; Wilson, 'Ecclesiastical History', p. 84.

338 William Jackson, 'The Curwens of Workington Hall, and Kindred Families', in Mrs Jackson, ed., William Jackson, *Papers and Pedigrees Mainly Relating to Cumberland and Westmorland* ... (Two Vols., Publications of the Cumberland and Westmorland Antiquarian and Archaeological Society, Extra Series, Vols. V and VI, London: Bemrose; Carlisle: Charles Thurnham, 1892), I, pp. 311-12; Hudleston and Boumphrey, *Cumberland Families and Heraldry*, p. 79.

339 Widdup, *The Story of Christianity*, p. 71; Hilton, 'The Cumbrian Catholics', p. 45; Wilson, 'Ecclesiastical History', p. 82; Mullett, *Dictionary of the Reformation*, p. 170.

340 Hilton, 'The Cumbrian Catholics', p. 44; Mullett, *Penrith II*, p. 44; Wilson 'Ecclesiastical History', pp. 82-3; Hylson-Smith, *The Churches in England*, p. 89; McGrath, *Papists and Puritans*, pp. 192-4.

341 *Concise Dictionary of National Biography*, II, pp, 2683, 1997.

342 Wilson, 'Ecclesiastical History', p. 83; Hilton, 'The Cumbrian Catholics', p. 47.

343 Wilson, *Ecclesiastical History*, p. 87; Godfrey Anstruther, O.P., *The Seminary Priests A Dictionary of the Secular Clergy of England and Wales 1558-1850 Vol I Elizabethan 1558-1603* (St Edmund's College, Ware, Ushaw College, Durham, nd. [c. 1968], p. 293.

344 Wilson, 'Ecclesiastical History', p. 87, n. 2.

345 Michael A. Mullett, '"This Irreligious Art of Liing": Strategies of Disguise in Post-Reformation English Catholicism', *The Journal of Historical Sociology*, Vol 20, Number 3 (September 2007), p. 334.

346 Mullett, '"This Irreligious Art of Liing"', p. 335.

347 Mullett, '"This Irreligious Art of Liing"', p. 335.

348 Wilson, 'Ecclesiastical History', p. 87, n. 3.

349 Anstruther, *Seminary Priests I*, pp. 106-7; Wilson, 'Ecclesiastical History', p. 87, n. 3 .

350 Wilson, 'Ecclesiastical History', pp. 87-8, n. 3.

351 Wilson, 'Ecclesiastical History', pp. 85-6.

352 Wilson, 'Ecclesiastical History', p. 86.

353 R. T. Spence, 'The Pacification of the Cumberland Borders, 1593-1628', *NH*, Volume XIII (1977), pp. 84-5, 147.

354 Bouch, *Prelates and People*, p. 217; Mullett, *Penrith II*, pp. 108-125; Bouch, Jones and Brunskill, *Economic and Social History*, p. 80.

355 Edward M. Wilson, 'Richard Leake's plague sermons, 1599', *CW2*, Volume LXXV (1975), pp. 155-6, 163.

356 Wilson, 'Richard Leake's plague sermons', p. 162.

357 Wilson, 'Richard Leake's plague sermons', p. 163; Bouch, *Prelates and People*, pp. 215-16; *The Compact Edition of the Oxford English Dictionary Reproduced Micrographically ... Volume II P-Z ...* (London: Book Club Associates, 1979), p. 3664; David Uttley, *The Anatomy of the Helm Wind The Scourge of the Cumbrian East Fellside* (Carlisle: Bookcase, 1998), p. 49.

358 *The Book of Common Prayer and Administration of the Sacraments ... of the ... Church of England ...* (Cambridge: Cambridge University Press, nd.), pp. 62, 616, 624.

359 Hugh Vaux, '"and all his Saintes and Electe": the will and declaration of John Vaux', *CW3*, Volume 20 (2020), p. 295.

360 Bingham, *Kendal A Social History*, p. 398; T.G. Fahy, 'The Philipson family: Part II. Philipson of Crook Hall', *CW2*, Volume LXXII (1972), p. 270.

361 Clark, 'Kendal: The Protestant exception', p. 149; T. G. Fahy, 'The Philipson family: Part II. Philipson of Crook Hall, *CW2*, Volume LXXIII (1973), pp. 279-80.

362 C. Roy Hudleston, 'Canon Winder Hall and its owners', *CW2*, Volume LXXXVII (1987), p. 161.

363 Thompson, 'Westmorland church bells', pp. 57-8.

364 Vaux, '" and all his Saintes and Electe"', p. 295; Boumphrey and Hudleston, *Cumberland Families and Heraldry*, p. 350.

365 Michael Mullett, *John Bunyan in Context* (Studies in Protestant Nonconformity Edited by Alan P. F. Sell (Keele, Staffs:. Keele University Press, 1996), pp.35, 38, 67; Reardon, *Religious Thought in the Reformation*, p. 195.

366 Mullett, *John Bunyan*, pp. 35, 67; Walsh, ed., *Dictionary of Christian Biography*, pp. 695, 707-8.

367 Duffy, *Stripping of the Altars*, pp. 237, 236.

368 Vaux, '"and all his Saintes and Electe"', p. 295.

369 McBrien, ed., *Encyclopedia of Catholicism*, p. 796; Duffy, *Stripping of the Altars*. p. 161; Cross, *Dictionary of the Christian Church*, p. 23; Vaux, '"and all his Saintes and Elect"', p. 295 .

370 *The Daily Missal and Liturgical Manual ... Compiled from the Missale Romanum ...* (Leeds: Laverty & Sons, 1954), p. 939; Mullett, *The Catholic Reformation*, p. 67.

371 Michael A. Mullett, *John Calvin* (Routledge Historical Biographies Series Editor: Robert Pearce, London and New York: Routledge, 2011), pp. 101-106; McBrien, ed., *Encyclopedia of Catholicsm*, p. 189.

372 Peter Burke, 'How to be a Counter-Reformation Saint', in Kaspar von Greyerz, ed., *Religion and Society in Early Modern Europe 1500-1800* (London: Routledge, 1984), pp. 45-55.

373 Vaux, '"and all his Saintes and Electe"', p. 290.

374 Spence, 'The Pacification of the Cumberland Borders', p. 147.

375 Hyde and Pevsner, *Cumbria*, p. 118; Spence, *The Pacification of the Cumberland Borders*, p. 148: there is some disagreement over the chronology of this restoration, Spence writing that the 'work began in 1602' [before the king's English accession] and Hyde and Pevsner recording that the monarch was moved by the dilapidation of Arthuret church in 1607 and that work on it was 'begun in 1609', with a new, nine-sided baptismal font installed in that year. Either way, a fine new church replaced the ruin as a result of the king's intervention.

376 Spence, 'The Pacification of the Cumberland border', p. 149; Hyde and Pevsner, *Cumbria*, p. 453.

377 Widdup, *Christianity in Cumbria*, p. 73; Spence, 'The Pacification of the Cumberland Borders', p.150.

378 Spence, 'The Pacification of the Cumberland Borders', pp. 150, 148; Bouch, *Prelates and People*, p. 245.

379 Bouch, *Prelates and People*, pp. 244-5.

380 Joseph B. Gavin, SJ, 'Handley v. Neubie alias Shields: A marriage at Farlam, Cumberland in 1605', *CW2*, Volume LXX (1970), pp. 263-5.

381 Mullett, *Penrith II*, p. 48; Bouch, *Prelates and People*, pp. 245-6.

382 Spence, 'The Pacification of the Cumberland Borders', p.148.

383 C. M. L. Bouch, 'The Visitation Articles of Bishop Robinson, 1612', *CW2*, Volume XLIX (1950), pp. 148-65.

384 Bouch, 'The Visitation Articles', p. 149.

385 Bouch, 'The Visitation Articles', p. 149. The Articles were published before Prince Henry's death in November 1612: Williamson, *British Royalty*, p. 205.

386 James Sharpe, *Remember, Remember A Cultural History of Guy Fawkes Day* (Cambridge, MA: Harvard University Press, 2005), p. 79.

387 Bouch, 'The Visitation Articles', p. 151.

388 Bouch, 'The Visitation Articles, p. 152.

389 Bouch, 'The Visitation Articles', pp. 150, 151-2.

390 Bouch, 'The Visitation Articles', p. 153.

391 Mullett, *John Bunyan in Context*, pp. 18, 212-13. In the cultural civil war over how Sunday should be spent, traditionalists found an ally in James I, whose Declaration of Sports of 1618 (later reissued by Charles) I condemned the suppression of 'honest mirth … exercise' and defended dancing and various sports 'or any such harmless recreation': Mullett, *John*

Bunyan in Context, pp. 18-19.

392 Bouch, 'The Visitation Articles', pp. 153-4.

393 Bouch, *Prelates and People*, p. 216; Gambles, *The Story of the Lakeland Dales*, p. 95.

394 Angus J. L. Winchester, 'Personal Names and Local Identities in Early Modern Cumbria', *CW3*, Volume XI (2011), pp. 41, 43-4.

395 Clark, 'Kendal: The Protestant exception', p. 145; Bingham, *Kendal A Social History*, pp. 256, 416; Andrew White, *A History of Kendal* (np.: Carnegie Publishing, 2013), p. 222; Joe Scott, 'The Kendal Tenant Right Dispute 1619-26', *CW2* Volume XCVIII (1998), p. 177; Anne C. Parkinson, 'Religious Drama in Kendal The Corpus Christi Play in the Reign of James I', *Recusant History*, 25 (October 2001), pp. 604-612.

396 Clark, 'Kendal: The Protestant exception', p. 145

397 Clark, 'Kendal: The Protestant exception', pp. 145, 146; www.visitoruk.com/Kendal/kirkland – c592-V27161.html.

398 Bouch, *Prelates and People*, p. 222.

399 Mullett, 'The Urban Reformation', p. 12; Edward M. Wilson,'Ralph Tyrer, B.D., Vicar of Kendal, 1592-1627', *CW2*, Volume LXXVIII (1978), p. 78.

400 Mullett, 'Urban Reformation', p. 12.

401 Mullett, 'Urban Reformation', p. 12.

402 Bouch, *Prelates and People*, pp. 221, 222.

403 Cross, ed., *Dictionary of the Christian Church*, p. 991; Diarmaid MacCulloch, *Reformation Europe's House Divided 1490-1700* (London: Allen Lane, 2003), p. 590.

404 Bouch, *Prelates and People*, pp. 221-2.

405 Clark, 'Kendal: The Protestant exception', p. 149.

406 Weston, *Carlisle Cathedral History*, pp. 142, 144.

407 Mullett, *Historical Dictionary of the Reformation and Counter-Reformation*, p. 241; Walsh, ed., *Dictionary of Christian Biography*, p. 620; John Warren, *Elizabeth I: Religion and Foreign Affairs* (Access to History General Editor: Keith Randell, London: Hodder & Stoughton p'back, 1993), pp. 58-9.

408 MacCulloch, *Reformation*, pp. 511, 594.

409 MacCulloch, *Reformation*, p. 511.

410 Cross, ed., *Dictionary of the Christian Church*, p.40; Kenneth Hylson-Smith, *The Churches in England from Elizabeth I to Elizabeth II Volume I:*

1558-1688 (London: SCM Press, 1996), pp. 147-156, quotations at pp. 153, 149.

411 https://en.wikipedia.org/wikiFrancis_White_ (bishop), 1/3, 2/3; Hylson-Smith, *The Churches in England I*, pp. 136, 146; Michael A. Mullett, *Carlisle in Revolution and Restoration, c. 1648-1688* (Kendal: Cumberland and Westmorland Antiquarian and Archaeological Society General Editor Colin Richards, Tract Series, Volume 30 (2012), pp. 52, 56.

412 Bouch, 'The Visitation Articles', pp. 149-55; Bouch, *Prelates and People*, p. 255.

413 Bouch, *Prelates and People*, p. 255.

414 Cross, ed., *Dictionary of the Christian Church*, p. 901; Bouch, *Prelates and People*, pp. 255, 256.

415 Bouch, *Prelates and People*, p. 256; MacCulloch, *Reformation*, p. 594.

416 Ian Green, 'Anglicanism in Stuart and Hanoverian England', in Sheridan Gilley and W. J. Sheils, eds., *A History of Religion in Britain Practice and Belief from Pre-Roman Times to the Present* (Oxford, and Cambridge, MA: Blackwell, 1994), p. 174.

417 Bouch, *Prelates and People*, p. 259; Nicolson and Burn, *The History and Antiquities*, II, p. 286; https://www.biblicalcyclopedia.comP/potter-barnabas.html, 1/2; *Concise Dictionary of National Biography*, III, p. 2428.

418 https://www.biblicalcyclopedia.comP/potter-barnabas.html, 1/2

419 Bouch, *Prelates and People*, pp. 257-8.

420 MacCulloch, *Reformation*, p. 511; Green, 'Anglicanism', p. 169.

421 Bouch, *Prelates and People*, p. 259.

422 Bouch, *Prelates and People*, p. 259; Weston, *Carlisle Cathedral History*, p. 19.

423 D. R. Perriam, 'The Demolition of the Priory of St Mary, Carlisle', *CW2*, Volume LXXXVII (1987), pp. 128-9.

424 Bouch, *Prelates and People*, p. 259; Weston, *Carlisle Cathedral History*, p. 19.

425 Perriam, 'The Demolition of the Priory', p. 130.

426 Mullett, *Carlisle in Revolution and Restoration*, pp. 15-16; Weston, *Carlisle Cathedral History*, p. 19; Perriam,'The Demolition of the Priory', p. 130; Hyde and Pevsner, *Cumbria*, p. 224.

427 Perriam, 'The Demolition of the Priory', pp. 132, 133, 130.

428 Nicolson and Burn,*The History and Antiquities*, II, p. 248.

429 Perriam, 'The Demolition of the Priory', p. 130.

430 Weston, *Carlisle Cathedral History*, p. 19; Mullett, *Carlisle in Revolution and Restoration*, p.8.

431 Weston, *Carlisle Cathedral History*, p. 19; Mullett, *Carlisle in Revolution and Restoration*, p. 21.

432 Michael A. Mullett, *A New History of Penrith Book III Penrith in the Stuart Century, 1603-1714* (Carlisle: Bookcase, 2018), p. 41.

433 MacCulloch, *Reformation*, p. 675.

434 Weston, *Carlisle Cathedral History*, p. 19.

435 Mullett, *Carlisle in Revolution and Restoration*, pp. 22, 31; Weston, *Carlisle Cathedral History*, p. 19.

436 Francis Nicholson and Ernest Axon, *The Older Nonconformity in Kendal A history of the Unitarian Chapel in the Market Place* ...(Kendal: Titus Wilson, 1915) p. 6.

437 Nicholson and Axon, *The Older Nonconformity*, pp. 12-13.

438 Bouch, *Prelates and People*, p. 266; B. Nightingale, *The Ejected of 1662 in Cumberland & Westmorland Their Predecessors and Successors* (Two Volumes, Publications of the University of Manchester Historical Series No. XII, Manchester: Manchester University Press, 1911), I, p.178; Nicholson and Axon, *The Older Nonconformity*, pp. 8, 15, 16.

439 Nicholson and Axon, *The Older Nonconformity*, p. 19, fn., 19-20.

440 Nicholson and Axon, *The Older Nonconformity*, p. 17.

441 Nicholson and Axon, *The Older Nonconformity*, p. 18.

442 Nightingale, *The Ejected of 1662*, II, p. 879; G. F. Trevallyn Jones, *Saw-Pit Wharton The Political Career from 1640 to 1691 of Philip, fourth Lord Wharton* (Stuart Historical Studies, Sydney: Sydney University Press, 1967), pp. 86, 106.

443 Nicholson and Axon, *The Older Nonconformity*, p. 19, fn., 19-20.

444 Mullett, *Penrith III*, pp. 34, 35.

445 Mullett, *Penrith III*, p. 36.

446 Mullett, *Penrith III*, pp. 36-7.

447 Austin Woolrych, *Britain in Revolution 1625-1660* (Oxford: Oxford University Press, 2002), pp. 271-2.

448 Woolrych, *Britain in Revolution*, pp. 272, 184; Cross, ed., *Dictionary of the Christian Church*, pp. 636-7.

449 Hilton, 'The Cumbrian Catholics', p. 48.

450 John Bossy, *The English Catholic Community 1570-1850* (London:

Darton, Longman and Todd, 1975), p. 96.

451 Hilton, 'The Cumbrian Catholics', p. 58.

452 Hilton 'The Cumbrian Catholics', pp. 49-50.

453 Lance Thwaytes, 'Catholics of the Seventeenth Century Barony of Kendal', in Marie B. Rowlands, ed., *English Catholics of Parish and Town 1558-1778 A Joint Research Project of the Catholic Record Society and Wolverhampton University* (London: Catholic Record Society, 1999), pp. 182-3.

454 Parkinson, *Catholicism in the Furness Peninsula*, p. 30. There is no record in the published collection of biographies of English Catholic priests of the 16th to 19th centuries that the Manor was served by the priest John Hudleston (or Huddleston 1608-98), second son of Joseph Hudleston of Farington Hall. It was this John Hudleston who protected Charles II after his defeat by Cromwell at Worcester in 1651 and who received Charles into the Catholic Church at the king's death. Hudleston had early Cumberland connections, having received schooling at Hutton John and Blencow: Godfrey Anstruther, O.P., *The Seminary Priests A Dictionary of the Secular Clergy of England and Wales 1558-1850 II Early Stuarts 1603-1659* (Great Wakering, Essex: Mayhew-McCrimmon, 1975), p. 163; Hudleston and Boumphrey, *Cumberland Families and Heraldry*, p. 172.

455 Parkinson, *Catholics in the Furness Peninsula*, p. 31.

456 Mullett, *Catholics in Britain and Ireland*, p. 26.

457 C. B. Phillips, 'The Royalist North the Cumberland and Westmorland Gentry, 1642-1660', *NH*, Volume XIV (1978), p. 169.

458 Phillips, 'The Royalist North' pp. 174-5; P.R. Newman, 'Catholic Royalists of Northern England', *NH*, Volume XV (1979), p. 92.

459 Mullett, *Catholics in Britain and Ireland*, p. 73.

460 Newman, 'Catholic Royalists, pp. 91, 92; Hudleston and Boumphrey, *Cumberland Families and Heraldry*, pp. 171, 172; Phillips, 'The Royalist North', p. 175, n. 18.

461 Phillips, 'The Royalist North', p. 175; Woolrych, *Britain in Revolution*, p. 453.

462 John Morrill, 'God's Englishman', 'The Tablet', 13 May 2023, pp. 4-5; Mullett, *Catholics in Britain and Ireland*, p. 75.

463 F. B. Swift, 'The old church of Allhallows', *CW2*, Volume LXXV (1975), p. 120.

464 Michael A. Mullett, *Patronage, Power and Politics in Appleby in the Era of Lady Anne Clifford, 1649-1689* (Kendal: Cumberland and Westmorland

Antiquarian and Archaeological Society, General Editor Colin Richards, Tract Series Vol. 25, 2015), p. 15; R. T. Spence, 'Lady Anne Clifford, Countess of Dorset, Pembroke and Montgomery (1590-1676): a reappraisal', *NH*, Volume XV (1979), p. 45.

465 George C. Williamson, *Lady Anne Clifford Countess of Dorset, Pembroke & Montgomery 1590-1676 Her Life, Letters and Work* ... (Kendal: Titus Wilson, 1922), p. 465, Appendix V; Richard T. Spence, *Lady Anne Clifford Countess of Pembroke, Dorset and Montgomery (1590-1676)* (Stroud, Glos.: Sutton Publishing, 1997), p. 213.

466 Williamson, *Lady Anne Clifford*, pp. 188, 199; *The Book of Common Prayer*, p.54; https://historicengland. org.uk/listing/what-is-designation/heritage-highlights/did-oliver-cromwell-really-ban-christmas/#:~:text=The rejection of Chri ...; D. J. H. Clifford, ed., *The Diaries of Lady Anne Clifford* (Stroud, Glos.: Alan Sutton Publishing p'back, 1990), p. 112.

467 Martin Holmes, *Proud Northern Lady Lady Anne Clifford 1590-1676* (Chichester, Sussex: Phillimore, 1984), p. 161.

468 Bouch, *Prelates and People*, p. 271. Edward Rainbow (or Rainbowe, 1608-84), bishop of Carlisle, 1664-84, was the preacher at Lady Anne's funeral.

469 Wilson, 'Ecclesiastical History', p. 94, n. 1.

470 Scott Sowerby and Noah McCormack, eds., *The Memoirs of Sir Daniel Fleming of Rydal Hall from 1633 to 1688* (Kendal: Cumberland and Westmorland Antiquarian and Archaeological Society, General Editor Colin Richards, Record Series Volume 23, 2021), pp. xv, 137.

471 Nicholson and Axon, *The Older Nonconformity*, p. 23.

472 *Chambers's Encyclopedia*, Volume XI, p. 180; Michael Mullett, *Sources for the History of English Nonconformity 1660-1830* (London: British Records Association Archives for the User no.8, 1991), p. 45; Cross, ed., *Dictionary of the Christian Church*, p. 329; *Concise Dictionary of National Biography*, I, p.903.

473 Michael A. Mullett, *Politics and Religion in Restoration Cockermouth* (Kendal: Cumberland and Westmorland Antiquarian and Archaeological Society, General Editor Colin Richards Tract Series Vol XXIV, 2013), pp.5-6; Nicholson and Axon, *The Older Nonconformity in Kendal*, pp. 106-7.

474 Wilson 'Ecclesiastical History', p. 94; Nightingale, *The Ejected of 1662*, I, pp. 88-9.

475 Nicholson and Axon, *The Older Nonconformity*, p. 33; Mullett, *Sources for English Nonconformity*, p. 93.

476 John Burgess, 'The Quakers, the Brethren and the Religious Census in Cumbria', *CW2*, Volume LXXX (1980), p. 103.

477 Peter Lucas, *The Rise of the Quakers Revaluing the Place of Preston Patrick in the Early Movement* (Kirkby Lonsdale, Cumbria: PJYL Publishing, 2017), pp. vii, 2.

478 Michael Mullett, 'Introduction: George Fox and the Society of Friends', in Michael Mullett, ed., *New Light on George Fox (1624-1691) A Collection of Essays...*(York: The Ebor Press, nd.), pp. 2-3; Nightingale, *The Ejected of 1662*, I, p. 123; *Concise Dictionary of National Biography*, II, p. 1502; I, p. 409; I, p. 448; III, pp. 3203-4.

479 Mullett, *Politics and Religion in Cockermouth*, p. 7.

480 Nightingale, *The Ejected of 1662*, II, p. 1077 and n. 1; *Concise Dictionary of National Biography*, III, P. 2151; Hylson-Smith, *The Churches in England*, I, pp. 221-2.

481 Nicholson and Axon, *The Older Nonconformity*, p. 33.

482 Bouch, *Prelates and People*, p. 267.

483 Bouch, *Prelates and People*, p. 267; *Concise Dictionary of National Biography*, I, p. 981; Hyde and Pevsner, *Cumbria*, p. 630; Hylson-Smith, *The Churches in England*, I, p. 220; Walsh, ed., *Dictionary of Christian Biography*, p. 458.

484 Nightingale, *The Ejected of 1662*, I, pp. 749-51.

485 Nightingale, *The Ejected of 1662*, I, p. 750.

486 Bouch, *Prelates and People*, p. 267; Mullett, *Carlisle in Revolution and Restoration*, p. 20.

487 Mullett, *Carlisle in Revolution and Restoration*, pp. 18, 19, 21.

488 Richard G. Bailey, 'The Making and Unmaking of a God: New Light on George Fox and Early Quakerism', in Mullett, ed., *New Light on George Fox*, p. 122, n. 6.

489 Woolrych, *Britain in Revolution*, p. 453; Bailey, 'The Making and Unmaking of a God', pp. 121-2, n. 6; David M. Butler, *The Quaker Meeting Houses of Britain ...* (2 vols., London: Friends Historical Society, 1999), I, p. 84.

490 Butler, *Quaker Meeting Houses of Britain*, I, pp. 83-4; Nightingale, *The Ejected of 1662*, I, p. 122.

491 Nightingale, *The Ejected of 1662*, I, pp. 98-9.

492 Nightingale, *The Ejected of 1662*, I, p. 122; Bouch, *Prelates and People*, p. 268.

493 Bouch, *Prelates and People*, p. 268.

494 Hylson-Smith, *The Churches in England*, I, pp. 240-1.

495 Hylson-Smith, *The Churches in England*, I, p. 240.

496 William Parson and William White, *A History, Directory, and Gazetteer, of Cumberland and Westmorland with that part of the Lake District in Lancashire, forming the Lordship of Furness and Cartmel* (Leeds and Newcastle: Edward Baines, 1829, Republished Beckermet, Cumbria: Michael Moon, 1976), p. 110; Robinson, 'Notes on Brampton Old Church', p. 75.

497 Mullett, *Politics and Religion in Restoration Cockermouth*, pp. 7, 5, 18-19, 21.

498 Mullett, *Carlisle in Revolution and Restoration*, pp. 18-19.

499 Bouch, *Prelates and People*, p. 269; Wilson, 'Ecclesiastical History', p. 96; Mullett, *Carlisle in Revolution and Restoration*, pp. 49-51.

500 C. B. Phillips, 'The Corporation of Kendal under Charles II', *NH*, Volume XXXI (1995), p. 163; Mullett, *Carlisle in Revolution and Restoration*, pp.33-3; Clark Stuart Colman, 'Sir Philip Musgrave and the Re-Establishment of the "Old Regime" in Cumberland and Westmorland *c*. 1660-1664: Local Loyalty and National Influence', *NH*, Volume XLVII (2010), pp. 247-70.

501 Antonia Fraser, *King Charles II* (Two volumes, London: Phoenix p'back, 1993), I, p. 279; Mullett, *Carlisle in Revolution and Restoration*, p. 36.

502 Michael A. Mullett, *Patronage, Power and Politics in Appleby in the Era of Lady Anne Clifford, 1649-1689* (Kendal: Cumberland and Westmorland Antiquarian and Archaeological Society, General Editor Colin Richards, Tract Series 25, 2015), pp. 38, 37.

503 Peter D. Clarke, 'The Sectarian "Threat" and its impact in Restoration Cumbria', *CW2*, Volume LXXXVIII (1988), pp. 160-175; Mullett, *Carlisle in Revolution and Restoration*, p. 36.

504 T. G.Fahy, 'The Philipson Family: Part II. Philipson of Crook Hall', *CW2*, Volume LXXIII (1973), pp. 242-3.

505 Carl Stephenson and Frederick George Marcham, eds. and transs., *Sources of English Constitutional History A Selection of Documents from A.D. 600 to the Present* (Harper's Historical Series, ed. Guy Stanton Ford, New York and Evanston: Harper & Row, 1937), pp. 553-4.

506 Mullett, *Politics and Religion in Restoration Cockermouth*, pp. 17-18, 26.

507 Mullett, *Politics and Religion in Restoration Cockermouth*, pp. 23, 24, 20.

508 Mullett, *Politics and Religion in Cockermouth*, pp. 27, 28; Hylson-Smith, *The Churches in England*, I p. 254; Mullett, *Carlisle in Revolution and Restoration*, p. 40; Mullett, *Penrith III*, 52; Wilson,'Ecclesiastical History', p. 99.

509 Mullett, *Penrith III*, pp. 52-3.

510 Mullett, *Carlisle in Revolution and Restoration*, pp. 50, 19; Mullett, *Penrith III*, p. 79.

511 Mullett, *Politics and Religion in Restoration in Cockermouth*, p. 27.

512 Mullett, *Politics and Religion in Cockermouth*, pp. 27, 28; Hylson-Smith, *The Churches in England*, I p. 254; Mullett, *Carlisle in Revolution and Restoration*, p. 40; Mullett, *Penrith III*, 52; Wilson,'Ecclesiastical History', p. 99.

513 Stephenson and Marcham, eds. and transs, *Sources of English Constitutional History*, pp. 560, 561.

514 Michael Mullett, *James II and English Politics, 1678- 1688* (Lancaster Pamphlets, General editors Eric J. Evans and P.D. King, London and New York: Routledge 1994), pp. 3-4; Wilson, 'Ecclesiastical History', p. 99; Hylson-Smith, *The Churches in England*, I, pp. 244-5.

515 Hilton, 'The Cumbrian Catholics', p.51; Nicolson and Burn, *The History and Antiquities*, I, p. 102; Wilson, 'Ecclesiastical History', p. 99.

516 Jackson, 'Curwens of Workington Hall', p. 315.

517 Hylson-Smith, *The Churches in England*, I, p. 247; Mullett, *Carlisle in Revolution and Restoration*, pp. 120, 79-82.

518 Mullett, *Politics and Religion in Restoration Cockermouth*, pp. 50, 49.

519 Sowerby and McCormack, eds., *Memoirs of Sir Daniel Fleming*, p. 310; Scott Sowerby, *Making Toleration The Repealers and the Glorious Revolution* (Cambridge, MA, and Cambridge: Harvard University Press, 2013), pp. 6, 12, 24, 25, 27, 35, 36, 41,58, 62, 65,77, 82, 89, 125, 199, 202, 214, 226, 257.

520 Mullett, *Politics and Religion in Cockermouth*, pp. 62-3; Butler, *Quaker Meeting Houses of Britain*, II, p. 654; Hyde and Pevsner, *Cumbria*, p. 400; Bingham, *Kendal A Social History*, p. 75; Michael Mullett, *Radical Religious Movements in Early Modern Europe* (Early Modern Europe Today Series Editor J.H. Shennan, London George Allen & Unwin, 1980), p. 134.

521 J. A. Hilton, ed., *Bishop Leyburne's Confirmation Register of 1687* (Wigan: North West Catholic History Society, 1997); Pers. Comm. Anthony Cousins.

522 Mullett, *Penrith III*, pp. 85-94.

523 Mullett, *Carlisle in Revolution and Restoration*, pp. 143, 146; Hilton, 'The Cumbrian Catholics', p. 51.

524 Bouch, *Prelates and People*, p. 236.

Index

Aachen, 115
Abbey Town, 25
Aberdeen, 121
Acorn Bank, 68
Act against Jesuits… , 163
Act for the Better Propagating … the Gospel .., 209
Act of Supremacy, 136, 149
  Oath of, 151-2
Acts of Uniformity, 1559, 149, 158, 184
Act of Uniformity, 1662, 231, 232, 236
Act of Union, 245
Adam , parson, 38
Addingham, 27, 231
Adelweld, prior of Nostell, 40
Aidan of Lindisfarne, 105, 177, 178
Ainstable, 245
Alan, lord of Allerdale, 38, 46
Aldingham, 23
Aldrich (Aldridge), Bishop Robert, 145, 148
Alexander Severus, 17
Allerdale, 57
Allhallows, 216
Allom, Thomas, 123
Alston, 8, 41
  Moor, 232

Altenbecken, Westphalia, 130
Ambleside (Galava), 19
Ambrose, Bishop of Milan, 100
Amiens, 50
Andrew, Apostle, 112
Andrew, Richard, 132
Anglicans, 206-7, 210, 216-220, 230-1, 232 233, 234, 235, 241, 244
Aglionby, Bernard, 147
  John, 151
Agnes, spouse, 61
Anne, Queen, 184
Anthony of Padua, 188
Antony of Egypt, 96, 98, 100, 103-105, 130, 188
Appleby, 18, 26, 37, 45, 55, 69, 71, 80, 81, 122, 123, 124, 132, 161, 167, 206, 217-218, 224, 233, 234
Appleby, Bishop Thomas, 76
Archer, Richard, 206
Arezzo, 35
Arles, Council of, 23
Armathwaite, 49, 74
Arminians, 194
Arnside, 27
Arthur, King, 66
Arthuret, 179-180
Asby, 159
Aske, Robert, 139

Askham, 161, 206, 231
Aspatria, 25, 26, 27, 34
Assheton, Nicholas, 147
Athanasius of Alexandria, 103
Atkinson, Captain Robert, 234
Audland, John, 222,223
Augustine of Hippo, 96-103, 104
Augustinian Canons, 38, 39-40, 42, 43, 49, 66-7, 95, 98, 119-120, 127
Augustinian (Austin) Friars, 69, 72-3, 142
Aurelia Aureliana, 19
Austria, 18, 117
Avignon, 70

Baden-Württemberg, 130
Baldwin, Roger, 209-210, 237
Balliol, John, 55
Bampton, 43
Bannockburn, battle, 77
Baptists, 227-8
Bardseys, family of, 213
Barnard Castle, 124
Barnes, Bishop Richard, 151,155-7, 159, 160, 163
Barnes, June, 91-2
Barrow-in-Furness, 46, 165
Bartholomew, Apostle, 116
Barton, 37, 231
'Basil', Bishop of Lindisfarne, 107
Bassenthwaite, 57

Beaufort, Lady Margaret, 135
Beaulieu, Abbot Hugh, 50, 51
Beaumont, 150
Becket, Thomas, 81, 122, 123
Beckermet, 27, 34, 56, 81
Bede, St, 105
Beetham, 27
Belatucadrus, 21
Belgium, 117
Bellingham, Sir Roger, 133
Benedict of Nursia, 46, 95
  Rule of, 59, 05
Benedict XII, Pope, 70
Benedictines, 38, 45, 47-9, 61, 64, 86, 88, 211
Benson, George, 232
Bernard, Archbishop of Ragusa, 50-1
Bernardino of Siena, 83
Best, Bishop John, 149-150, 151-3, 155
Bewcastle, 27, 29, 30, 33, 34, 162, 179, 181
  Fort, 18
Bewly, Thomas, 228
Birdoswald, 17, 18
Black Death, the, 70, 77
Blasphemy Act, 288
Blois, Stephen of, count of Mortain, 45-6, 61
Bolingbroke, Henry, duke of Hereford, 87-8
Bollandists, 177, 178

284

Bolton, 157
Book of Common Prayer, 7, 146-7, 149, 184, 185, 197-8, 210, 216, 217, 218, 219, 230, 231
Bootle, 48, 225
Bosch (van Aken), Hieronymus, 103
Bost (Boste), Andrew, 163
  Janet, 162
  John, 162-3
  Nicholas, 155
Bouch, Canon, 127-8, 219
Bough, Sam, 79
Bowes, 22
Bowness-on-Solway, 33, 73, 80, 231
Boyvill, William de, 54
Brampton, 19, 24, 25, 42, 78, 231
Branthwaite, 239
Brathwaite, Richard, 190
Breda, Declaration of, 233, 234, 238
Bricquessart, Randolp de (le Meschin), 38, 45
Bridekirk, 27, 36, 148, 231, 232
Briggs, Robert of Cowmire Hall, 129
Brigham, 27, 122, 128, 143, 221, 226
Bristol, 127, 147
Bromfield, 25, 26, 27, 38, 143
Brookland, 92
Brough-under-Stainmore, 22, 77, 123, 124, 129, 137, 141, 161, 206
Brougham (Brocavum), 16, 21, 24, 159
Broughton, John, 138
Brown, Henry, 150
Browne, Mabell, 170
Brueghel, Jan, the Elder, 115
Brunskill, John, 124
Brussels, 116
Buchanan, George, 207
Buck, Nathaniel, 44, 47, 48, 56, 67
  Samuel, 44, 47, 48, 56, 67
Bunyan, John, 174-5
Burgh-by-Sands, 55, 73, 74
Burgkmair, Hans, 118
Burgundy, 46
Burnand, Nathaniel, 231
Burneside, 180
Burrough, Edward, 223
Burton-in-Kendal, 27, 206
Byland, 47
Calamy, Edmund, 231
Caldbeck, 25, 54, 226, 228
Calder Abbey, 46-7, 56, 60
Calvin, John, 115, 171, 173, 174, 177, 194, 220
Cambridge, 127, 147, 190, 191, 194
Camm, John, 23
Camsgil, 223
Canon Winder, 173
Canterbury, 92, 194

285

Capella (de la Chapelle), John de, 71, 121
Carlatton, 42
Carleton, 155
Carlisle, 6, 14, 16, 17, 18, 19, 20, 21, 22, 23, 25, 26, 27, 34, 36, 37, 38, 42, 45, 46, 49, 51, 52-4, 55, 67, 69-70, 75, 82, 86, 91, 92, 112, 120, 128-9, 132, 143, 150, 155, 157, 160, 163, 164, 167, 168, 198, 201, 204 ,210, 219, 226, 227, 228-9, 231, 232, 233, 235, 237, 238 ,244, 245
Castle, 129
Cathedral ,6 ,41, 49, 50, 52, 76-7, 84-119-121, 122, 151, 199-203, 232-3
Dean and Chapter, 54, 201
Deanery, 73, 237
Diocese, 39-41, 51, 68, 143-4, 149, 161, 162, 166, 222, 240
Old, 17, 19
Priory, 39-40, 42, 51
Treaty of, 167
Carmelites, 69, 71
Carthusians, 133, 175
Cartmel, 26, 41, 43, 165
Fell Chapel, 130-131, 178
Priory, 44, 55, 132
Carvetii, 17, 21
Castlerigg, 9, 10, 11
Castlesteads, 18, 19
Castle Carrock, 161

Castle Sowerby, 54, 79-80
Catherine de Valois, 135-6
Catherine of Alexandria, 100, 121
Catherine of Aragon, 136
Catholics, 7, 8, 126, 128, 133, 137, 148, 151, 152, 160-167, 173-4, 196, 205, 211-216, 230, 237, 239-240, 243, 244
Catterlen, 173
Cavendish, William 1st duke of Newcastle, 216
Caxton, William, 65
Cecil, Robert, 164
   William, 153, 155
Chambers, John, 216
Chantries, 121-5, 131-3, 142-4
Charles I, 180, 195, 198, 200, 201, 202, 204, 214
Charles II, 217, 230, 233, 238, 240, 241
Chartres, 50
Chatton, Walter de, 70
Cheshire, 71
Chester, diocese, 64, 65, 167, 189, 222
   deaneries, 207
Chester-le-Street,108
Cicely, countess of Albemarle, 47
Cimabué, Giovanni, 35
Cistercians, 47, 49, 50, 56, 57, 61, 64-5, 95, 119
Cîteaux, 46
Claife, 57

'Clarendon Code', 233, 234
Cleator, 56
Cliburn, 206
Clifford, barons, 71
  Henry, 2nd earl of Cumberland
Clifford, Lady Anne, 122, 217-219
Clifton, 206
Cocidius, 21
Cockermouth, 13, 18, 25, 27, 29, 123, 128, 150, 221, 223, 225, 227, 231, 232, 236-7, 238, 241, 242
Cockersand, 43
Coledale, Richard, 151
Collingwood, W. G., 18, 21, 27
Colmar, Alsace, 104, 130
Cologne, 50
Colthouse, 242
Colton, 180, 239
Comber, Thomas, 200-201
Committee for Sequestration of ... Estates, 207-8, 209
Compositions, the, 214
Compostela, Galicia, 113
Comyn, John 3rd earl of Buchan, 53, 74
Conishead Priory, 42, 55, 132
Coniston, 57
Constantine, Emperor, 113-114
Conventicle Act, 1664, 235, 236, 241, 245
Cookson, William, 237

Cooper, Anthony Ashley, 1st earl of Shaftersbury, 240
Copeland, 46
Corby, 45, 77, 215, 243
Corecrumruadh, 60
Coremac Gille Becoe, 37
Corporations Act, 233, 244
Corpus Christ play, 156, 189, 191
Council of the North, the, 159
Countess Joan, 86
Coupland, 40, 207
  deanery, 59, 167, 207, 222
Courcy, John de, 64
Coventry, 127
Coventry and Lichfield, Bishop of, 48
Craister, Thomas, 203
Crécy, battle, 65
Crescentius, 15, 16
Cressingham, Hugh de, 53
Croglin, 231
Cromwell, Oliver, 201, 204, 216, 220, 227, 230, 234
Cromwell, Thomas, 136, 144
Crook, 81, 224
Crook Hall, 172
Crosby, 231
Crosby Garrett, 37, 80, 81
Crosby Ravensworth, 37, 159, 161

Crossby-on-the-Hill, 231
Crosscanonby, 26, 27

287

Crosthwaite, 25, 39, 65, 80, 143, 156-7, 231
'Cult of a King, A', 86-92
Cumberland, 6, 8, 26, 34, 37, 38, 39, 40, 41, 42, 46, 47, 70, 72, 78, 84, 86, 105, 121, 122, 126, 127, 128, 141, 142, 147, 148, 151, 152 154, 155, 160, 161, 162, 169, 170, 179, 199, 204, 204, 209, 214, 215, 221, 225-6,229, 230, 231, 233, 238, 244
Cumberland and Westmorland Association, 221, 229
Cumbria, 9, 11, 26, 27, 31, 34, 36, 37, 39, 49, 64, 68, 73, 79, 82, 92, 125, 126, 127, 129, 142, 146, 147, 152, 154, 156, 160, 162, 165, 166, 179, 180, 182, 188, 206, 207, 211, 214, 215, 220, 221, 229, 234, 237-8, 239
Cummersdale, 83
Curwen, family of, 211, 239, 240
  Henry, 299
  Katherine, 239
  Nicholas, 162
  Sir Christopher, 81
  Sir Henry, 162
  Sir Patricius, 240
  Sir Thomas, 142
Cuthbert of Lindisfarne, 6, 23, 26, 42, 81, 83, 96, 98, 104, 105-110, 120, 177, 178, 179
cyfarwyddon, the, 66

Czech Republic ,the, 117
Dacre, 27, 29, 37, 108, 159
Dacre, Elizabeth, 152
  family of, 151-2, 153
  Leonard, 153-4
  Thomas, 2nd Lord, 61-2
  Thomas, 4th Baron, 152, 153
  William, 3rd Lord, 151
Dalston, 51, 75, 161
Dalton-in-Furness, 39, 60
Darmstadt, 112
David I, 46
David II, 68, 74
Dean, 13
Dearham, 25, 27
Declaration of Indulgence, 1672, 239
Declarations of Indulgence, 1687, 1688, 241-2, 245
Declaration (Book) of Sports, 187, 195
Denton, 37, 42
Denton, Thomas, 219
Derwentfells, 128
Derwentwater, 26, 57, 161
Devon, 238
Directory for the Public Worship ..., 210, 218
Dissenters, 234, 235, 238, 241, 242, 244, 245
Dissolution of the Monasteries, 44, 48, 70, 138, 140, 142 143
Distington, 27, 39, 42, 56, 81

288

Dodding Green, 243
Dolfin, 37
Dominicans, 69, 70-1, 98
Dorset, 90
Douai, 162, 179
Dudley, Catherine, 165
  Edmund, 165
  family of, 170
  Richard, 165-6
  Robert, earl of Leicester, 165
Dufton, 161, 162
Dumfries and Galloway, 24
Durham, 105, 120, 147, 163, 196
  County, 209, 211, 234
Dutch Republic, 238
Dynes, Ingram de, 68

Eadred, Bishop of Lindisfarne, 108
Eaglesfield, 29, 33, 127
Eaglesfield (d'Eglesfield), Robert, 127
Eamont Bridge, 9, 11
Ecgfrith, 26
Edenhall, 143, 231
Edinburgh University, 209
Edward, earl of Carrick, 75
Edward I, 43, 53, 66, 67, 69, 71, 72
Edward III, 57, 64, 65
Edward VI, 135, 142, 146
Edward, Prince, 135, 137
Edwards, Thomas, 220

Egremont, 27, 46, 47, 143
Eldredsson, Ketel, 38
Eleanor, Queen, 67
Elizabeth I, 147, 149, 153, 154, 158, 159, 161, 165, 199, 203, 216
Ellerton, Thomas, 150, 151
Elmeden, Thomas de, 70
Embleton, 223
Ennerdale, 81
Erasmus, Desiderius, 144, 145
Erfurt, 13
Eskdale, 81
Eskead, Sir Thomas de, 80
Esseby, William de, 47
Esslingen, 115
Eugenius III, Pope, 61
Everdon, Bishop Silvester de, 51-2
Exclusion Acts, 241
Exeter, 119

Farlam, 42
Fehmarn Castle, 130
Fell, Leonard, 133
Fell, Margaret, 225
  Thomas, 224-5
Fermoy, 60
Firbank Fell, chapel, 222, 223, 224
Fitzarthur, Henry, lord of Millom, 48
Flavius Martius, 19

Flavius Romanus, 19
Fleming, Daniel, 219, 235
Fletcher, Sir George, 232
Florence, 86
Fountains Abbey, 57, 65
Fourth Lateran Council, 128
Fox, George, 224-9
France, 65, 86, 92, 239
Francis of Assisi, 69
Franciscans, 69-70, 82-3, 103
  Conventuals, 69
  Spirituals, 69-70
Freising, 112
Friends, the, 221, 222, 232, 234, 242-3
Fuller, Thomas, 149, 198
Furness, 41, 140, 161, 225
  Abbey, 6, 47, 54, 56-66, 67, 132, 138, 140, 142
  deanery, 59, 222

Gardiner, Stephen, Bishop, 137
Gaul, 11, 23, 24
Gaunt, John of, duke of Lancaster, 87, 88
Geneva, 194, 220
Gerald, Abbot, 46
Germany, 18, 117, 145
Gernun, Richard, 55
Gilbertine Canons Regular, 44, 49
Gilcrux, 47, 56
Gilpin, 221

Gilpin, Allan, 208
Gilsland, 42, 152, 161, 168, 229
Giovanni da Fiesole (Fra Angelico), 86
Glasgow, diocese of, 40
  University of, 209
Gnosticism, 22
Gododdin, the, 66
Gondicourt, Prior Thomas, 120, 121
Gordianus Pius (Gordian III), 17
Gosforth, 37, 167
  Cross, 26, 31-2, 34
Graham, Richard, 181
Graham, Sir Richard, 1st Viscount Preston, 244
Grange-over-Sands, 27, 43
Grasmere, 206
Grayrigg, 161
'Great Bible', 145
Great Langdale, 13
Great Orton, 82
Great Salkeld, 73, 143, 146, 157
Gregory I, Pope, 95
Gregory IX, Pope, 45
Gregory XIII, Pope, 90
Greystoke, 78-9, 143, 152, 161, 182, 221, 231, 243, 245
Greystoke, John, Lord, 78
Greystoke, Ralph, Lord, 78
Greystoke, William 14th Baron, 78
Grindal, Archbishop Edmund,

290

150-151, 152, 159, 192
Grinsdale, 25, 42
Grünewald, Matthias (Mathis Nithardt), 103-4
Guisborough Priory, 36
Gunpowder Plot, 161, 184, 189
Guzmán, Domingo de, 69

Hadrian's Wall, 14, 17, 18, 42
Haile, 46 55
Haile, Custance de, 55
Halton, Bishop John de, 70, 75
Hampton Court Conference, 182, 185
Hardred, Abbott, 47
Haringtom, William 5th Lord, 55
Harrington, 27
Harrison, Anna, 170
Harrison, Thomas, 218
Hastings, battle, 36
Hastings, Henry, 3rd earl of Huntingdon
Hawkshead, 39, 57, 242
Helen, Empress, 64
Helm Wind, 170
Henry, Prince, earl of Huntingdon, 46
Henry I, 40, 45, 200
Henry II, 44, 46, 50, 55
Henry III, 51, 55, 69
Henry IV, 88, 91
Henry VII, 135, 136
Henry VIII, 44, 70, 133, 135, 136, 137, 138, 140
Henry Frederick, Prince, 184
Hesilrige (Haselrig), Arthur, 210
Hesket, 161
Hesket Newmarket, 25
Heversham, 27, 38, 150
Hexham Priory, 67-8, 98
Heysham Head, 23
Higden, Ralph (Ranulph), 65, 66
Higginson, Francis, 223-4
Highhead, 122
High Commission, the, 150, 170, 211
Hilton, Andrew, 163
Hilton, J. A., 212
Hippo, North Africa, 102
Historia regum Britanniae, 65-6
Hodgson, Agnes, 164-5
Hodgson, Hugh, 150, 151-2
Holm Cultram, 229
  Abbey, 46, 47, 55-6, 74, 119, 121, 141
Holy Cross, 60
Holy Land, the, 54, 68
Homer, 65
Hooker, Bishop Richard, 193-4
Horncastle, 51
Hoton, John, 136
House of Commons, 234, 244
House of Lords, 149
Howard, Charles, 204, 210, 226-7, 228
Howard, family of, 211f

291

Lord William, 161
Thomas, 3rd duke of Norfolk, 137, 141, 142
Howard, of Corby, Anne, 239
 Francis, 239
 Sir Francis, 215
 Thomas, 215
Howgill, Francis, 222
Hubert, 26
Hudleston, Andrew, 215
Hudleston, Sir John, 56, 58
 Sir William, 215
Huggen, Anthony, 170
 Jannet, 170
Hundred Years War, the 65
Hutchinson, William, 11
Hutton, Anthony, 155
 family of, 143, 162
Hutton-in-the-Forest, 122, 143, 231, 232
Hutton John, 215

IHS, 83, 129,135, 178
Independency, Independents, 220-1, 223-4, 230, 232, 236, 237, 238
Inglewood, Forest, 49
Inislaunaght, 58, 60
Innocent III, Pope, 69
Ireby, 38
Ireland, 27, 29, 43, 64, 108, 165, 211
Ireleth, 180

Irthington, 42
Irton, 26, 27, 48
Irton, Bishop Ralph de, 50
Isel, 159, 221
Isenheim Altarpiece, 103-4
Isis Parlis, 24
Isle of Man, 29, 58, 60
Italy, 92, 100, 117

James, Apostle, 81, 112-113
James, 'the Less', Apostle, 115
James I, 91, 179-180, 187, 198, 211, 216
James II, 241, 243, 245
James, duke of York, 239, 240-1
Jerusalem, 113, 224
Jews, 113, 117
Jocelin, Bishop of Glasgow, 64
Jocelyn of Furness, 25, 64
John, Apostle, 113-114, 118, 176
John XXII, Pope, 69-70
Johnby Hall, 161,163, 178-9
Johnson, Mr, 206
Jollie, Francis, 202
Judas Iscariot, 116, 117
Julian of Norwich, 175

Kaber Rigg, 234
Kempe, Margery, 175
Kendal (Kendale), 27, 38, 42, 82, 83, 123, 124, 129, 131-3, 135, 137, 147-8, 157, 161, 168 , 172, 173, 182,189-192, 198, 205,

206-209, 223, 224, 229, 233, 234, 242, 243
  deanery, 149-150, 161, 167, 207, 222
Kendal, Issabil, 128
Kent, 92
Kentigern (Mungo), 5, 23, 25, 39, 64, 83, 177, 178, 188
Keswick, 9, 11, 25, 167, 229
Killington, 168
King Arthur's Round Table, 11
King John, 50, 53, 55
Kip, Johannes, 52
Kirk Maughold, 58
Kirk Michael, 58
Kirkandrews-on-Eden, 25, 179-180, 231
Kirkbride, 16
Kirkby, Bishop John, 75
Kirkby Ireleth, 60
Kirkby Lonsdale, 37, 38, 78, 122, 157, 168, 207
Kirkby Stephen, 26, 27, 37, 38, 44, 77, 234
Kirkby Thore, 18, 37, 161, 206
Kirkbys, family of, 213
Kirkcambeck, 25
Kirklinton, 37, 159
Kirkoswald, 168, 238
Knights Hospitallers of St John, 68
Knipes, family of 213
Knights Templar, 68

Knockross, 3-4

Lake Counties, District, region, Lakeland, 6,7, 9, 23, 49, 50, 57, 72, 73, 84, 126, 127, 143, 156, 171, 214, 221, 238
Lancashire, 6, 41, 43, 65, 71, 138, 165, 167, 215, 238
Lancaster, 48, 59, 71
Lancaster Thomas, 164, 166
Lancaster, House of, 88
Lancaster, William de, I, 38, 42
  II, 38
  III, 61
Lanercost Priory, 25, 42-3, 61-2, 66-7, 74, 78
Langdale, 42
Langhorne, Thomas, 210, 237, 238
Langlands, 229, 230
Langwathby, 17
Larkham, George, 221, 223, 232, 236, 238
Laud, Archbishop William, 194-5, 196
Laudians, 194-5, 199-200, 217, 231, 233
Lawsons, family of, 221
Lazonby, 231
Leake, Richard, 168-9
Legenda Aurea ('Golden Legend'), 98
Leicester, 127

293

L'Engleys, Sir William, 122
le Fleming, Annabel, 56
　John, 56
le Franceys, John, 55
le Meschin, William, 38, 46
le Scrope, Henry, 4th Baron, 163
Leonard, St, 130
Leyburne, Bishop John, 243
　family of, 179
Limburg, Johan, de, 92
Lincolnshire, 51, 140
Lindale, 180, 224
Lindisfarne, 26
Lisbon, 103
Little Salkeld, 9, 77
Liutprand (Luitbrand), Bishop of
　Cremona, 102
Lollards, 127-8, 145
Lombardy, 102
London, 89, 90, 127, 134, 150,
　152, 154, 190, 194, 232, 238,
　240
Longtown, 27, 179
Long Marton, 43, 45, 81, 206
Long Parliament, the 205, 207,
　209, 211
Lonsdale, 161
Long Meg and Her Daughters, 9,
　10, 11-12
Losh, Sarah, 74
Loweswater, 81
Lowther, 26, 45, 161
Lowther, family of, 45

Gerard, 154
Leonard, 182
Low Countries, 86, 121, 163
Lübeck, 130
Ludolph of Saxony, 175
Lumley, Bishop Marmaduke, 76
Luther, Martin, 144, 147, 171

M. Censorius Cornelianus, 16
Machell, Thomas, 83
Mallerstang, 80
Manichaeans, 100-101
Marcus Aurelius Syrio, 17
Marcus, Licinius Ripanus, 19
Marcus Ulpius Trajanus (Trajan),
　16, 114
Marshall, William, 1st earl of
　Pembroke, 43
Martindale, 24, 180
Martin of Tours, 24
Mary Magdalene, 33, 42, 176
Mary Queen of Scots, 153, 154,
　162
Mary I, 135, 148, 159, 162, 214
Mary II, 245
Maryport (Aulana), 16, 19 22,
　25, 26
Masham, North Riding, 90
Masy (Massey), 209-210
Mather, Cotton, 23-4
Matilda, countess, 61
Matilda, Queen, 40
Matthew, Apostle, 116

'Matthew Bible', 145
Matthias, Apostle, 116-117
Mauclerk, Bishop Walter, 51, 71
Mayburgh, 9, 11
May (Meye), Bishop John, 163, 166, 167, 181
Melmerby, 159, 231
Melrose, 105
  Abbey, 46, 64, 105, 120
Mendicant friars, 49, 55, 68-72
Merke, Bishop Thomas, 76, 86-91
Methodists, 7
Michael, St, 43-4
Middleton, 180
Middleton, John, 164-5
Middleton, Dr William, 122
Milbourne, Bishop Richard, 193
Milburn, 37
Milecastle 51, 17
  73, 18
  79, 18
  59, 19
Millenary Petition, 185
Millom, 9, 11, 12, 47, 54, 56, 58, 60, 215, 225
Mithras, 20
Monica, St, 98
Monmouth, Geoffrey, of, 65-6
Moor Divock, 9
More, Thomas, 137, 145
Morland, 36, 38, 151, 161, 206
Moses, 104

Mosser, 143
Mortmain, Statute of, 67
Motherby, Nicholas de, 79
Mountford, priest, 163
Mount Grace, Yorkshire, 133
Multon, Thomas de, 56
Muncaster, 26, 42, 55, 81
Mungrisdale, 25
Munich, 112, 113, 116
Münster, 130
Musgrave, 80, 81, 206
Musgrave, Leonard, 161, 163
Musgrave, Sir Philip, 234-5

Naworth, 19, 152
Nayler (Nailer), James, 223, 224
Neile, Bishop Richard, 196
Netherby, 20
Nenthead, 8
Netherlands, the, 18, 194
Nether Denton, 34, 83, 129
Neville, Charles, 6th earl of Westmorland, 153
Neville's Cross, battle, 65
Newbiggin, 161, 206
Newcastle upon Tyne, 67, 71
Newton Arlosh, 73, 74
Newton in Cartmel, 224
New England, 220, 223
New Model Army, 204 220
Nicea, 114
Nicene Creed, 114
Nicolson, William, 245

295

Nicolson and Burn, 123, 202
Ninian, 6, 23, 24, 83, 108
Noble, John, 237
Nominated Assembly ('Barebones Parliament'), the, 227
Nonconformists, Nonconformity, 230, 231, 233, 234, 236, 237, 238, 241, 244, 245
Norbert, Archbishop, 43
Norfolk, 79, 82, 137
Normandy, 46, 85
Normans, 6, 29, 36, 37, 40, 49
Northampton, 127
Northumberland, 51, 98, 204, 209
North Riding, 234
North Wales, 88
Northumbria, 26, 105, 107
Norwich, 199
Nottinghamshire, 130
Nutter, Matthew Ellis, 110

Oates, Titus, 240
Oddendal, 9
Offler, H. S., 40
Oglethorpe, Bishop Owen, 148, 149
Ormside, 81, 148, 206
Orton, 55, 173, 223
Oswald, king of Northumbria, 108
Ouds, Thomas, 80
Oxford, 127

Pamplona, 113
Papcastle, 18
Pardsey Crag, 229
Pardshaw, 128
Paris, 166
Park, James, 243
Parr, Catherine, 145-6, 147
  Sir Thomas, 145
  Sir William, 123
Patraic, 31
Patrick, St, 64
Patterdale, 31
Paul, St, 145, 147
Paul III, Pope, 136
Pavia, 102, 103
Pennington, 42, 55, 60
Pennington, Adam, 124
Pennington, Gamel de, 42, 55
Penrith, 9, 16, 17, 18, 25, 26, 27, 34, 36, 49, 55, 69, 71-2, 86, 112, 123, 132, 136, 140-2, 143, 148, 150, 151, 154, 155, 161, 162, 167-8, 169, 173, 209-210, 231, 236-7, 238, 244
Penruddock, 237
Penton, 112
Percy, Algernon, 10th earl of Northumberland, 221
  barons, 71
  Sir Henry ('Hotspur'), 75
  Sir Thomas, 7th earl of Northumberland, 153, 154
Perkins, William, 187

296

Persia, 19
Peter, Apostle, 44, 110-112, 117
Pevsner, Nicholas, 27
Philip, Apostle, 115-116
Philippa, Queen, 127
Philipson, family of, 173
  Hudleston, 173
  Miles, 172
Philipson, Sir Christopher (d. 1709), 235
Pietro Matteo d'Amelia, 116
Pilgrimage of Grace, 7, 135, 137, 138, 139-142, 156, 178
Pilkington, Bishop James, 147
Pius, V, Pope, 158
Plumbland, 26 231
Pol, Hermann, 92
Polychronicon, 64-5, 66
Pontefract Castle, West Riding, 90, 91
Pontius Pilate, 113-114
Porters, family of, 239
Potter, Bishop Barnabas (Barnabie), 193, 198, 200-201
Postimius Acilianus, 16
Premonstratensians, 43, 49
Presbyterians, Presbyterianism, 7, 205-6, 207, 208-211, 214, 217, 220-1, 223, 227, 230, 237
Preston, 45, 71
Preston, Anne, 173
Preston Patrick, 43, 222, 224
Preston, family of, 213
  Sir John, 214
Prestwich, Margaret, 48
Primitive Methodists, 8
Protestants, Protestantism, 126, 133, 142, 144, 146, 147, 148, 149, 151, 155, 158, 161, 162, 171, 173, 174
Publius Aelius Hadrianus (Hadrian), 16
Pyne, James Baker, 10

'Quaker Act', 233
Quakers, Quakerism, 7, 221-229, 230, 235, 238, 243
Queen's College, Oxford, the, 127
Quintus Petillius Cerialis, 14

Radcliffe, family of 161
  Lady Katherine, 167
  Sir Francis, 161, 167
Ralph, 6th Baron Neville of Raby, 86
Rampside, 180
Ravenglass, 20
Ravenstonedale, 13, 44
Rawlinsons, family of 213
Reformation, Catholic, the, 110, 160, 177
  Protestant, the 82, 118, 127, 145, 146, 150, 156, 159, 174, 195
Reginius Justinus, 18

297

Regnans in Excelsis, 158
Reims, 163
Reisbach, Lower Bavaria, 130
Revolt of the Northern Earls, the, 153-4
Richard II, 86-92
Richardson, William 206
Richmond, 168
  archdeaconry, 41, 222
Richmondshire, 141
Rickerby, Robert, 232, 236
Robert I (Bruce), king of Scots, 68, 75, 77
Robinson, Bishop Henry, 166-7, 180-187, 193, 196, 197, 199
Robinson, Christopher, 163-4, 165-6, 179
Robinson, Richard, 147
Rodde, Christopher, 138
Roman Empire, 6, 19, 22, 113
Rome, 6, 24, 90, 110-111, 165, 177, 178, 194
Roos, Thomas de, 123
Rose Castle, 74, 155, 233
Ross, Bishop John de, 55
Rostock, 130
Rottenhammer, Hans, 114
Roxburghshire, 46
Rubens, Peter Paul, 91
Rumelli, Alice (Alicia) de, 57
Russell, Margaret, countess of Cumberland
Ruthwell Cross, 27

St Bees, 27, 37, 150
  Priory, 38, 47-8, 55
St Botoph, 56
St John's Chapel, 231
St Mary's Abbey, York, 38, 45, 47, 55, 78
Salisbury, 50
Salkeld, John de, 77
Salkeld, Lancelot, 133-4, 137, 148
Salkeld, Sir Francis, 239
Salkeld screen, 133-6
Salley, Henry, 138
Sanderson, Robert, 170
Sandford (Sandforth), Anne, 162
  family of, 161-2
  Martha, 167
  Thomas, 162, 167
Santon Bridge, 20
Sardinia, 102
Savigny, Savigniacs ,47
Sawley Abbey, 138
Saxony, 130
Scaleby Castle, 18, 21
Scotland, 24, 38, 40, 41, 46, 64, 65, 75, 78, 91, 112, 121,153, 154, 165, 179, 185, 200, 205, 211, 245
Seascale, 27
Sedbergh, 37, 222
Sebergham, 161, 218
Sedgwick, George, 218
Seekers, the, 222-3

Sellafield, 46
Selside, 157
Sempringham, Gilbert of 44
Senhouse, Bishop Richard, 193
Seton, 48
Sextus Severius Salvator, 19
Seymour, Jane, 135
Shakespeare, William, 88
  Richard II, of, 88-9
Shap, 9, 11, 82
  Abbey, 43, 44, 82
Shapbeck, 11
Simeon of Durham, 108
Simon, Apostle, 116
Simpson, Robert, 206
Six Articles of Religion, 136
Sizergh, 155, 239, 243
Skelsmergh, 157
Skelton, 143, 150, 151
Skelton, family of, 239
Skipton, 218
Sleigh, Anthony, 237
Smith, Augustine, 211
Smith, Bishop Thomas, 219-220
Smith, Sir Thomas, 148, 150
Snoden (Snowden), Bishop
  Robert, 193
Society of Jesus (Jesuits), 162,
  163, 164, 165, 177, 211
Solemn League and Covenant,
  205-6, 210, 211, 214, 216, 220,
  231, 232
Solway Plain, 16

Somerset, 79
Southampton, 147
Spain, 18, 113, 117
Spence, Richard, 218
Spenser, George, 162
Stainmore, 180
Stanwix, 18
Stapleton, 181
Starr, Comfort, 232, 237
Staveley-in-Cartmel, 180
Sterne, Bishop Richard, 233, 237
Strickland, Bishop William, 75,
  76, 84, 123, 143
Strickland, family of, 179, 211
  Sir Robert, 215
  Sir Thomas, 239
  Walter, 155
Strickland Head, 229
Studholme, Barbara, 238, 203,
  277
Swarthmoor, 224-5
Swetten, 10
Swindle, 180
Swinehead, 60
Swinside, 9

Taillebois, Ivo de, 37-8
Tallentire, Thomas, 147
Temple Sowerby, 68, 231
Test Act, 1673, 243
Test Act, 1678, 243
Thaddaeus, Apostle, 116-117
Thirty-Nine Article of Religion,

299

159, 171-2, 174
Thomas, Apostle, 114-115
Thomas (Tommaltach), Archbishop of Armagh, 64
Thomson, Robert, 150
Thornburghs, family of, 179
Thrace, 17
Threlkeld, Robert, 122
Thursby, 231
Thwaytes, Lance, 213
Tiberius Claudius Drusus Germanicus (Claudius), 14, 16
Titus Aurelius Fulvius (Antoninus Augustus Pius), 16-17
Todd, Hugh, 201
Todd, John M., 66-7
Toleration Act, 7, 230, 245
Tolhurst, Jeremiah, 204
Tonge, Israel, 240
Tories, 241
Torpenhow, 143, 231
Torphin, son of Robert, 44
Trent, Council of, 177, 178
Très riches heures du Duc de Berry, the, 92
Trevisa, John of, 65
Trinity College, Cambridge, 191
Troutbeck, 173
Tübingen, 116
Tudor dynasty, 120, 135
 Owen, 135
Tullie, Timothy, 232
Tyndale, William, 145, 146

Tyrer, Ralph, 182, 190-1

Uldale, 77-8, 230
Ullinus, 21
Ullswater, 9, 24, 31, 161
Ulpius Apolinaris, 19
Ulster, 64
Ulverston, 12, 37, 60, 133, 224
Urban VI, Pope, 48
Urswick, 23, 60

Vatican, 112, 116
Vaux (de Vallibus), Robert, 42
Vaux, John, 173-4, 175-6, 178, 179, 188
 Rowland, 172, 175
Vaux, Hugh, 176
Vesey, barons, 71
Vienna, 15
Voragine, Giacomo de, 98, 100

Waberthwaite, 26, 27, 81
Wallace, William, 75
Walney Island, 57
Walsingham, 82
Walsingham, Sir Francis, 163
Walter the Priest, 40
Waltheof (Waldef), 64
Walton, 42
Warcop, 43, 83, 161, 163
Warrington, 71
Wars of the Roses, 120, 136
Warwick, 45

Watton, East Riding, 44
Welton, Bishop Gilbert, de, 75
Wesley, John, 7
Western March, 75, 76, 163
Westminster Assembly of
  Divines, 210, 220
Westmorland, 6, 7, 13, 36, 38, 41, 43, 44, 72, 80, 121, 126, 127, 142, 148, 151, 154, 155, 160, 164, 165, 169, 173, 204, 205, 206, 207, 209, 214, 215, 222, 223, 224, 225, 229, 231, 233, 234, 239, 243, 244
West Riding, 234
Weston, David, 204
Wetheral, 38, 45, 74, 161, 231
Wharton, 143
Wharton, Philip Lord, 209, 210, 223
  Sir Thomas, 44
Whelpdale, Gilbert, 142
  John, 155
Whicham, 91
Whigs, 240, 241
White, Bishop Francis, 193, 194, 196-7,199
Whitehaven, 8,181
Whitehead, George, 223
Whithorn, 24, 108
Wigton, 19, 21, 46, 143, 157, 163, 221, 226, 229
William I, 36
William II Rufus, 37, 42, 49

William III (of Orange), 244-5
William the Lion, 38
William, son of Gillercrist de
  Alnebank, 55-6
Wilkinson, John, 226
Wilkinson, Thomas, 132
Wilson, Henry, 206
Wiltshire, 43
Winchester, 137
Windermere, 43, 57, 58, 206, 235
Windsor, 148
Wiseman, W. G, 53
Witherslack, 243
Wood, Rita, 43
Workington, 27, 38, 108, 142, 162, 240
  Thomas de, 43
Wotherney, 60
Wyclif, John, 127, 128
Wyse, Agnes, 170

Yanwath, 165
York, 23, 38, 120, 150, 159, 206, 236
  Archbishop, 40, 44, 74, 159
  diocese, 41
  Minster, 232
  province 21
York, Elizabeth of, 135
Yorkshire, 36, 47, 57, 139, 140, 141, 215

Zoschau, 130